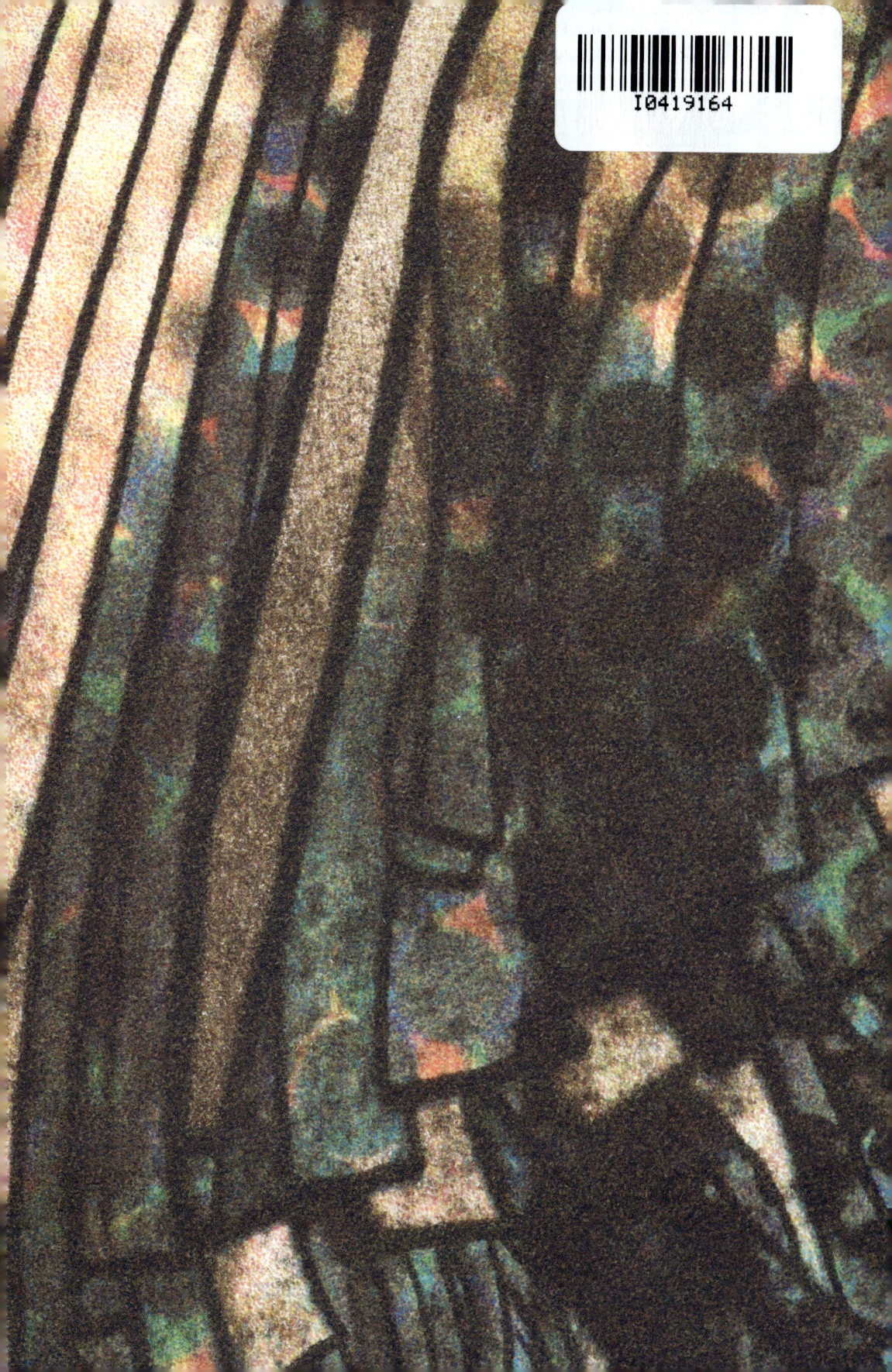

Dripping Earth

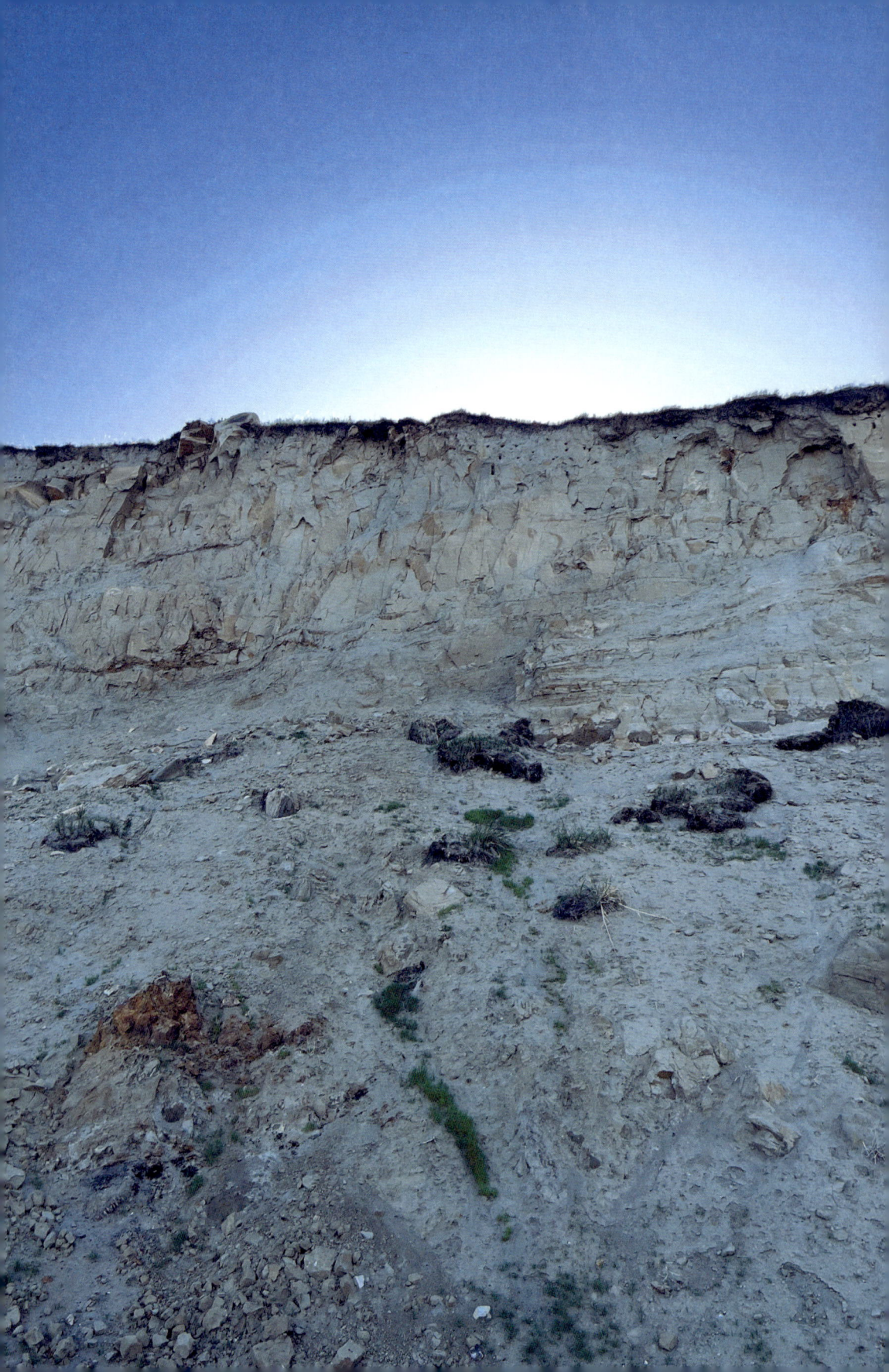

Dripping Earth

Cannupa Hanska Luger

**Karin Campbell and
Annika K. Johnson**

With contributions by
Cannupa Hanska Luger
Taylor J. Acosta
Michael Barthelemy Jr.
Alisha Deegan
Paul Farber
Josie Lopez
Steve Tamayo

**Margre H. Durham Center
for Western Studies**

Joslyn Art Museum

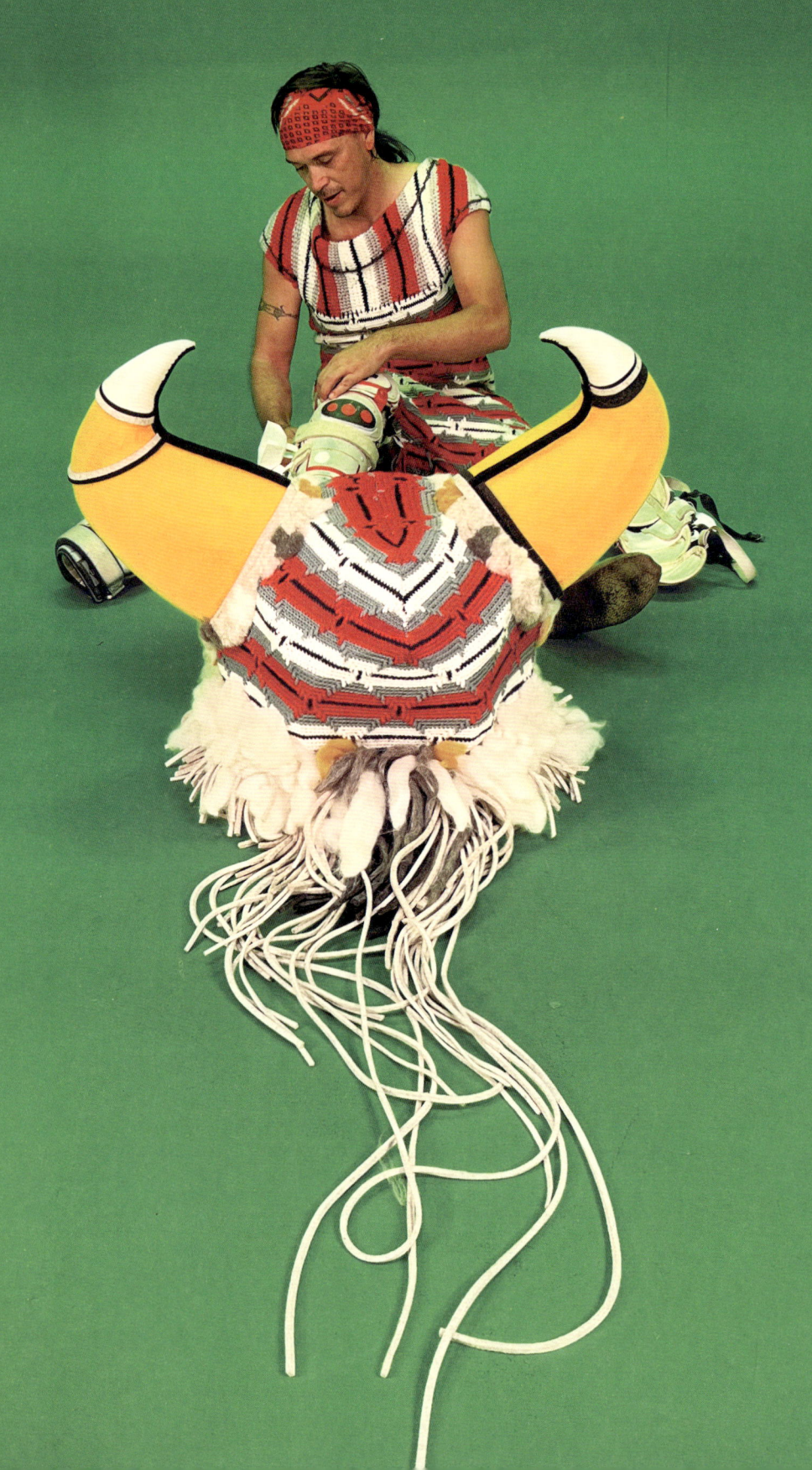

Contents

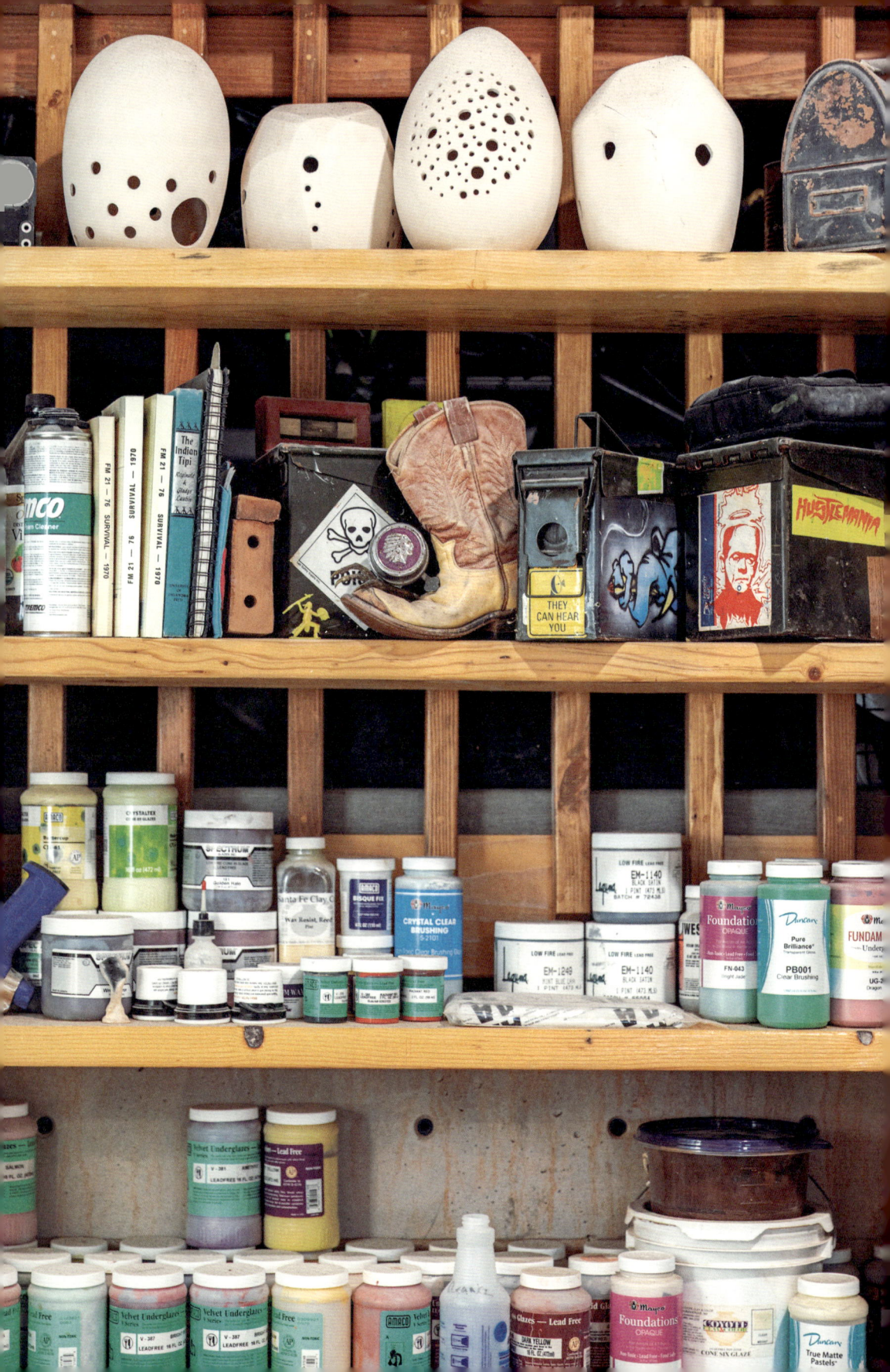

Director's Foreword

Joslyn Art Museum is located in present-day Omaha at the heart of Turtle Island. The city's name reflects the Umónhon people's ancestral connection to this region, which remains home to Indigenous people from many nations. We pay our respects to elders of the past, present, and future.

Flipping through the pages of this book, I am struck by the merging of history with futuristic storytelling. Landscapes, portraits, and spaces seem at once familiar and utterly transformed, evoking in the reader a sense of both recollection and discovery. These qualities characterize much of Cannupa Hanska Luger's process and art. Born on the Standing Rock Reservation in North Dakota, Luger is an enrolled member of the Three Affiliated Tribes of Fort Berthold Reservation and is Mandan, Hidatsa, Arikara, and Lakota. A multidisciplinary artist, he creates monumental sculptures, installations, and performances, combining insightful critique with a reverence for the diverse materials, environments, and communities he engages. His work reflects on universal human experiences while foregrounding an Indigenous worldview.

An ambitious and immersive exhibition, *Dripping Earth: Cannupa Hanska Luger* presents new work by the acclaimed artist. Joslyn Art Museum is especially honored to have originated this project. In the winter of 2024, Luger traveled to Nebraska, where he met with Joslyn staff, Indigenous community members, and educators at the Umónhon Nation Public School. He also toured the studio of ceramicist Jun Kaneko, with whom he discussed the past, present, and

future of sculptural ceramics. With the exhibition curators, he took a day trip to the Omaha and Winnebago
Reservations, losing cell service but finding connection.
And he spent a memorable evening at a reception hosted
by Bluebird Cultural Initiative, sharing a meal and many
stories with youth, elders, and relatives.

Back at The Joslyn, Luger pored over the watercolors,
prints, journals, and archives that comprise the Museum's
renowned Maximilian-Bodmer Collection. Preserved in the
Margre H. Durham Center for Western Studies, these materials document the 1832–34 North American expedition of the
German prince Maximilian of Wied and the Swiss artist Karl
Bodmer. Their work reflects European sensibilities of their
era—the intellectual curiosity of the patron, a prince and
amateur naturalist, and the traditional artistic training of
the painter. Bringing the cultural, scientific, and philosophical principles of the Enlightenment to bear on the Missouri
River Basin, they created a literary and visual impression
of the nineteenth-century American interior. Maximilian's
account of their journey, *Reise in das innere Nord-America in
den Jahren 1832 bis 1834* (*Travels in the Interior of North America,
1832–34*), accompanied by eighty-one hand-colored prints
after Bodmer's original watercolors, defined the American
landscape and its Indigenous peoples for generations of
European and American audiences. In many ways, the central questions of the present exhibition grew out of Luger's
study of Bodmer's iconic portrait of a Mandan Buffalo Bull
Society leader, specifically concerning what is discernible
and what is not.

Employing a vibrant mix of found and repurposed
materials, such as afghan blankets and vintage sports equipment, Luger reimagines depictions of his Mandan and
Hidatsa ancestors found in Bodmer's work. Situating visitors
within Missouri River landscapes now submerged by colonial damming projects, Luger reveals how such interventions
continue to shape the land and its people. The exhibition
and this accompanying publication challenge conventional
narratives and ask us to envision a future where land, identity, and culture are reclaimed and transformed.

Dripping Earth: Cannupa Hanska Luger was curated by
Karin Campbell, Phil Willson Curator of Contemporary
Art, and Annika K. Johnson, Stacy and Bruce Simon Curator
of Native American Art, who worked closely with the artist for more than two years to shape the exhibition. Their

thoughtful essay in the pages that follow offers new insights into Luger's practice. They have gathered an exceptional roster of writers for this catalogue, and I extend my admiration and gratitude to Taylor J. Acosta, Alisha Deegan, Paul Farber, Josie Lopez, and Steve Tamayo for their poignant reflections. The catalogue also includes an engaging conversation between the artist and Michael Barthelemy Jr., director of Native American Studies at Nueta Hidatsa Sahnish College.

The Joslyn is fortunate to have a talented and dedicated staff. Karin and Annika's acknowledgments of those crucially involved in this project follow; I would like to add my thanks to Taylor J. Acosta, chief curator and director of collections; Nancy Round, director of learning and engagement; Jim Sullivan, director of development; and Amy Rummel, director of marketing and public relations, for their leadership of the institution and guidance on all aspects of ambitious projects such as this one. I also thank the Museum's Board of Governors.

We are enormously grateful for the cooperation and support of the artist's studio, especially Ginger Dunnill, and gallery, Garth Greenan Gallery, New York.

Lastly, I extend my personal thanks on behalf of The Joslyn to Cannupa Hanska Luger. He has been generous with his time, attention, creativity, and spirit. We feel immensely privileged to have benefited from his participation in our planning, his contribution of new work to the exhibition and text to the catalogue, and his earnest engagement with our community.

Jack Becker
Executive Director and CEO

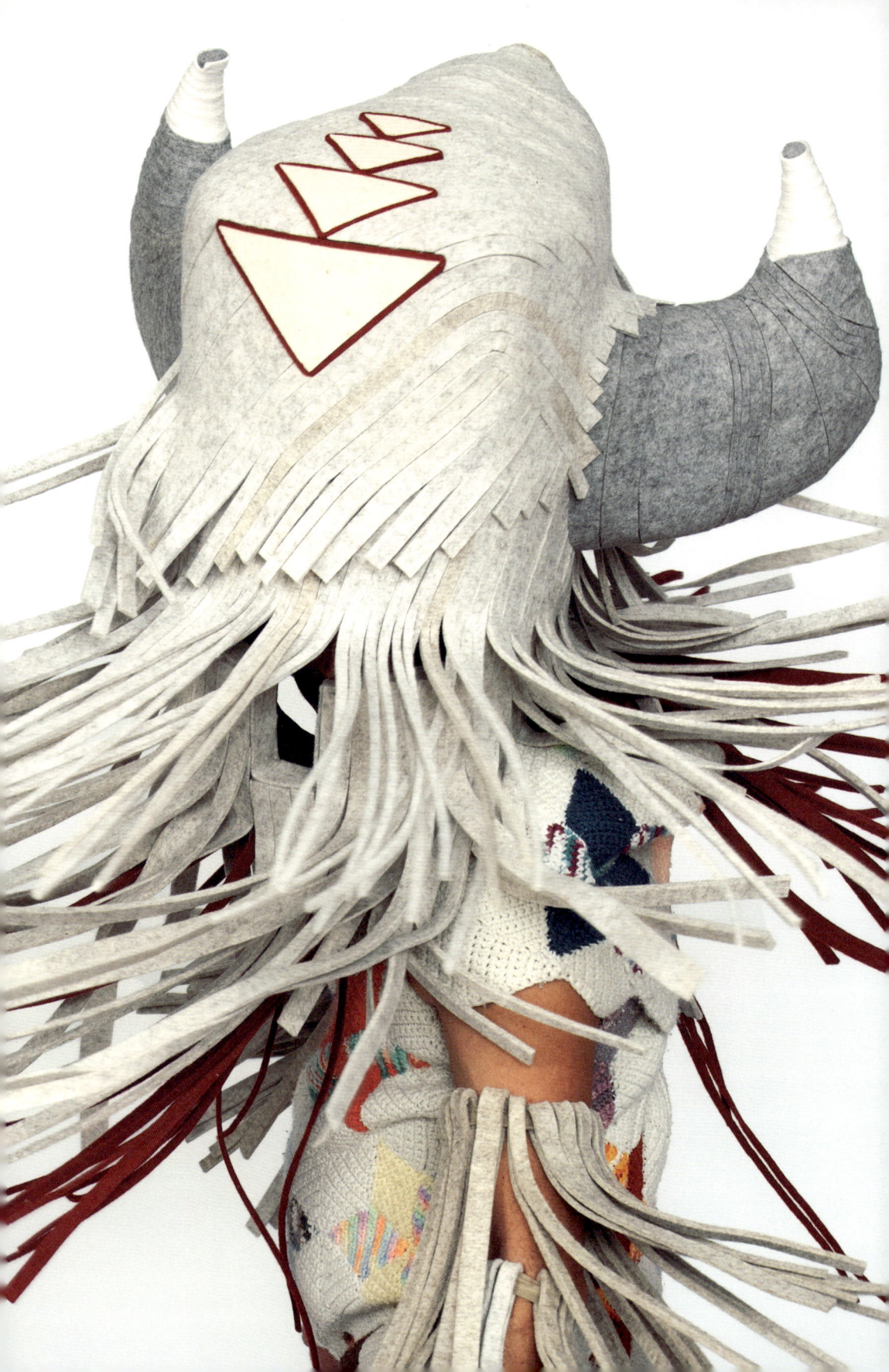

Acknowledgments

Bringing *Dripping Earth* to life required the dedication and commitment of many individuals and organizations. First and foremost, we extend our heartfelt gratitude to Ginger Dunnill, Cannupa Hanska Luger's studio manager and collaborator. Her grace, thoughtfulness, and good humor were invaluable throughout this process. The diverse perspectives of the catalogue contributors—Taylor J. Acosta, Alisha Deegan, Paul Farber, Josie Lopez, and Steve Tamayo— enrich this publication in meaningful ways. We are especially thankful to Michael Barthelemy Jr. for sharing Mandan and Hidatsa stories with Cannupa and readers. Shayla Blatchford photographed Cannupa's work in the studio and Z Long documented *Bison Bead Project* workshops, providing essential visual complements to the catalogue's written contributions.

Organizing an exhibition of this magnitude is no small feat, and many individuals aided Cannupa in transforming his ambitious vision into tangible and important work. We would like to thank Corson Androski, 3D designer, for their pivotal role in envisioning and realizing a complex exhibition layout. Corson also helped to bring the sculpture *Census* to life, alongside John Hilton of Quality Custom Manufacturing and Etta Salzman and Paulina Salzman. Printmaker Mitchell Marti worked closely with Cannupa over the course of many months to produce a new series of lithographs. We are grateful to Logan Schmit and Casey Duncan, who assisted in welding and powder coating *A Nation*, and to Rico Ramirez for his help in sewing the afghan "hides" of *Nahxibi I* and *II*. Special thanks to Kathy Elkwoman Whitman, Heather Baker, Graycee Gillis, Erica Giron, and Twila Jerome, Cannupa's relatives in North Dakota, who participated in harvesting and stripping willow branches for *Máadiraxbi I* and *II*. Additional thanks to filmmaker Justin Deegan for working with the artist to document their ancestral homelands. Garth Greenan, Hugh O'Rourke, and Julian Corbett of Garth Greenan Gallery, New York, were great champions of this project. The gallery's assistance in fabrication, installation, and logistics ensured that *Dripping Earth* was a success.

This project benefited greatly from the talents and efforts of individuals across departments at The Joslyn. Jack Becker, executive director and CEO, saw the cultural and intellectual value in *Dripping Earth* from its inception and offered his unwavering support throughout its planning. In addition to writing for the catalogue, Taylor J. Acosta, chief curator and director of collections, guided and encouraged us at every step with an unflappable upbeat spirit. Ingrid Cho, former curatorial assistant for Native American art, was invaluable in the early stages of organizing both the exhibition and the publication, and Camryn Moore, Rae and Bill Dyer Curatorial Assistant, provided essential support in the final months of preparations. Sarah Haines, registrar, and Candace Berger, associate registrar, were thorough and precise in their management of logistics. Kevin Salzman, exhibition design and installation manager, and Jordan Cairncross, assistant preparator, skillfully brought months of dreaming and planning to fruition in the galleries. We offer special thanks to our colleagues in Learning and Engagement, Kristin Bergquist, head of community programs, and Janie Helt, adult programs manager, who were instrumental in coordinating *Bison Bead Project* workshops. We are also grateful to the workshop participants, who, as Cannupa so eloquently put it, offered their life force to this ongoing endeavor.

Many individuals warmly greeted Cannupa upon his arrival to Omaha and the region. We thank Ree and Jun Kaneko for their hospitality during Cannupa's visit to their Omaha studio, and Nicole Benegas of Bluebird Cultural Initiative for hosting a Native community gathering, where elder Rudi Mitchell welcomed Cannupa on behalf of the Umónhon people. The Joslyn's Native American Art Advisory Committee and Ricardo Ariza, Michelle Blackbird, Ed Encinas, and Vida Stabler of the Umónhon Nation Public School on the Omaha Reservation offered essential guidance on pathways for engaging Native youth in the project.

ACKNOWLEDGMENTS

For the production of this catalogue, we extend our thanks to the team at Marquand Books, including Gina Broze, Leah Finger, Ryan Polich, and Kestrel Rundle. We are grateful, as well, to Kristin Kearns for editing the written contributions with precision and expertise.

Finally, we extend our deepest thanks to Cannupa Hanska Luger. In October 2024, he asked two *mashii* curators, "What do you see when you think of an Indian?" After an exchanged glance, followed by laughter and hours of conversation, Cannupa and the curators developed a plan to conceive a sixteen-foot-tall sculpture that features a figure wearing bison regalia to serve as the centerpiece of *Dripping Earth*. The rhythm of working with Cannupa— in a process that was thought-provoking, collaborative, and full of sparkle—made this an unforgettable and rewarding project.

Karin Campbell
Phil Willson Curator of Contemporary Art

Annika K. Johnson
Stacy and Bruce Simon Curator of Native American Art

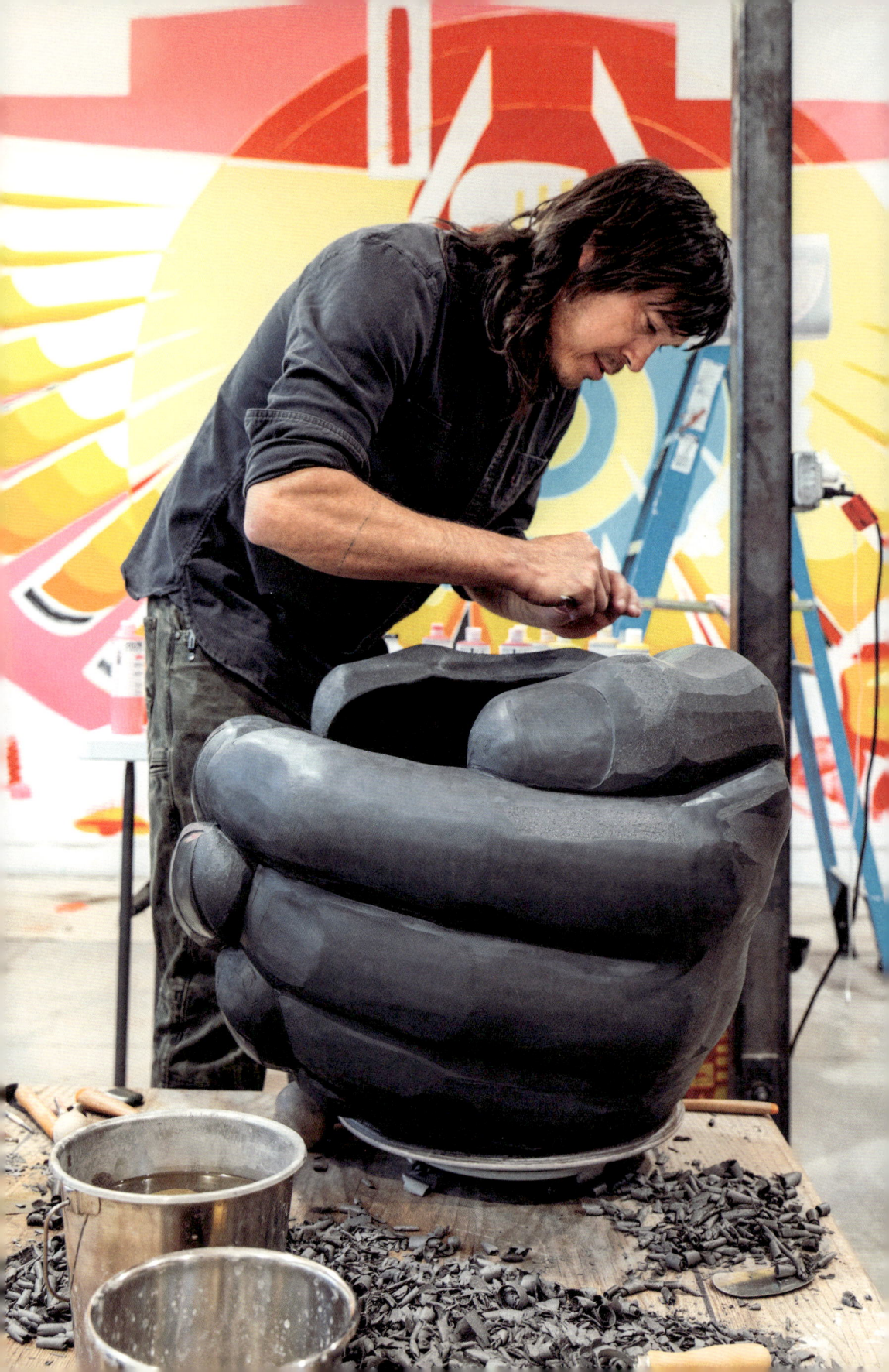

Dripping Earth

Karin Campbell and Annika K. Johnson

As a trained ceramicist, Cannupa Hanska Luger marvels at the complexity and capabilities of the human hand (fig. 1). Many artists cite their hands as their first and most important tools. For Luger, they offer something more: a conduit to the earth, and specifically to home. Following his mother's lineage, Luger is an enrolled member of the Mandan, Hidatsa, and Arikara (MHA) Nation, known as the Three Affiliated Tribes of Fort Berthold Reservation, located in North Dakota along the northern Missouri River. Raised on his father's homeland, the Standing Rock Reservation, just south of Fort Berthold along the same river, Luger grew up in a place deeply affected by the Dawes Act of 1887, federal legislation that fractured vast tribal lands and enforced a settler approach to agriculture that hinged on individual land management, rather than collective stewardship. This history and its impact drive Luger's experimentation in *A Way Home* (2020–), the artist's ongoing effort to reconnect with ancestral ceramic traditions by gathering clay from the shores of the Missouri River and creating vessels deriving from the land (fig. 2).

Luger's material sensibilities have expanded beyond ceramics in recent years to encompass steel, canvas, and acrylic, as well as found objects, from thrifted sports equipment and crocheted blankets to discarded industrial textiles. Yet he always returns to clay. Made on the occasion of Luger's solo exhibition *Dripping Earth*, *Irabágu* comprises thirteen ceramic vessels that reflect customary Mandan clay practices, in which the act of making and the resulting object are inseparable (pp. 14, 17, 94–95). Shaped using a specialized paddling

Fig. 1 Luger and his family gather clay on the banks of the Missouri River near Lucky Mound, North Dakota, 2022

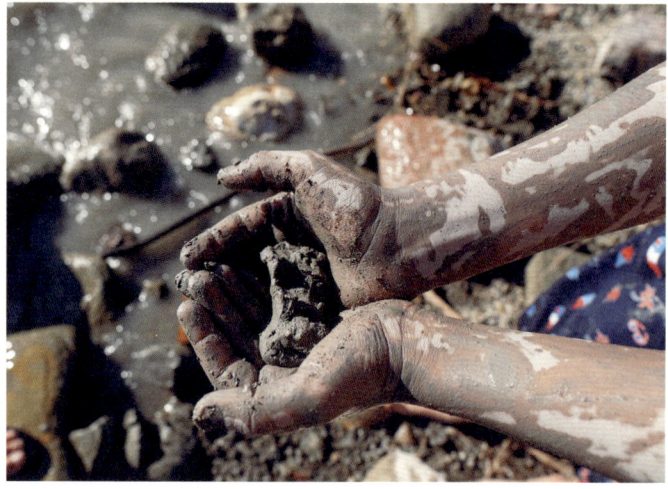

Fig. 2 Installation view of *Nǫ́ǫxįįhe (Grandmother I and II)*, 2022, ceramic, from the exhibition *Mįhǫ́pmǫk*, Center for Craft, Asheville, North Carolina, August 2022– January 2023

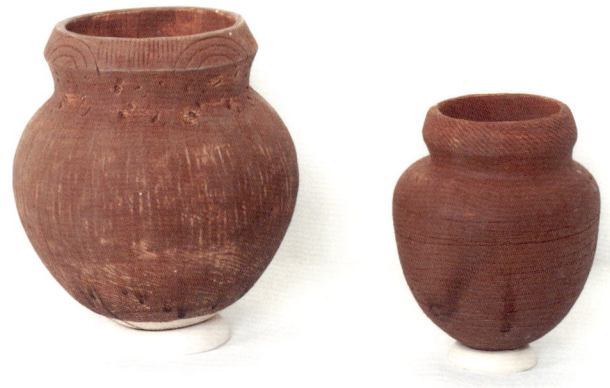

technique, pottery in the northern Missouri River region traditionally served utilitarian and aesthetic purposes, with incised and stamped patterns that indexed the prosperity of the larger community. Luger's play on these containers is rooted in the motif of cupped hands, a universal gesture that suggests holding or offering something precious. In displaying thirteen vessels, Luger references the number of moons in the lunar calendar—an Indigenous system of marking time through natural cycles—while their arrangement in a four-pointed star evokes the cardinal directions, referring to cosmological symbolism while grounding the work in the physical world. Though separated from their body, Luger's impressions of human hands in clay are assuredly present.

DRIPPING EARTH

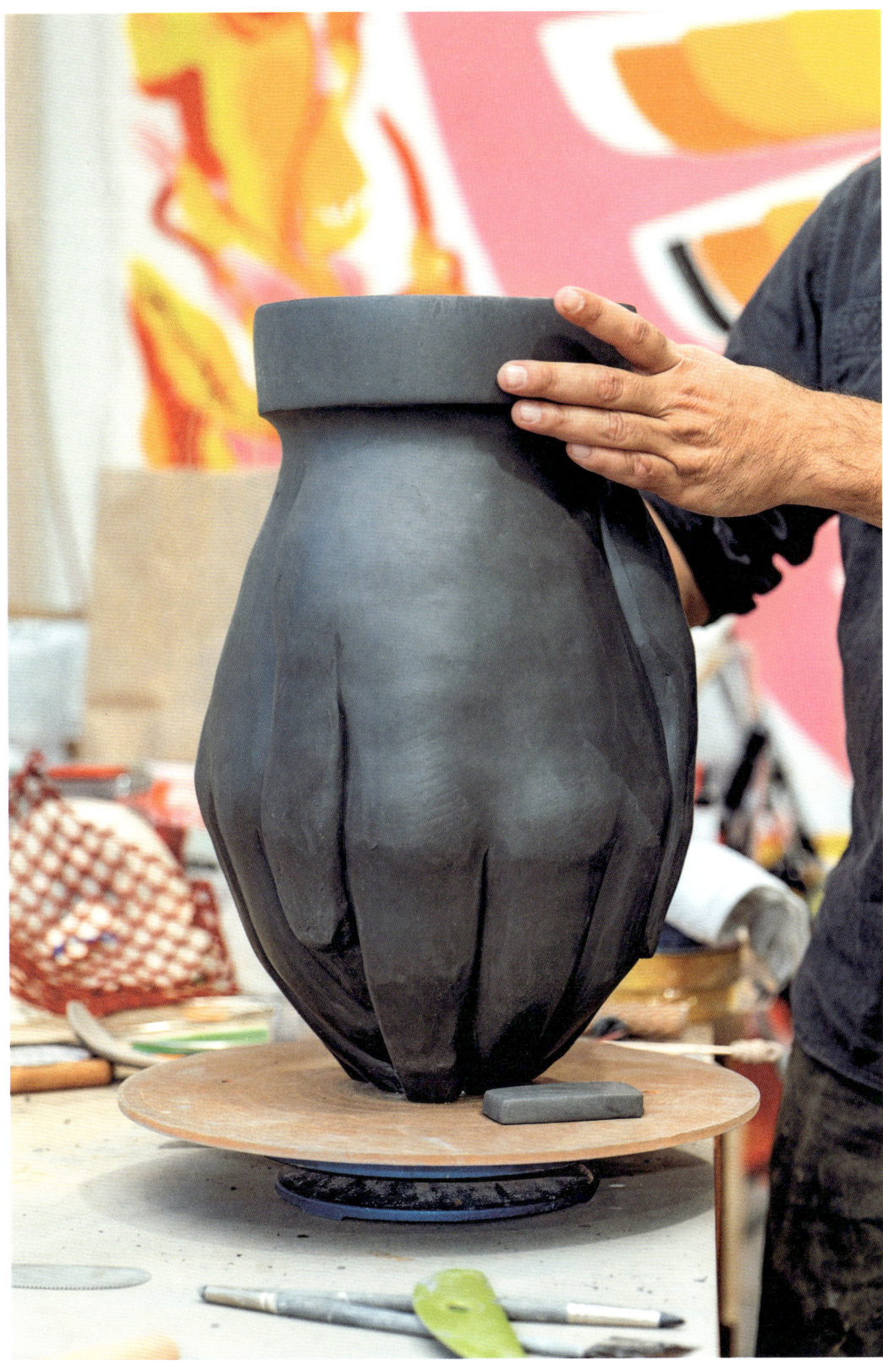

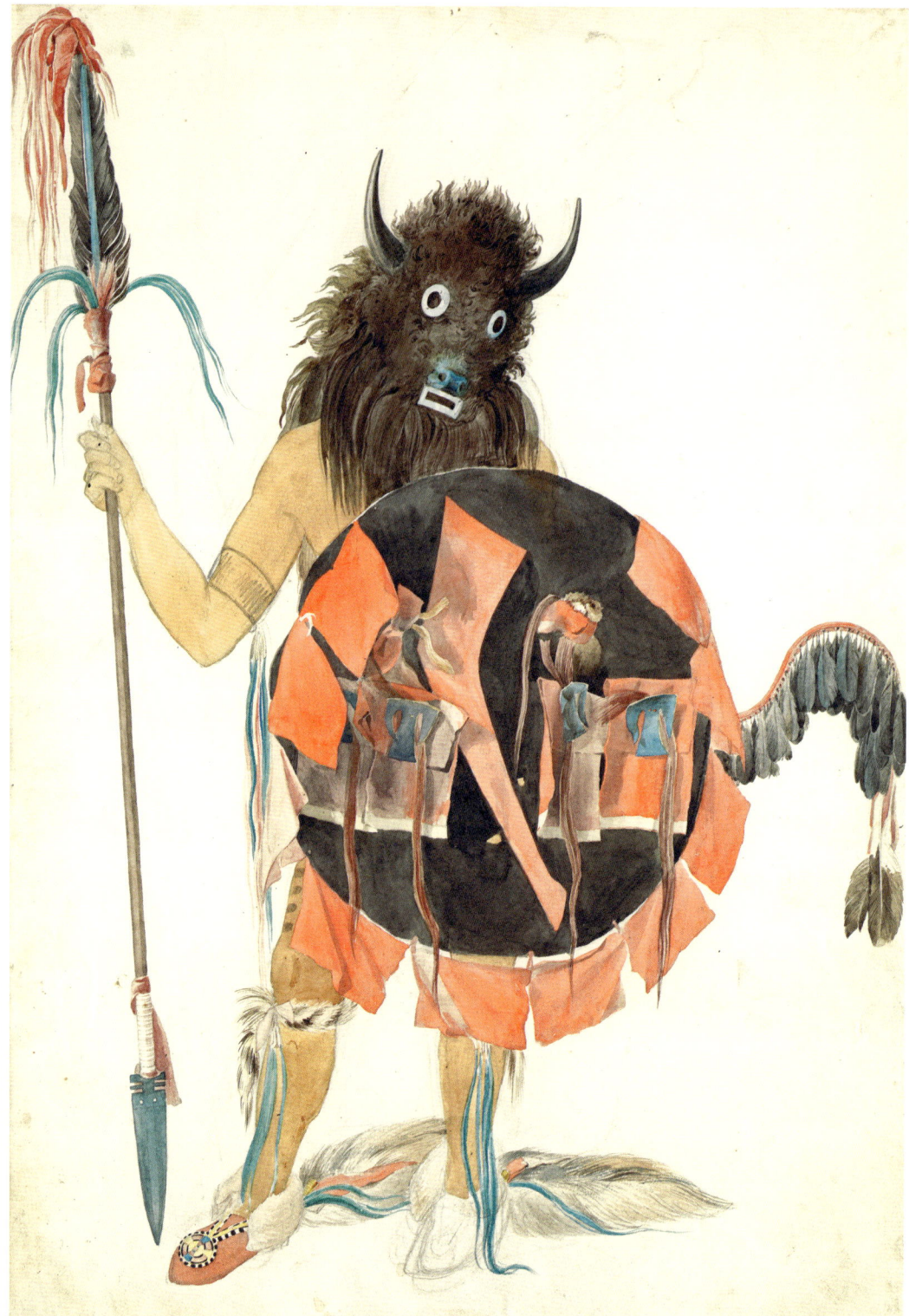

Luger's creative inquiry into the connections between the body and the earth gained new meaning upon a visit to the Joslyn Art Museum in early 2024. While in the Margre H. Durham Center for Western Studies, he surveyed a selection of images produced by the Swiss artist Karl Bodmer during his 1832–34 travels to the North American interior in the company of German prince and naturalist Maximilian of Wied. Bodmer made nearly four hundred watercolors and drawings that document settlements, bodies of water, flora and fauna, and Native leaders and lifeways with remarkable clarity.[1] For Luger, Bodmer's numerous portrayals of Mandan and Hidatsa people and their lands present an opportunity to connect with ancestors. One exquisitely detailed portrait, *Leader of the Mandan Beróck-Óchatä* (Buffalo Bull Society), stood out (fig. 3). Positioned in subtle contrapposto, the figure wears a headdress fashioned from an entire buffalo head, with glimmering tin-lined eyes and mouth. Unique and uncanny, the portrait is perhaps the most iconic image Bodmer made during his travels to Mandan and Hidatsa villages along the Missouri River. Just a few years later, the 1837 smallpox epidemic severely impacted specialized societies, along with their regalia, which were buried with the dead or burned, prompting Native people to regard the singularity of Bodmer's meticulous archive with both respect and thoughtful skepticism. Culture bearers have placed particular emphasis on what is missing: women, scenes from everyday life, songs and stories, and, crucially, cultural knowledge. For all the visual splendor of the portrait of the Buffalo Bull dancer, it was the omissions that struck Luger most deeply. While Bodmer depicted the society member's right beaded moccasin in full detail, its left counterpart is little more than a ghostly sketch. And while each pigment and material is discernible, the figure's visible hand lacks definition. In the face of glorious presence, Luger saw absence.

Bodmer was among the first European observers of a Buffalo Bull Society dance. This group of male elders was one of several specialized societies organized by age and status, with ceremonial duties to ensure the health of the community. On a spring day in 1834, Bodmer worked quickly to record the society gathering in real time, eschewing anatomical accuracy in favor of the visual information he deemed essential.[2] His talent for draftsmanship shines through in

Fig. 3 Karl Bodmer, *Leader of the Mandan Beróck-Óchatä*, 1834, watercolor and graphite on paper, Joslyn Art Museum, Omaha, Nebraska, Gift of the Enron Art Foundation, 1986.49.264

KARIN CAMPBELL AND ANNIKA K. JOHNSON

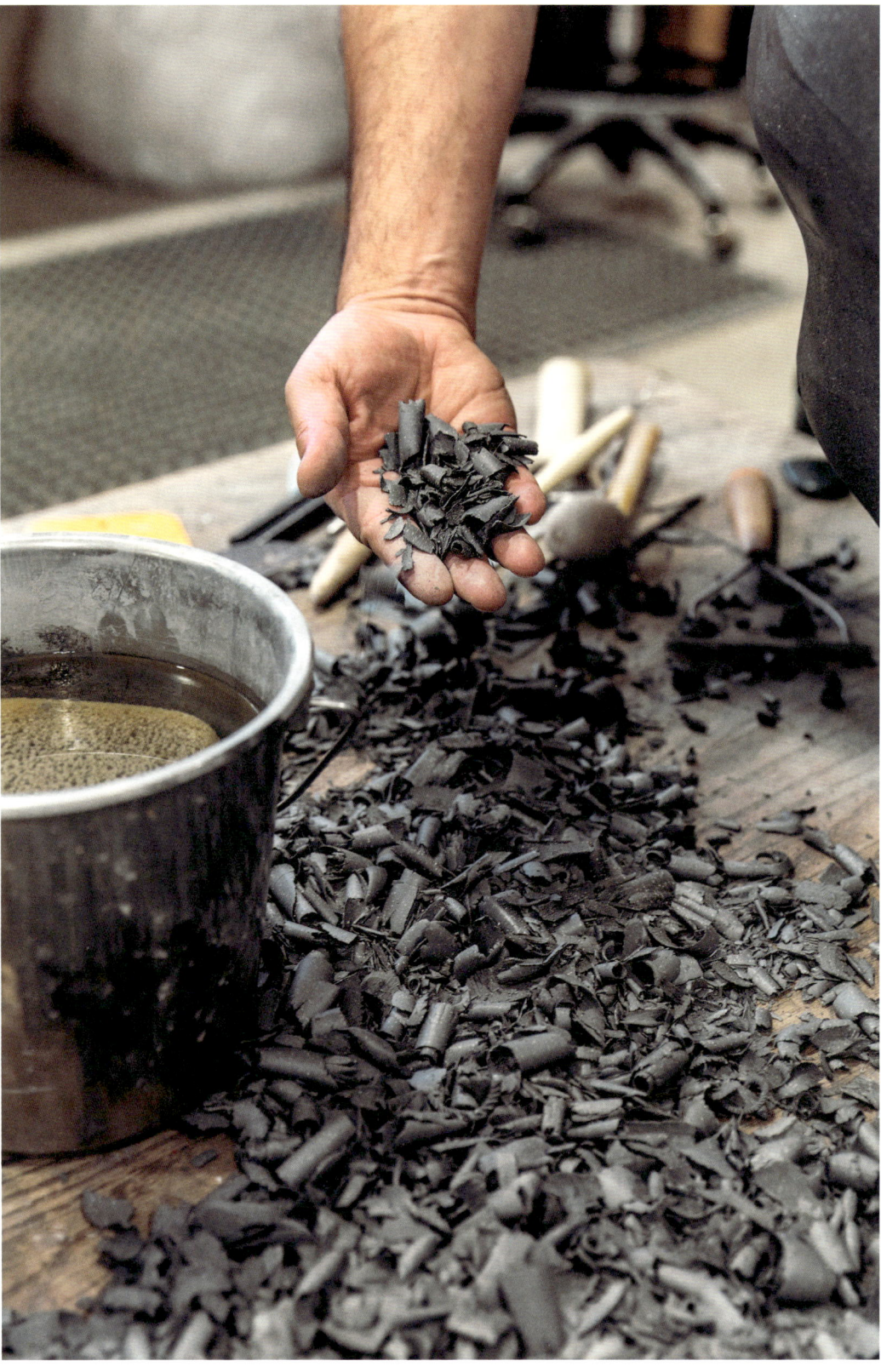

his sitters' distinct facial features and the exceptional color, patterning, and materials of their regalia. However, Bodmer was a landscape printmaker with no formal training in anatomy or life drawing, and his technical facility suffered when it came to the human body. Many of his portraits show distinguished individuals with their hands tucked into elegant robes or grasping tools or weapons with imprecise, jointless fingers. He treated feet similarly, often portraying his subjects from the torso up. When feet do appear, they are either concealed in moccasins or simply sketched ovals.

Feet often serve as metaphors for the human condition. To "plant one's feet" is to hold one's own, to refuse to yield. Having "both feet on the ground" suggests practicality, a clear-eyed way of viewing the world. "Finding your footing" indicates the gaining of confidence in a new situation. Each of these expressions acknowledges greater elemental forces and describes a kinship between humanity and the earth. What happens when this connection is severed? Given how thorough Bodmer was in his portrayals, it might be tempting to dismiss the absences as anomalies in the work of an otherwise fastidious artist. However, by eliminating these body parts, Bodmer removed the possibility that his sitters could touch the places that shaped their culture, lifeways, and belief systems. Luger's sculptures attempt to repair that connection, literally and figuratively completing the picture. "I am activating touch sensory organs on a human body that a landscape painter omitted," the artist says (fig. 4).[3] Although Bodmer may not have been fully cognizant of his positionality, he was a product of a Eurocentric discourse that located Indigenous people in the faraway "west" rather than in their homelands. His omission of hands reinforces this disconnection of Indigenous people from their communities, overlooking the significance of the acts of creation, repair, care, honor, and offering through which individuals contribute to their societies according to clan and society affiliation.

A Collective Question

Mandan and Hidatsa clans extend kinship ties beyond immediate family, offering structured support systems, with distinct responsibilities that collectively strengthen the community. Luger belongs to his mother's clan, the Awa xee, or Dripping Dirt Clan. The Awa xee oversaw the construction and repair of earth lodges, semipermanent domed dwellings

Fig. 4 Luger in his studio with clay shavings from the production of *Irabágu*, 2025

KARIN CAMPBELL AND ANNIKA K. JOHNSON

Fig. 5 Karl Bodmer, *Mandan Earth Lodges*, c. 1833–34, graphite on paper, Joslyn Art Museum, Omaha, Nebraska, Gift of the Enron Art Foundation, 1986.49.334

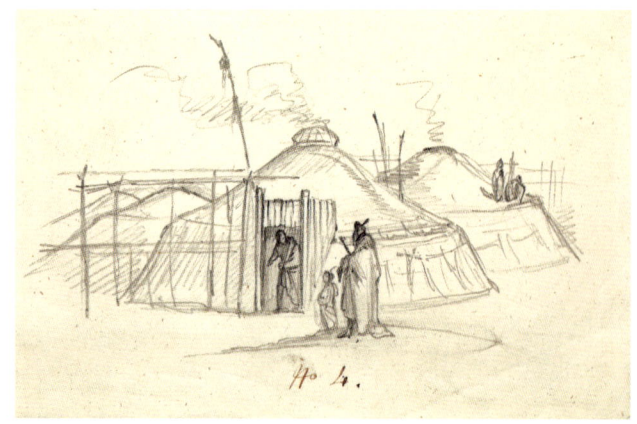

made from branches, grasses, and earth layered over sturdy cottonwood frames (fig. 5). The circular design of earth lodges accommodated multiple generations of extended family and fostered a strong sense of community. Many tribes, including the Mandan, Hidatsa, Arikara, and, downriver, Otoe and Umóⁿhoⁿ peoples in present-day Nebraska, built these dwellings to protect against the harsh weather conditions of the Northern Plains. When earth began to drip from the lodges' ceilings, the community called upon the Awa xee. Although the few lodges built today serve as teaching tools at cultural institutions and visitor centers at historic sites, the values embedded in their design continue to resonate with Native people living in modern housing.

In the exhibition *Dripping Earth*, Luger centers his clan and tribal affiliations, sharpening his articulation of belonging and responsibility to align with the broader purpose of his creative work and his deep connection to clay. The title conveys multiple meanings. Luger appreciates the paradox it encapsulates, of a material that is at once solid and liquid, symbolizing transformation within stability. Speaking with Luger on the topic of cultural fluidity, Michael Barthelemy Jr. noted that the shared process of self-definition lies at the heart of Mandan and Hidatsa culture. The cultural hero Macéruwacash (Lone Man) first contemplated the question of identity when he witnessed the earth's emergence from a world covered in water, and the topic has resurfaced after every profound disruption to Mandan and Hidatsa lives brought on by colonization. From smallpox epidemics to forced removals and prophecy-fulfilling topographical changes to their homelands, its significance endures.[4]

As an artist who engages in what he calls "make-believe," Luger is in a unique position to address the question of cultural belonging: Who are we, where do we come from, and where are we going? He understands the question of identity as a collective one. Being Awa xee does not define him as an individual but, rather, speaks to who he is in the context of his community—locally and globally—and affirms how he may meaningfully contribute to that community. In a time when the art world and American society writ large are shining a renewed light on Native stories in very generalized terms, Luger's work challenges viewers to engage more deeply with the complexities of cultural identity by recognizing that it is not fixed. While some knowledge of stories, medicines, and ceremonies is proprietary, by virtue of operating in a contemporary context, Luger opens the door for a more global application of cultural lessons, especially in the face of ecological collapse. The work in *Dripping Earth* asks: What makes Mandan art Mandan? What makes Hidatsa art Hidatsa? Guided by this inquiry, Luger cites his application of clay as a natural extension of the labor of his lodge-building forebears, even if his work serves a purpose far removed from the essential human need for shelter. When Luger uses his hands to shape and transform wet earth, he is not just pursuing a creative outlet. He believes this work, as a manifestation of a responsibility to community, locates him on a continuum that connects ancestors past, present, and future. As such, he refuses to gaze longingly at the past. While the possibility of repair inspires Luger, nostalgia most certainly does not. Embracing his platform as an artist, he envisions how ancestral arts and ways of knowing and being might inform the next chapter for humanity.

Reorienting Indigenous identity around the land and bodies of water is a significant aspect of this endeavor. Luger frames this approach as a direct contrast to the colonial concept of land-as-territory, which fueled policies of forced displacement, led to the establishment of the reservation system, and continues to promote lateral oppression and erode tribal sovereignty today. He focuses on the connections among communities on the Missouri River, including the Umónhon people, on whose ancestral homelands the Joslyn Art Museum resides. "We're river people," he noted during a conversation with teachers and elders at the Umónhon Nation Public School.[5] In illuminating the

KARIN CAMPBELL AND ANNIKA K. JOHNSON

connection between people and the waterway that gives them life, *Dripping Earth* fosters solidarity among river communities that are navigating contemporary challenges of identity and belonging.

One such challenge stems from large-scale industrial interventions in the landscape. Situating audiences within the layered histories of the Missouri River Basin, Luger calls attention to the cultural and ecological consequences of these initiatives. In 2016, he launched the *Mirror Shield Project* in response to the construction of the multibillion-dollar subterranean Dakota Access Pipeline (DAPL), which carries millions of barrels of oil across the Upper Plains (fig. 6). DAPL starts in the Bakken Formation, where fracking taps reserves beneath the Fort Berthold Indian Reservation, his mother's homeland, and crosses Lake Oahe near the Standing Rock Reservation, his father's ancestral land. DAPL was originally routed to cross the Missouri River north of Bismarck, but the city objected, voicing concerns that its water supply could be contaminated. A successful lobbying campaign prompted DAPL's owner, Energy Transfer Partners, to relocate the pipeline downstream, just north of Standing Rock. The pipeline's environmental risks and disregard for ancestral burial sites drew water protectors from around the world to assemble the Oceti Sakowin (Seven Council Fires) encampment on the reservation. Conceived in solidarity with the protectors, *Mirror Shield Project* drew

Fig. 6 Action at Oceti Sakowin Camp, Standing Rock, North Dakota, November 18, 2016. Pictured: *Mirror Shield Project*, 2016–, social collaboration, video, sculpture, and land art performance, featuring shields made from wood, reflective Mylar, and paracord

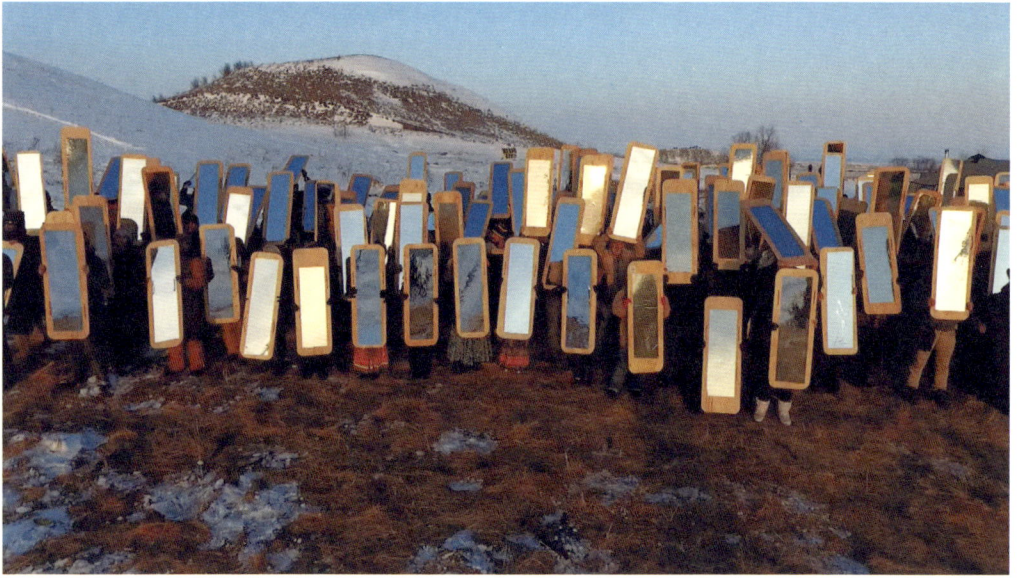

inspiration from images of 2014 protests in Ukraine, where demonstrators formed human barricades and held small mirrors, forcing approaching riot police to witness their own actions in real time. Luger designed body-length plywood shields with reflective surfaces and produced an instructional video that invited activists at Standing Rock and beyond to create their own protective gear. When used during protest actions, the shields reflected not only the pipeline's construction but also the landscape, the sun, and the gathered community of water protectors, offering both physical and symbolic protection. Referencing the customary use of mirrors in regalia to deflect spiritual harm, the shields became powerful tools of resistance.

Remarkable Landscapes

Perhaps nothing has impacted river communities more than the Pick-Sloan Missouri Basin Program, a mid-twentieth-century federal initiative that built a chain of reservoirs and dams from present-day Montana to South Dakota. Ironically referred to as "reclamation projects," these endeavors displaced Native communities in pursuit of stemming flooding and boosting hydroelectric power output. Today, energy from the dams serves several hundred thousand customers at a great cost. On the shores of Lake Sakakawea, a reservoir formed by the 1953 construction of the Garrison Dam, sits New Town, North Dakota, the headquarters of the Three Affiliated Tribes. As its name implies, New Town was established in anticipation of displacement. Garrison is one of the world's largest earthen dams, and like many US Army Corps of Engineers projects, it has had an outsize and lasting impact on Native populations. The dam fundamentally altered the Missouri River Basin, drowning entire villages, cultural sites, and the fertile river bottomlands where generations of Mandan, Hidatsa, and Arikara families grew corn, beans, squash, and sunflowers that fed the community and provided income. Approximately one-third of the Fort Berthold Reservation now lies underwater. The dam's creation fractured communities and challenged the extent of tribal sovereignty, forcing difficult choices between adaptation and resistance. In the early 1980s, Luger's grandfather Carl Whitman Jr. gave a lecture titled "The Past, Present and Futures of the Three Affiliated Tribes," accompanied by slides featuring images of the Garrison Dam, the reservoir,

KARIN CAMPBELL AND ANNIKA K. JOHNSON

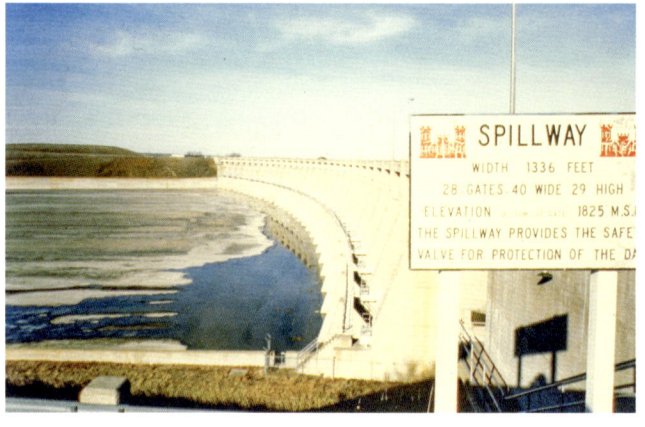

and communities around Fort Berthold. Luger discovered the lecture script, slide carousel, and related recordings in his family's archive and saw the opportunity to re-present the material in a new work titled *A/V Presentation: Past, Present + Future of FB Res* (fig. 7 and pp. 86–87, 90–91). Named after a cassette tape label handwritten by his grandfather, the work pairs audio with photographs projected onto the surface of a tipi cover in a powerful assertion of the dam's ongoing impacts.

Tipis are ingenious technologies that allow for mobility and resilience. Customarily crafted from tanned buffalo hides stretched over lodgepoles, these portable, easy-to-assemble dwellings reflect a deep understanding of plains and prairie environments. Following the Great Plains bison massacre of the nineteenth century, Native communities adapted by using industrially produced canvas, which remains a typical tipi cover today. Luger nods to this legacy when he employs canvas tipi covers as substrates for his abstract paintings. Life-size works like *Kill Time* hearken to the monumental scale that became popular in painting following the Second World War (fig. 8). Luger also disrupts prevailing understandings of the tipi by deploying unexpected materials that do not have a relationship to the structure's history. In 2024, visitors to *Even Better Than the Real Thing*, the eighty-first Whitney Biennial at the Whitney Museum of American Art, in New York, encountered a massive tipi made from sheer magenta crinoline that Luger inverted and suspended from the gallery ceiling. *Uŋziwoslal Wašičuta*, titled after a Lakota language phrase meaning "the fat-taker's world is upside down," challenges the assumed perspective of the viewer: The installation is not upside down—our world is (fig. 9). *Wašiču*, a name for colonizers, more broadly encapsulates the consumerist, individualist mindset that Luger upends in his vision of a postcolonial and postcapitalist future.

Dripping Earth continues Luger's ongoing *Transportable Intergenerational Protection Infrastructure (TIPI)* series, introducing *Remnant* (2022), which uses light to transform a tipi cover into a space for processing the past and imagining the future.[6] Whitman's slides flicker on a tipi cover made from repurposed ripstop—a durable, woven material commonly used in modern camping tents, athletic gear, sails, and hot-air balloons—unfurled from its traditional conical shape and flattened into a semicircle. Like memories of lived experiences, the flashing snapshots illustrate the resilience of those who, once again, survived catastrophe. Angela K. Parker's history of the Garrison Dam preserves the devastating testimony of elders who faced the impending flood: "Tribal members found unfathomable not only the loss of the physical soil but also the loss of landmarks and places that indexed crucial cultural and community histories. This shared history—and, in the case of cemeteries, literally interred in the landscape—structured their tribal and

Fig. 8 *Kill Time*, 2022, acrylic on canvas and mixed media, Tia Collection

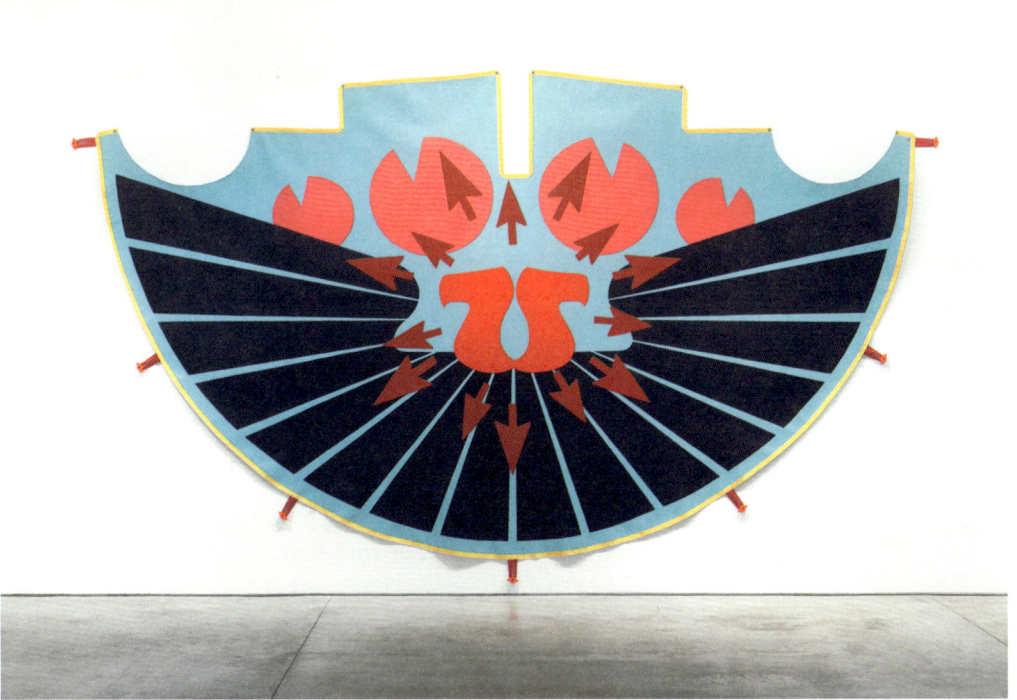

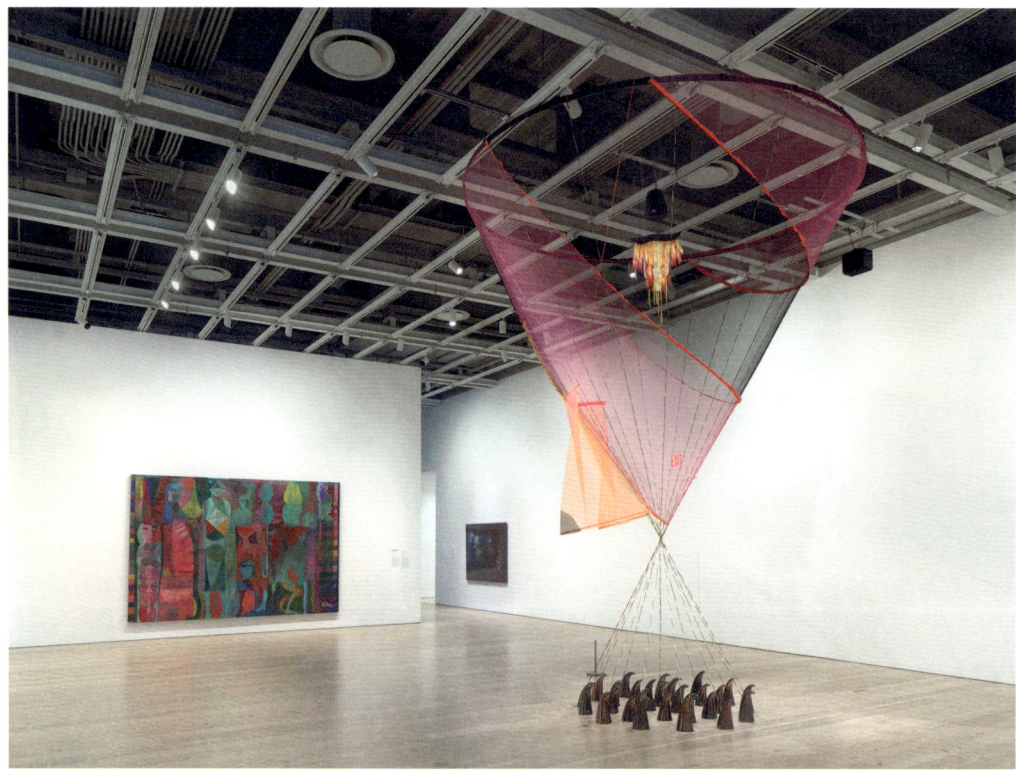

Fig. 9 Installation view of Whitney Biennial 2024: *Even Better Than the Real Thing*, Whitney Museum of American Art, New York, March 20–August 11, 2024. Pictured, from left: Maja Ruznic, *The Past Awaiting the Future/Arrival of Drummers*, 2023; Dora Budor, *Dominoes*, 2023; Cannupa Hanska Luger, *Uŋziwoslal Wašičuta*, 2021, from the ongoing series *Future Ancestral Technologies*, 2018–

community identities, and how they defined themselves as human beings."[7] The upheaval of the lands that contained this history compounded generations of trauma, further eroding cultural continuity. In her short essay in this catalogue, "Living Landscapes," MHA Nation citizen Alisha Deegan reflects on the enduring blood ties to these lands—an embodied sense of connection that has persisted through many changes.

The images of the Upper Missouri that Bodmer created during his travels with Prince Maximilian hold value as early visual records of places now submerged under reservoirs. Sketches of fantastical geological outcroppings near the present-day Fort Belknap, Fort Peck, and Fort Berthold Reservations are particularly meaningful to Luger (fig. 10). Bodmer compiled vignettes of landforms silhouetted against a white sky into two hand-colored aquatints titled *Remarkable Hills on the Upper Missouri* (figs. 11, 12). Published to accompany Maximilian's journal, *Travels in the Interior of North America*, Bodmer's prints gave visual form to the so-called American West in the European collective imagination. Reflecting on what is now the Upper Missouri

Fig. 10 Karl Bodmer, *Rock Formations on the Upper Missouri*, 1833, watercolor and graphite on paper, Joslyn Art Museum, Omaha, Nebraska, Gift of the Enron Art Foundation, 1986.49.190

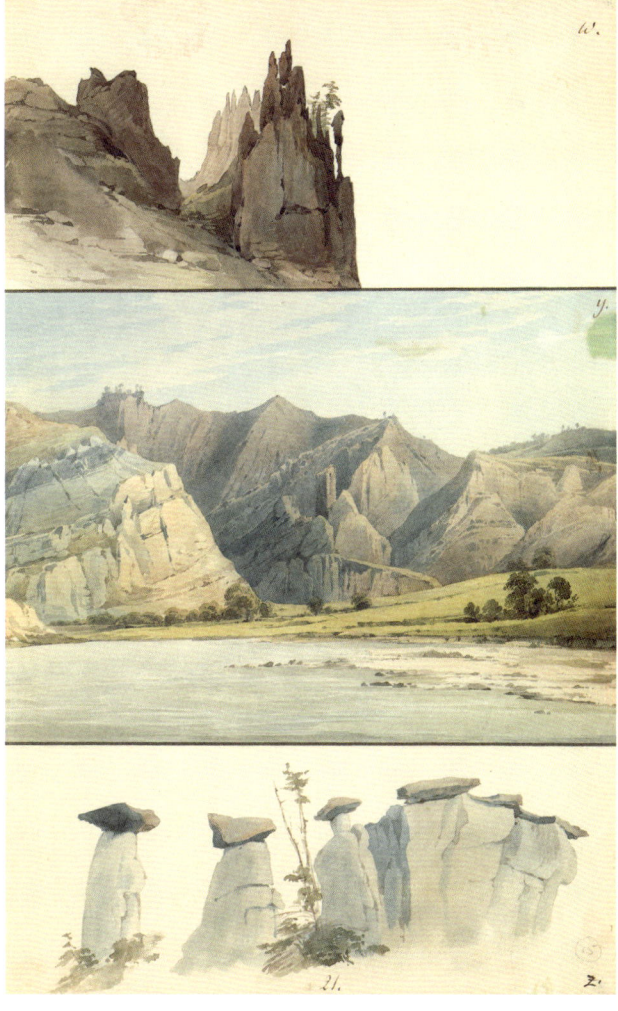

River Breaks National Monument in north-central Montana, Maximilian wrote:

> *We once more admired the white fortresses, turrets, old castles, churches, and rock pillars, to which we now had to bid farewell forever. Like a dream, these marvelous figures streak past the eyes of the astonished traveler, and only through direct sketches of the most striking ones do these later still survive in [our] rewarding recollection of this remote, forgotten, marvelous world of nature. Only individual trappers, beaver hunters, and the boats of the Fur Company observe these wonders of nature.*[8]

KARIN CAMPBELL AND ANNIKA K. JOHNSON

Fig. 11 Friedrich Salathé, after Karl Bodmer, *Remarkable Hills on the Upper Missouri*, 1839, hand-colored aquatint, Joslyn Art Museum, Omaha, Nebraska, Gift of the Enron Art Foundation, 1986.49.542.34

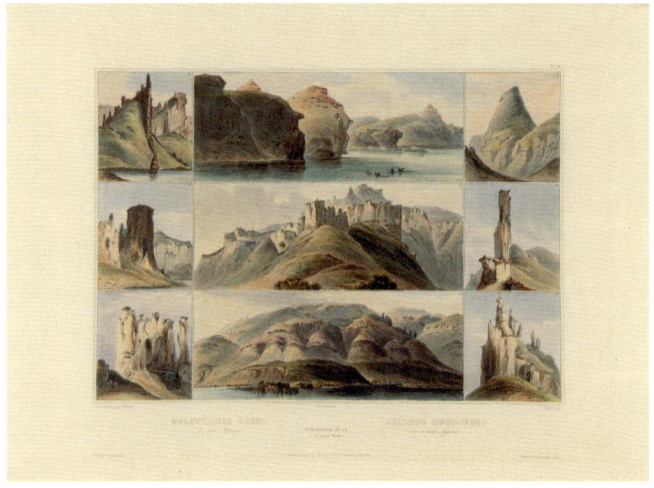

Fig. 12 Friedrich Salathé, after Karl Bodmer, *Remarkable Hills on the Upper Missouri*, 1837–43, hand-colored aquatint, Joslyn Art Museum, Omaha, Nebraska, Gift of the Enron Art Foundation, 1986.49.517.35

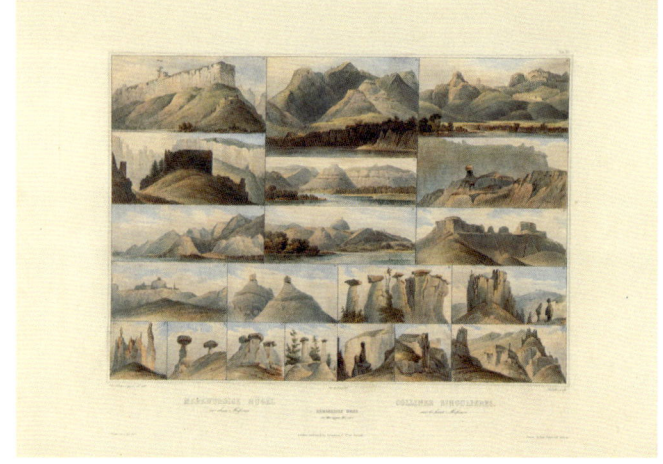

Indigenous lands are inseparable from the stories they hold. Lacking knowledge of those stories, Maximilian and Bodmer composed parallels, comparing the colorful buttes and sandstone shields to European castles and churches. For Luger, the geological formations do not resemble monoliths of the built environment. Rather, the land came first, and it carries generations of stories, making it a repository of cultural memory.

Future Ancestral Technologies

At the center of Luger's practice lies *Future Ancestral Technologies*, an ongoing project spanning sculpture, print-making, video, and performance. As its name suggests, the project embraces a speculative approach to storytelling by engaging the customary arts and practices of his ancestors to envision futures rooted in Indigenous knowledge. Luger draws inspiration from his ancestral connection to the Missouri River, particularly through technologies that exemplify lifeways tied to water. One such technology is the bullboat, a circular, personal watercraft made from a single buffalo hide stretched over woven willow branches, steered with a paddle with a hole carved into its center. These versatile vessels were used to take short trips between villages. During his visit to The Joslyn, Luger pored over Bodmer's intricate sketches of bullboats, admiring the ingenuity of his ancestors, who crafted the boats from everyday materials (fig. 13). Just as bullboats once facilitated the movement of people along waterways, Bodmer's drawings of them transport Luger into the world of his ancestors, becoming "sources of [his] imagining."[9]

With *Máadiraxbi I* and *II*, Luger reimagines life-size bullboats using willow branches he sourced in present-day North Dakota, emphasizing the delicate yet sturdy architecture of their frames (pp. 98–99). Luger deconstructs the vessels, replacing their customary coverings with afghan blankets mounted on the wall in the shape of bison hides. The exposed tracery of the bullboats highlights the inventiveness of ancestral engineers, while their skeletal appearance serves to embody cultural loss. Suspended overhead, the bullboats immerse viewers in an underwater landscape that is at once historical and imaginary.

Future Ancestral Technologies explores the role of imagination in shaping cultural narratives. As part of this process, Luger reflects on the assumed authority of historical

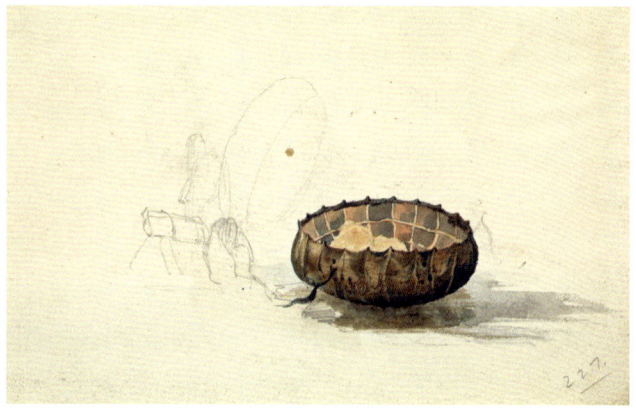

Fig. 13 Karl Bodmer, *Bullboats and Figures*, c. 1833, watercolor and graphite on paper, Joslyn Art Museum, Omaha, Nebraska, Gift of the Enron Art Foundation, 1986.49.365

KARIN CAMPBELL AND ANNIKA K. JOHNSON

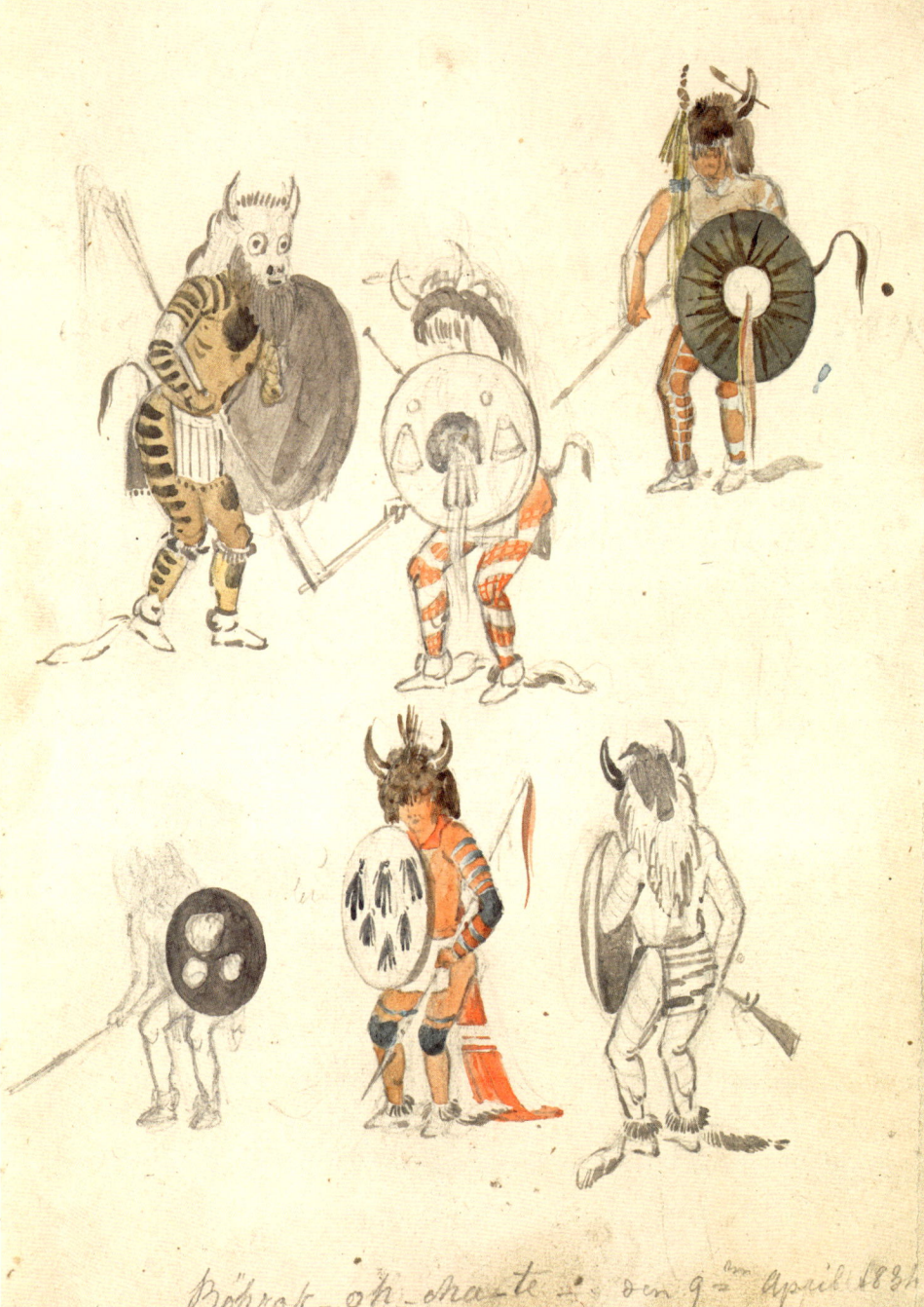

Böhrok-oh-charte den 9ᵗᵐ April 1834
Fort Mandan

Fig. 14 Karl Bodmer, *Men of the Mandan Buffalo Bull Society*, 1834, watercolor and graphite on paper, Joslyn Art Museum, Omaha, Nebraska, Gift of the Enron Art Foundation, 1986.49.265.a

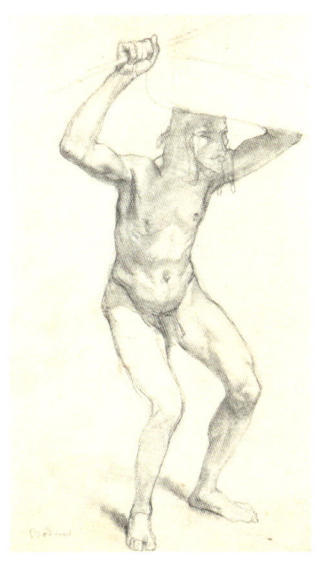

Fig. 15 Karl Bodmer, *Man and Shield (Sketch for "Bison Dance of the Mandan Indians")*, c. 1832–41, graphite on paper, Joslyn Art Museum, Omaha, Nebraska, Museum purchase with funds from Susan and Michael Lebens, Anne and John Nelson, Annette and Paul Smith, and the General Art Endowment Fund in honor of Rhonda and Howard Hawks, 2021.5.4

images produced by cultural outsiders and critically engages with Bodmer's legacy. Bodmer never intended to share his sketches and outdoor studies with the public. In *Men of the Mandan Buffalo Bull Society*, created during the Buffalo Bull Society dance in the spring of 1834, he focused on society members' shields and dance steps—or, more specifically, his impressions of these aspects of the ceremony as it unfolded (fig. 14). Upon his return to Paris, Bodmer synthesized his observational drawings, supplemented with figure studies of French models, to produce the print *Bison Dance of the Mandan Indians* (1842), a dynamic, multifigure tableau that resonates with the tenets of the European Romantic movement of his time (figs. 15, 16). This print circulated among wealthy Europeans, accruing cultural import as one of the first images of America's Northern Plains. Luger's interest lies in *Bison Dance*'s visual legacy, which spans historical and cultural applications, from museum dioramas and Buffalo Bill's sham battles to Disney's 1953 animated film *Peter Pan*. In the song "What Makes a Red Man Red?," Wendy and the Lost Boys whoop and dance around a fire with a cast of Indian caricatures, projecting large shadows on a backdrop of tipis. Noting the pervasiveness of these popular images, Luger acknowledges that they even inform his own perception of Native identity.

Luger's *Midéegaadi* ("bison" or "buffalo" in Hidatsa) are so vibrant and spirited as to transcend the weight of historical trauma (pp. 66–79). With this body of work, which he initiated in 2021, the artist reimagines the regalia's form and materials to evoke the bison dance, yet cleverly shifts away from a strictly ceremonial context. To create these elaborate works, Luger replaces buffalo hides and horns with repurposed afghan blankets, jingle bells, hockey gloves, and industrial-grade felt. The afghans, with their loud, unexpected colors and intricately crocheted "granny square" and chevron patterns, are original compositions that showcase the artistic play of their makers (fig. 17). Luger sources them from estate sales and thrift stores, drawn to these quintessential icons of Americana. By incorporating the textiles into *Midéegaadi* regalia, Luger honors the practicality and warmth that buffalo hides once offered, while forging a connection between the hands that lovingly crocheted the blankets and their emerging role in shaping future narratives.

While Luger's chosen materials may be familiar, their reassembly creates an otherworldly effect, embodying the

KARIN CAMPBELL AND ANNIKA K. JOHNSON

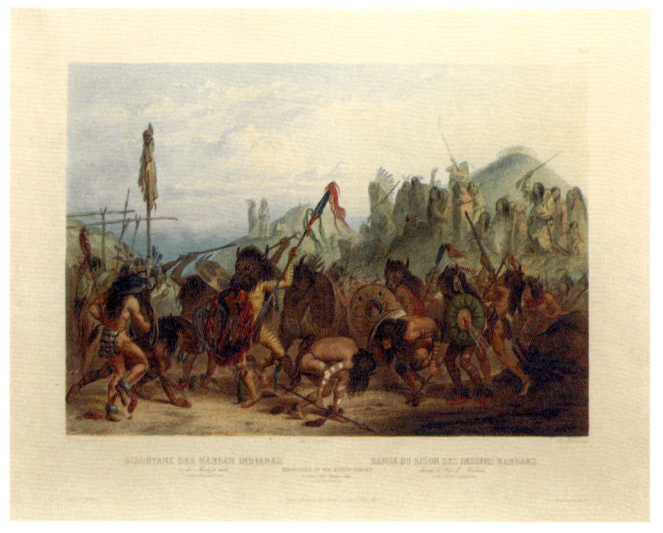

Fig. 16 Alexandre Damien Manceau, after Karl Bodmer, *Bison Dance of the Mandan Indians in front of their Medicine Lodge in Mih-Tutta-Hankush*, 1842, hand-colored aquatint, Joslyn Art Museum, Omaha, Nebraska, Gift of the Enron Art Foundation, 1986.49.542.18

artist's concept of a "new myth" (fig. 18). For Luger, myths are more than fairy tales; they provide a means to reckon with the past—including the violence enacted against bison and the people who relied on them for survival—and chart a new path in which society "once again lives in reverence and respect for more than human kinships."[10] As stand-alone art objects, the *Midéegaadi* are visually captivating and fantastical, but they are not static. Designed specifically for Luger's body, they take on an active presence when he wears them in photographs and videos, breathing life into both the materials and the traditions they reference. In *Dripping Earth*, the mannequins strike what Luger calls "editorial poses," intentionally contrasting with the static portrayals of Native people in historical images, including Bodmer's watercolors.

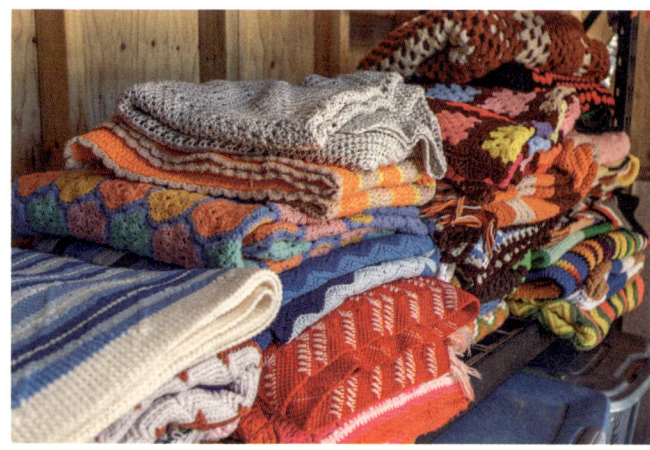

Fig. 17 Luger's collection of afghan blankets in his studio, 2025

While these historical representations often aimed for accuracy, in retrospect, they resemble the dioramas found in later ethnological museums—fixing their subjects in a single moment and adding a layer of remove from their vitality and cultural significance.

Luger challenges these images and museum display conventions, critiquing their limitations while finding pathways to restore Native people's ability to tell their own stories and activate their histories. Staging the *Midéegaadi* figures in deliberate, dynamic poses, Luger wrests back power and challenges the tendency to present Native people as cultural relics. The dressed mannequins appear against an immersive projection of *... We Are Its People ...* (2025), featuring drone footage of the Missouri River landscape, a region of great natural beauty blotted with fracking rigs, power lines, highways, and reservoirs. This layered presentation collapses timelines, grafting Luger's aspirations for the future onto the realities of a disrupted present.

One way in which Luger has activated the *Midéegaadi* is by filming himself dancing in the regalia against a green screen, allowing the landscapes in the background to shift and adapt (fig. 19). Luger frames this as an act of reclamation, emphasizing that Mandan and Hidatsa land is defined

Fig. 18 Still from *New Myth*, 2021, from the ongoing series *Future Ancestral Technologies*, 2018–, single-channel video with sound

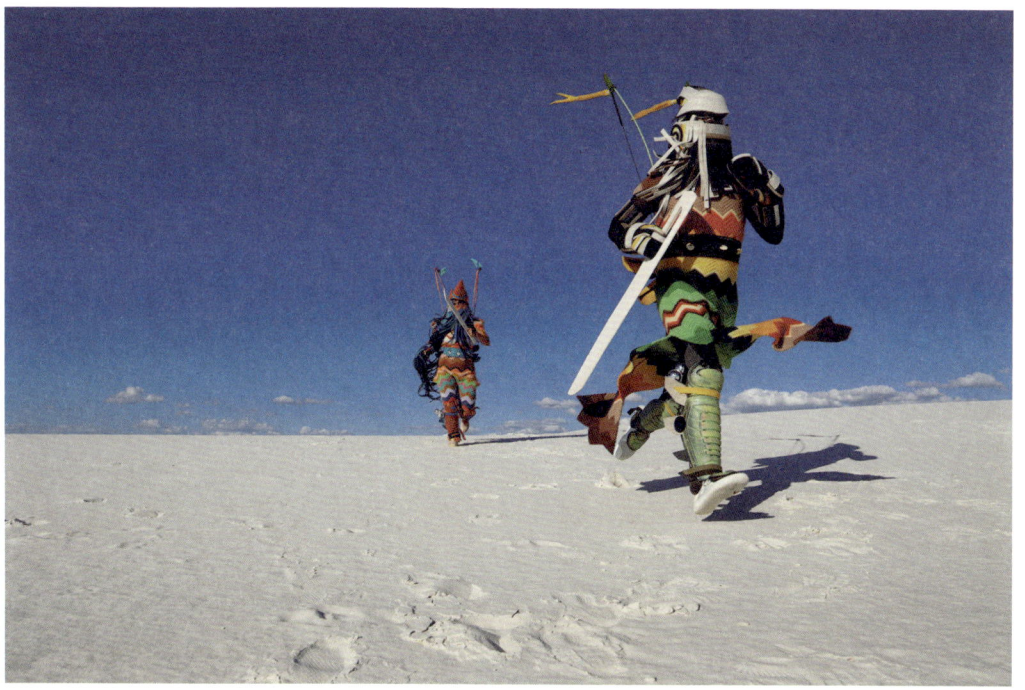

KARIN CAMPBELL AND ANNIKA K. JOHNSON

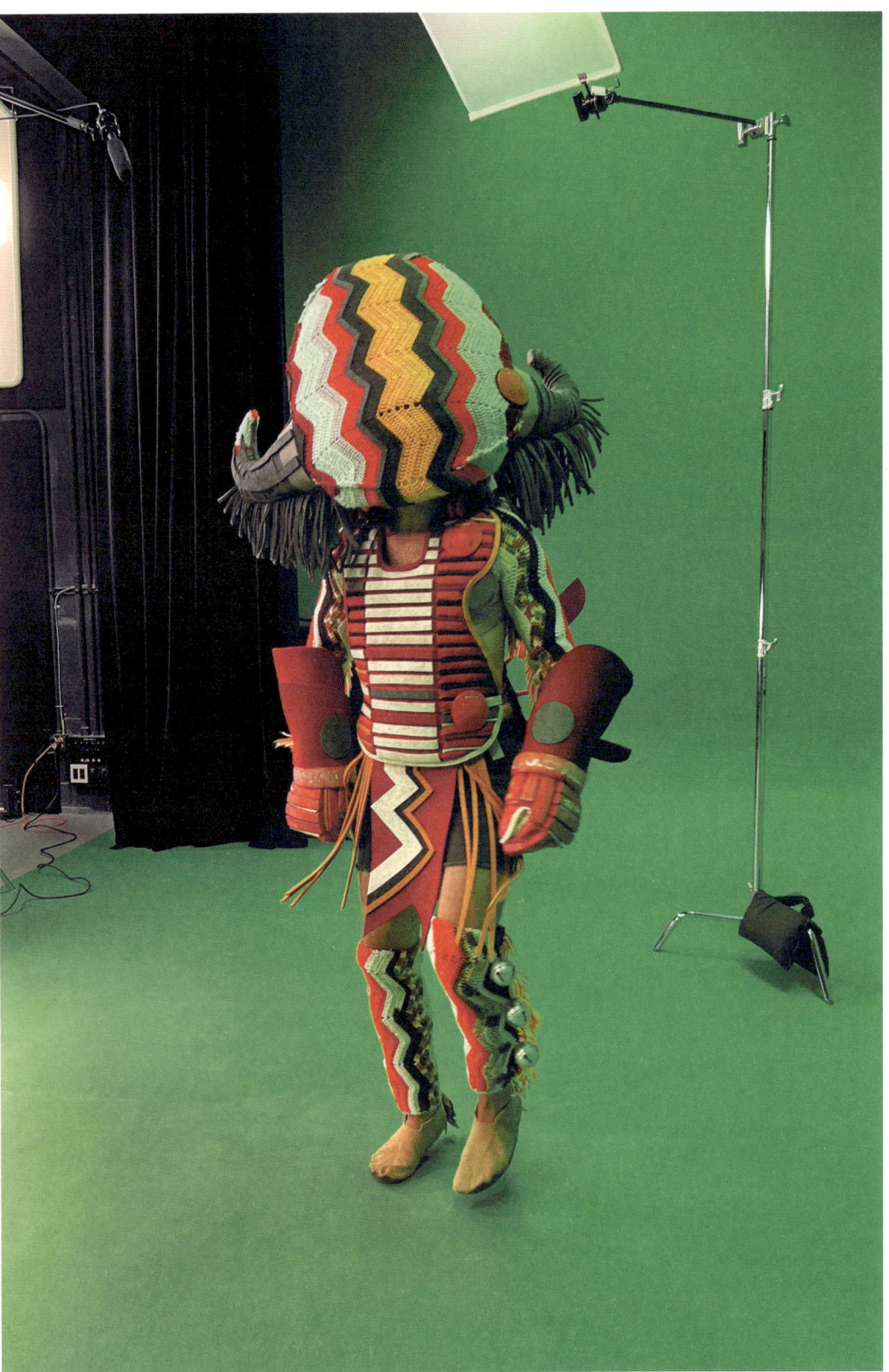

Fig. 19 Luger filming with green screen for *Midéegaadi* video series, 2022

not by imposed borders but by where its people and stories thrive. This exploration continues in a new series of lithographs that reflect on the landscape as it once was and how Luger's futuristic avatars might traverse it. Collaborating with the Santa Fe–based printmaker Mitchell Marti, Luger created dreamlike lithographs that superimpose the *Midéegaadi* over Bodmer's renderings of landscapes now submerged beneath reservoirs (pp. 104–17). Each print places one of seven *Midéegaadi* figures in the extreme foreground, casting the dancer as a superhero figure who commands the viewer's attention. Moving fluidly across media, Luger amplifies presences that have been erased by colonizer narratives and crystallizes the relationship between a place now called America and the people who have always made it home. Curator and art historian Josie Lopez provides further insights into this print portfolio later in this catalogue, highlighting how Luger repurposes a medium shaped by colonial history as a means of resistance.

Monumentality

Luger invites customary Mandan and Hidatsa storytelling into his work, particularly the teachings of the culture hero Coyote Chief, which impart warnings about the consequences of human folly. The artist says, "I've been thinking a lot about how we need to rebuild these stories because there's new things, new ways that we've screwed up. How do we add to the lineage and history of Coyote tales?"[11] By embedding such narratives in his work, Luger enlists art to rebuild and renew stories that address contemporary environmental challenges. This approach underpins much of his practice, in which play and critique are essential tools. In *Dripping Earth*, Luger explores these ideas with *A Nation*, a monumental *Midéegaadi* sculpture that the artist informally calls "the giant" (pp. 82–83). Measuring sixteen feet tall, *A Nation* dwarfs viewers and seems almost too large for a museum to contain. Featuring a ceramic face, feet, and hands that call back to the thirteen vessels in *Irabágu*, the giant lounges atop a base reminiscent of a classical column, apparently unconcerned that its likeness is being consumed by strangers. In The Joslyn's installation, it faces the ripstop tipi, *Remnant*, on which mid-twentieth-century images of the Garrison Dam and Fort Berthold scroll past.

KARIN CAMPBELL AND ANNIKA K. JOHNSON

Luger's contemplation of physical monumentality, particularly within an American context, evokes a well-known colossus: the Lincoln Memorial, in Washington, DC. Dedicated in 1922, the memorial features a grand temple modeled after the Parthenon, in Athens. Thirty-six fluted Doric columns, one for each state in the Union at the time of Abraham Lincoln's death, stand at the perimeter of the structure, at the center of which a towering statue of the sixteenth president sits on a tiered marble base. His head tilts down slightly, his gaze resting on those who stand before him, indicating that he is alert even though he is at rest. Luger finds it striking that a figure in a relaxed, seated position can command such reverence. *A Nation*'s undeniable presence also conveys power, but does so through a confident pose and nonchalant demeanor. The tension between the giant's grandeur and irreverence evokes the presence of a cultural hero steeped in generations of storytelling. If the power of the Lincoln Memorial derives in part from the statue's acknowledgment of the people who have come to behold him, the power of Luger's giant resides in its casual indifference and refusal to acknowledge being seen.

In another monumental endeavor, initiated in 2022, Luger harnesses the power of scale to collectively comprehend the loss of tens of millions of plains bison that once roamed North America. These majestic animals, also commonly called buffalo, made life possible on the Great Plains. In providing food, shelter, and tools, bison served as sources of spiritual and physical sustenance. Euro-American settlers systematically culled bison to near extinction in the late 1800s. The federal government reversed course in the early twentieth century with conservation efforts, and today, the US Fish and Wildlife Service manages approximately twenty thousand plains bison as a public resource. Luger's collaborative *Bison Bead Project* gives physical form to current bison statistics, which hold little practical meaning for most Americans. Through community workshops, the artist invites people to make small beads from one-inch blocks of earthenware clay in contribution toward the goal of amassing twenty thousand individual beads, one for each federally managed bison (fig. 20 and pp. 118, 122–25). Over the months that *Dripping Earth* is open to the public, new beads will be added to an abacus-like steel structure in the shape of a buffalo, resulting in a living sculpture that tracks bison data.

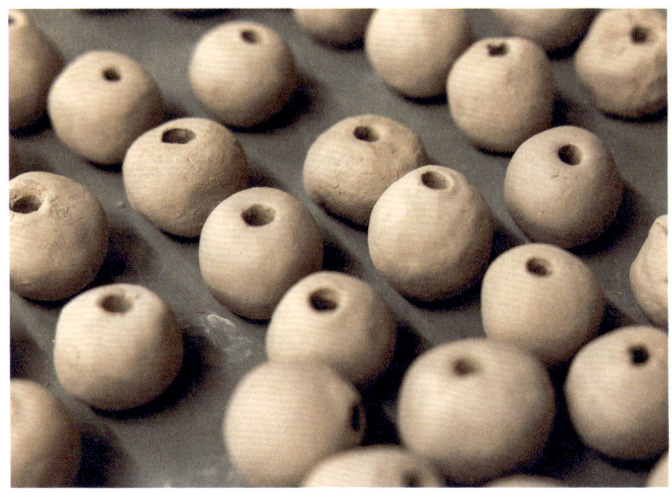

Fig. 20 *Bison Bead Project* workshop held at the Joslyn Art Museum, Omaha, Nebraska, February 6, 2025

Luger recognizes that plains bison herds will never return to their presettlement numbers; waning genetic diversity appears to be irreversible, and much of their natural habitat has been lost to human development. With the bead project, he aims to elevate and reanimate the buffalo in the American imagination. Beadmaking is a contemplative activity, one Luger compares to repetitive prayer rituals associated with many global faith-based practices, such as reciting the rosary in Catholicism. Just as the act of prayer is intended to make manifest expressions of faith and gratitude, crafting beads is an embodied way of making sense of loss and resilience. For Luger, the act of creating beads is as significant as the knowledge project participants might gain about buffalo in the process of rolling clay between their hands. He refers to beadmaking as a "record of effort" and lauds collaborators' willingness to contribute their life force to the story of the bison. In this catalogue, Sičaŋǧu Lakota culture bearer Steve Tamayo shares a Lakota creation story that contextualizes the *Bison Bead Project* within longstanding oral traditions.

The *Bison Bead Project* and all the varied forms of *Midéegaadi* harness one of the earliest functions of the bison dancer: to call the bison forward. Luger's practice is not limited to one gender role or identity, and he does not advocate for a strict traditionalist reading of ceremonial protocols and specialized knowledge. Instead, his work poses the idea that cultural revitalization is a matter of asking how people gained cultural knowledge in the first place. Relational living,

KARIN CAMPBELL AND ANNIKA K. JOHNSON

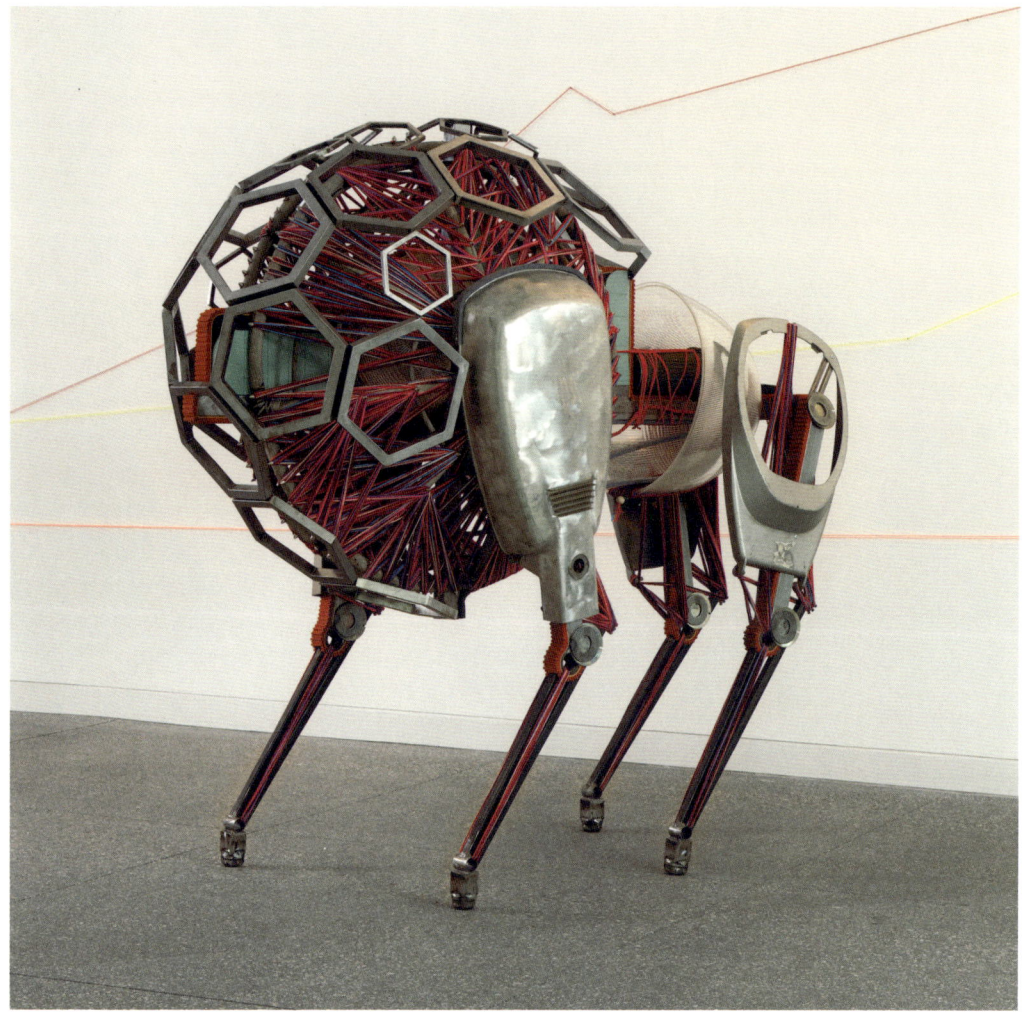

Fig. 21 Installation view of *Breath(e): Toward Climate and Social Justice*, Hammer Museum, Los Angeles, September 14, 2024–January 5, 2025. Pictured: *Red Rover*, included in the large-scale installation *Sovereign*, 2024, from the ongoing series *Future Ancestral Technologies*, 2018–, ceramic, steel, glass, fiber, detritus, three-channel video projection, and sound installation

the current needs of the community, and visions for the future will guide the customs needed to address the challenges of our era.

Continuum

According to Luger, "*Future Ancestral Technologies* is Indigenous science fiction—a methodology, a practice, a way of future dreaming rooted in continuum."[12] The artist recently began replacing the word "history" with "continuum" when discussing his art. This is more than mere semantic slippage. Perhaps the most well-known application of the notion of continuum is Albert Einstein's space-time theory, introduced to Western science in 1915. A polymath who draws from diverse disciplines in his work, Luger leverages the broad acceptance of this concept to amplify a much older understanding of our relationship to time and disrupt settler-colonial frameworks. Luger's embrace of ancestral storytelling in his practice activates a deep and enduring relationship between land, time, and existence. Deploying the concept of continuum allows Luger's "make-believe" to blur the boundaries that separate reality and fantasy, artist and audience, and past, present, and future (fig. 21). The films, regalia, and sculptures included in *Dripping Earth* are part of ongoing series that have no beginning or end. These works may read as artifacts by virtue of their presentation in a museum, yet they also document the artist's lived experiences in a world of his own making.

Luger asserts that the museum is not the subject of his work. Rather, he conceives of museums as stages for otherworldly encounters, giving visitors permission to suspend their disbelief and urging them to consider how they are connected to the stories he references. Luger explains, "My work is a radical and speculative way to interact with white interpretations of my culture."[13] Museum displays have long distorted scale and time, often presenting Native people as if they existed only in a distant past. Luger upends museums' proclivities for containment—literally, placing objects and the histories they hold in display cases—and tidy, linear narratives. In *Dripping Earth*, viewers enter a future in which they lose the power associated with colonial retrospect and instead are cast as ghosts witnessing the emphatic survival, resistance, and presence—a concept known as "survivance"— of Indigenous people.[14] Not every aspect of Indigenous knowledge in Luger's work is meant for audiences to understand or claim as their own. Yet the artist invites those engaging with his work to take their experiences beyond the museum—to pursue a future where land, identity, and culture are reclaimed and transformed.

KARIN CAMPBELL AND ANNIKA K. JOHNSON

1. These works, along with the prince's three handwritten travel journals and extensive archive, survived two transatlantic journeys and two world wars before arriving at The Joslyn in 1961. Since its founding in 1980, the Museum's Margre H. Durham Center for Western Studies has housed the collection and fostered ongoing research efforts. Scholars, knowledge bearers, and, more recently, artists continue to find new and relevant ways to interpret the collection.

2. Prince Alexander Philipp Maximilian of Wied, *The North American Journals of Prince Maximilian of Wied*, vol. 3, *September 1833–August 1834*, ed. Stephen S. Witte and Marsha V. Gallagher, trans. Dieter Karch (Norman: University of Oklahoma Press, 2012), 166.

3. Cannupa Hanska Luger, conversation with the authors, June 26, 2024.

4. Annika K. Johnson, "Bringing the Story Back: An Interview with Gerard Baker, Part I: The Earth Lodge," in *Faces from the Interior: The North American Portraits of Karl Bodmer*, ed. Toby Jurovics (Omaha, NE: Joslyn Art Museum, 2021), 98–100.

5. The conversation, for which the authors and other Joslyn staff were also in attendance, took place at the Umóⁿhoⁿ Nation Public School, Macy, NE, on January 26, 2024.

6. Cannupa Hanska Luger, "Uŋziwoslal Wašičuta: Transportable Intergenerational Protection Infrastructure (TIPI)," Future Ancestral Technologies, accessed January 1, 2025, https://www.cannupahanska.com/fat/tipi-1.

7. Angela K. Parker, *Damming the Reservation: Tribal Sovereignty and Activism at Fort Berthold* (Norman: University of Oklahoma Press, 2024), 133.

8. Prince Alexander Philipp Maximilian of Wied, *The North American Journals of Prince Maximilian of Wied*, vol. 2, *April–September 1833*, ed. Stephen S. Witte and Marsha V. Gallagher, trans. William J. Orr et al. (Norman: University of Oklahoma Press, 2010), 452.

9. Cannupa Hanska Luger, conversation with the authors, July 31, 2024.

10. Cannupa Hanska Luger, "Midéegaadi," Future Ancestral Technologies, accessed January 1, 2025, https://www.cannupahanska.com/fat/midegaadi.

11. See "Awa xee: Cannupa Hanska Luger and Michael Barthelemy Jr. in Conversation," in this catalogue, 134.

12. Cannupa Hanska Luger, "Future Ancestral Technologies Ethos," Future Ancestral Technologies, accessed January 1, 2025, https://www.cannupahanska.com/fat/ethos.

13. Luger, conversation with the authors, July 31, 2024.

14. See Gerald Vizenor, *Manifest Manners: Narratives on Postindian Survivance* (Hanover, NH: University Press of New England, 1994).

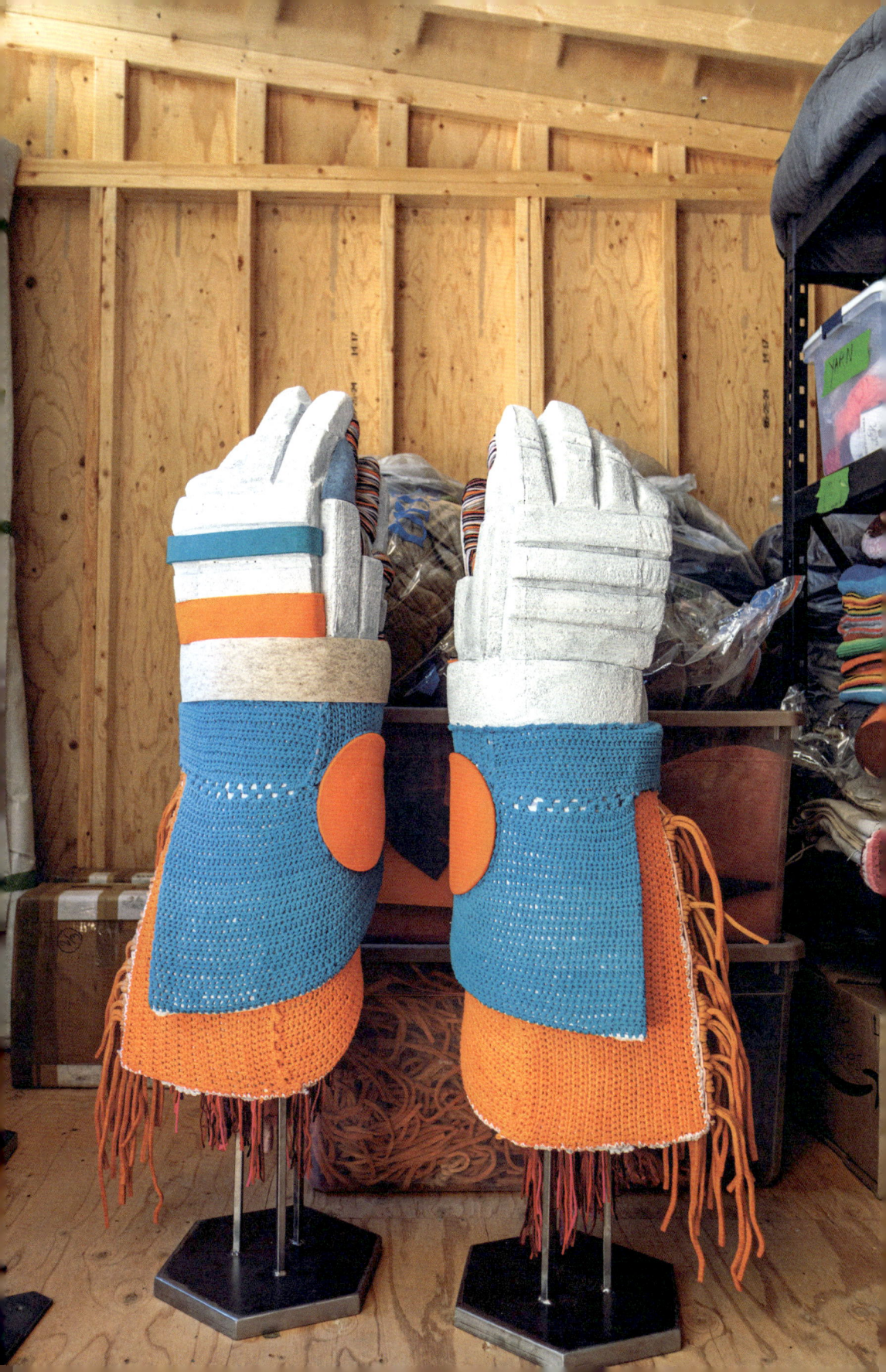

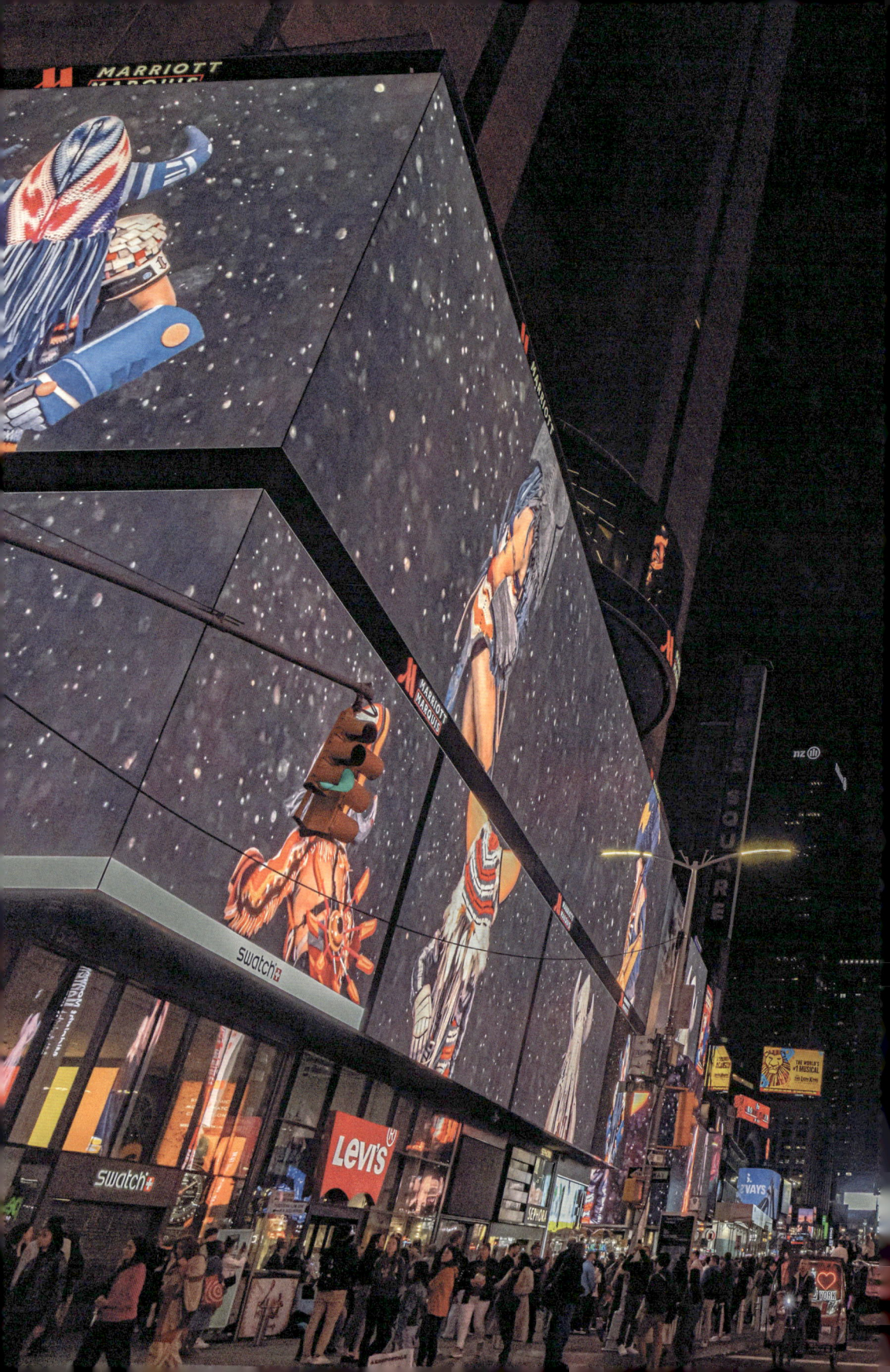

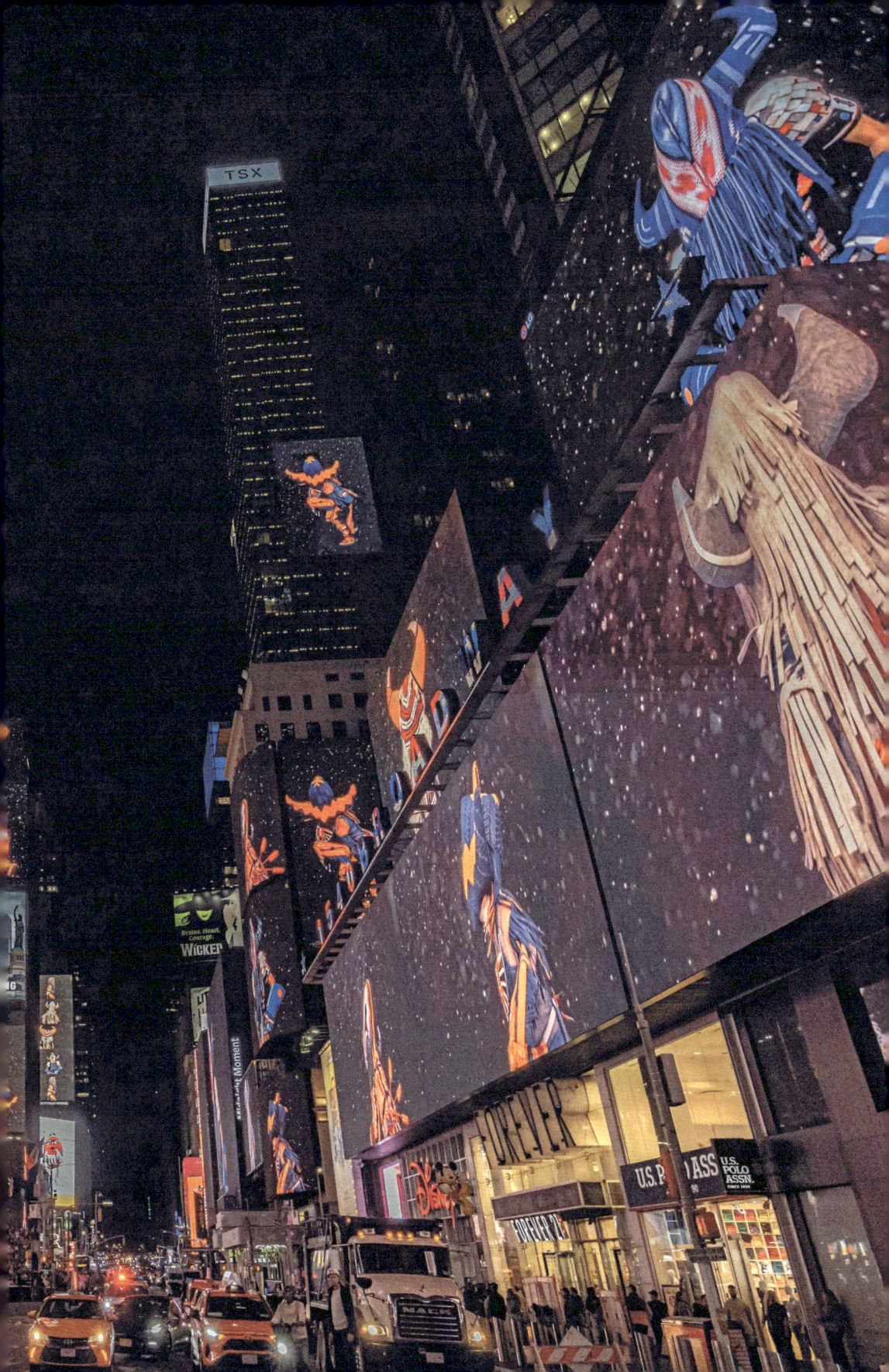

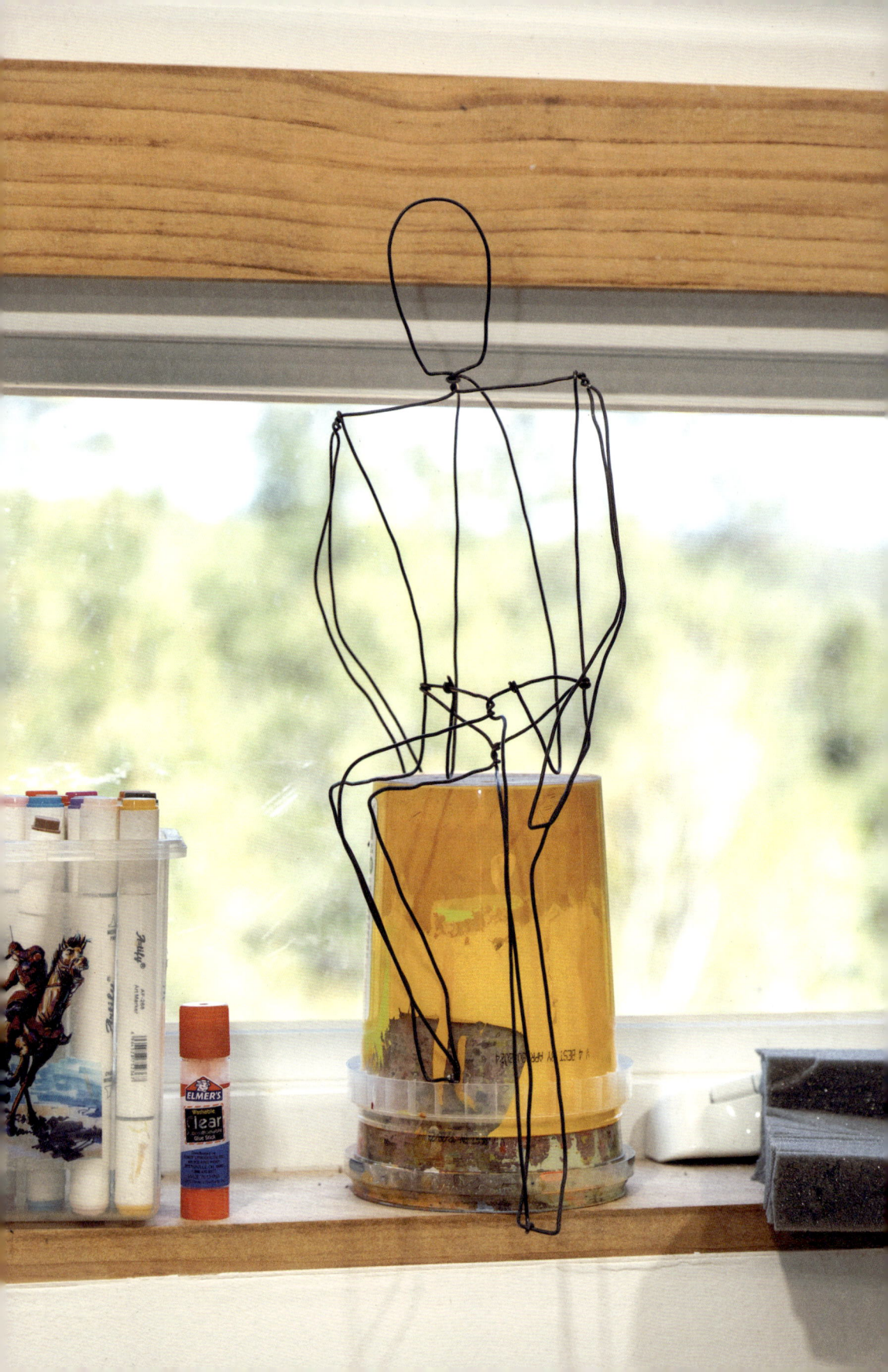

Studio Notes

Cannupa Hanska Luger

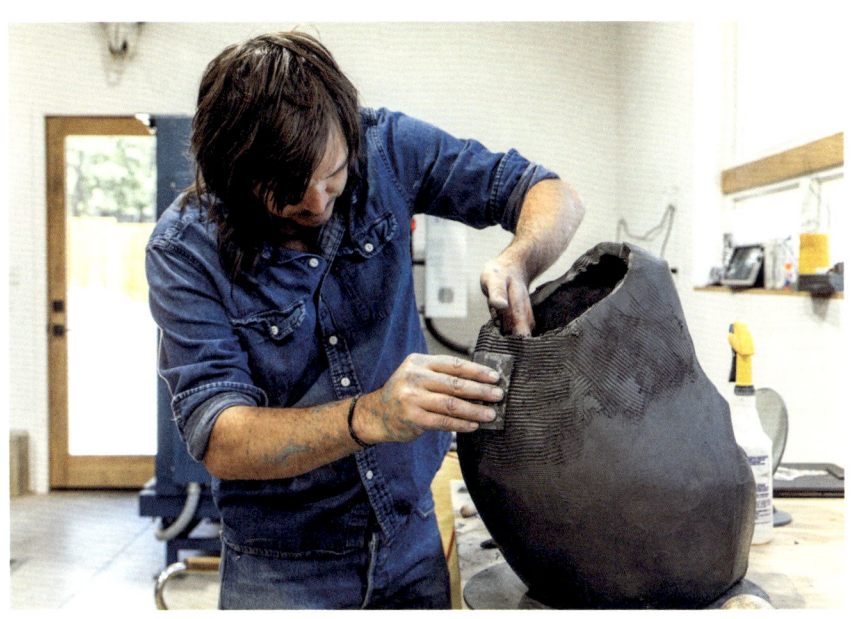

Acknowledging and recognizing the
components of Mandan life in the
1830s informed what materials
I was interested in using for
this exhibition.

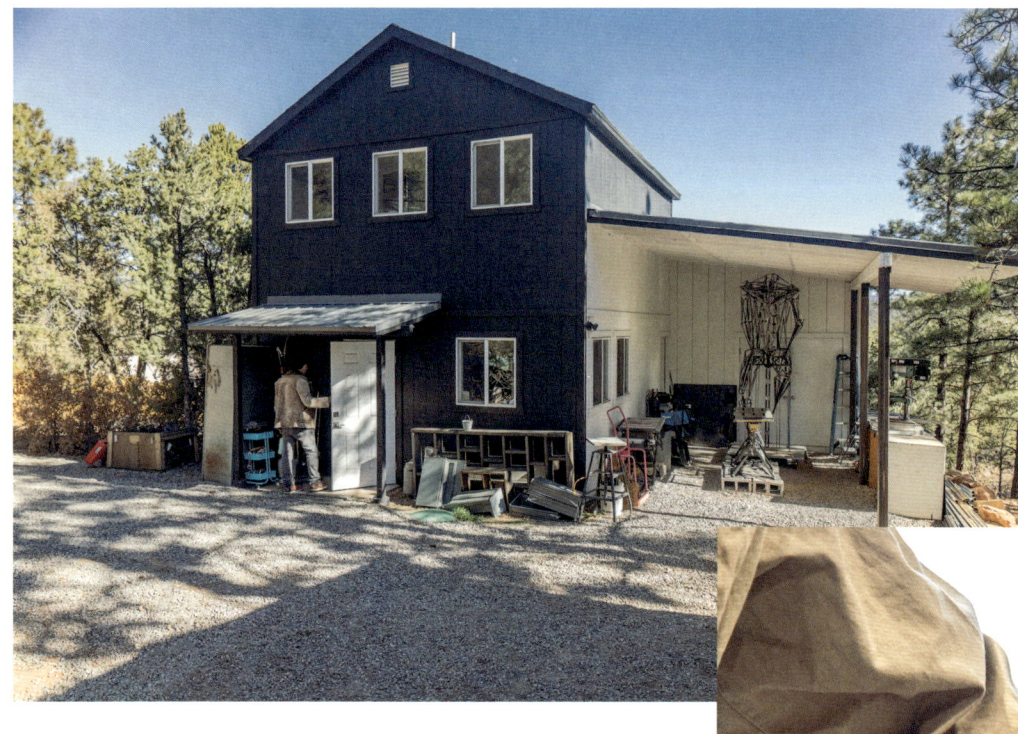

Land is always significant. The river is always significant. But so are ceramic vessels, regalia, colorways, and customary cultural practices. All of these things were documented by Karl Bodmer. They were also a part of my knowing, just growing up as a Mandan person.

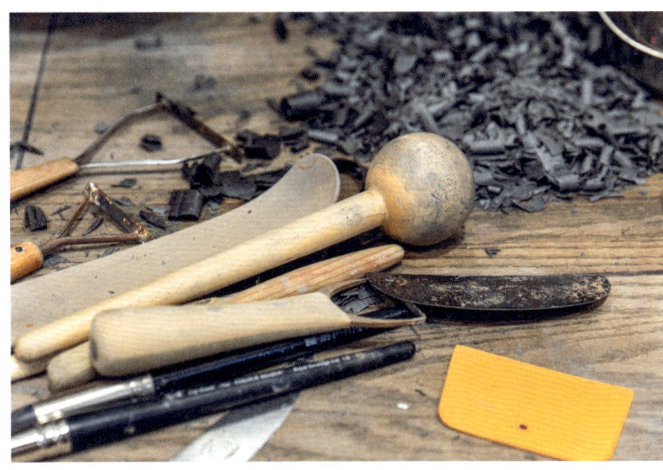

The clay techniques I use are based on our customary practices, including slab and anvil techniques. I build vessels the way that I would build them. And that's exactly how Mandan pottery would exist in the present. Does exist— is existing—because I'm doing it.

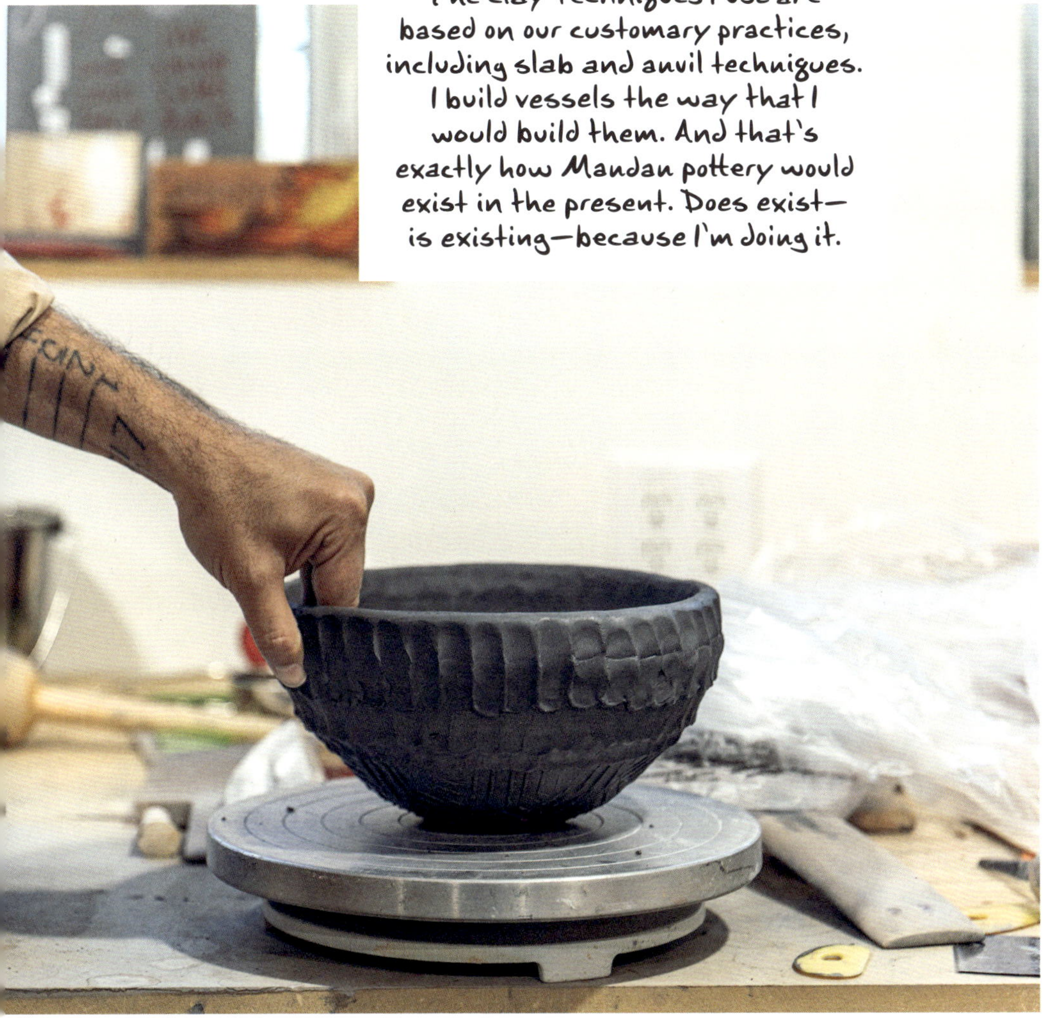

CANNUPA HANSKA LUGER

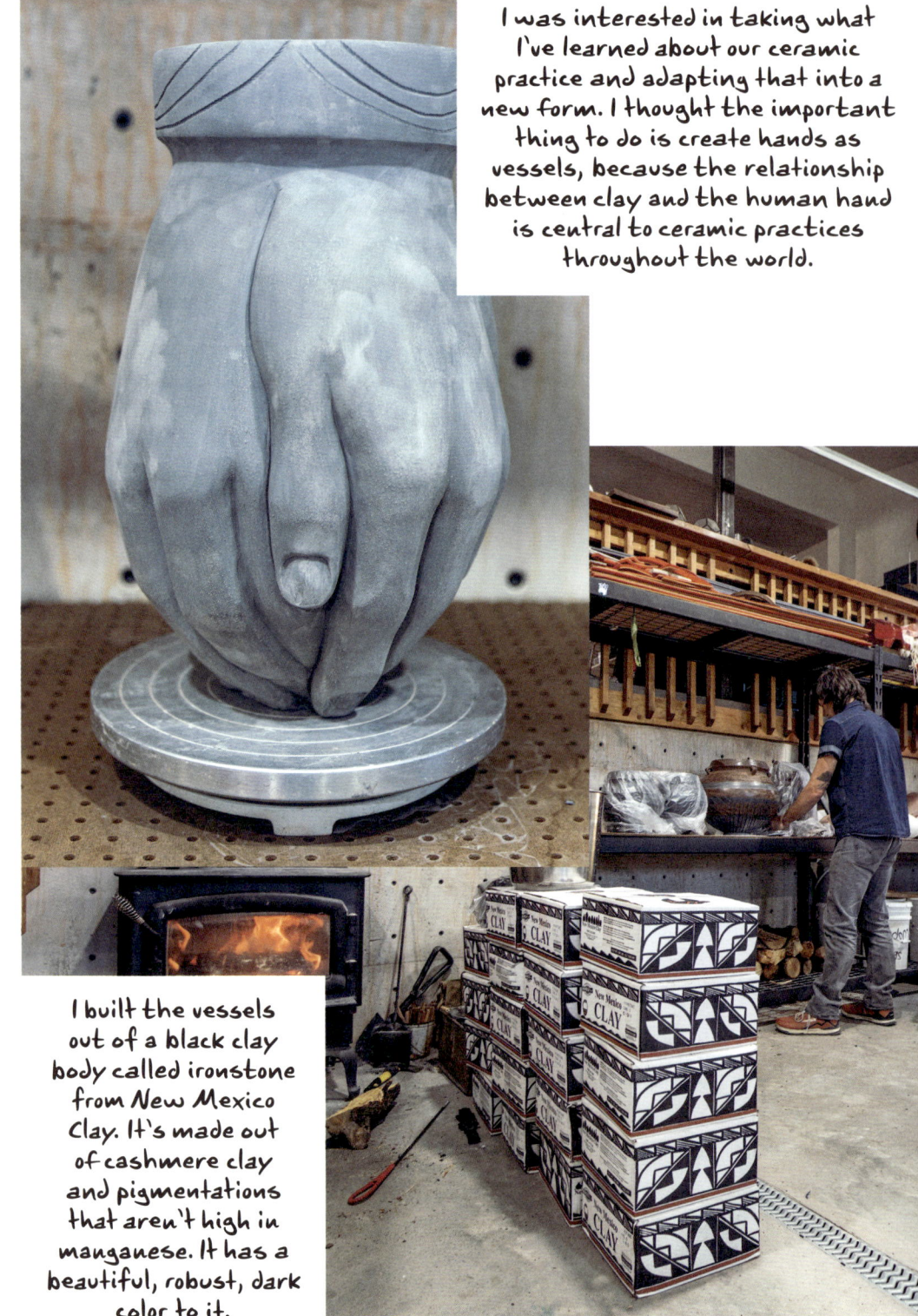

I was interested in taking what I've learned about our ceramic practice and adapting that into a new form. I thought the important thing to do is create hands as vessels, because the relationship between clay and the human hand is central to ceramic practices throughout the world.

I built the vessels out of a black clay body called ironstone from New Mexico Clay. It's made out of cashmere clay and pigmentations that aren't high in manganese. It has a beautiful, robust, dark color to it.

STUDIO NOTES

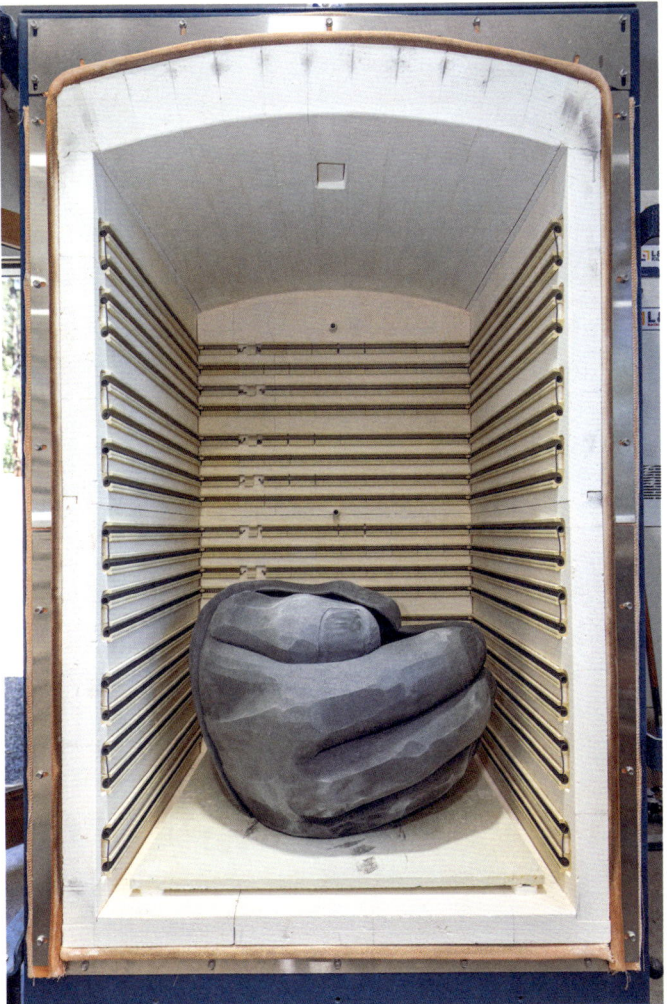

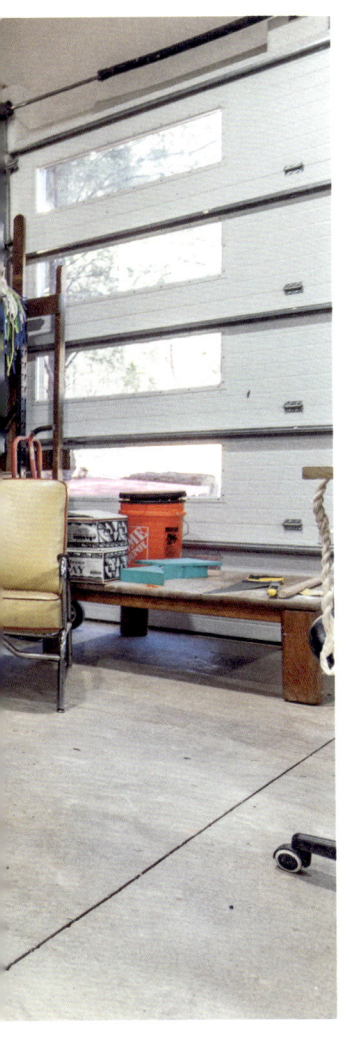

I wanted it to have a utilitarian aesthetic. The vast majority of our ceramic vessels were used for cooking. I thought that this would be a great way to embed the carbon-rich soot of use into new vessels without their actually doing what they would have been designed for.

CANNUPA HANSKA LUGER

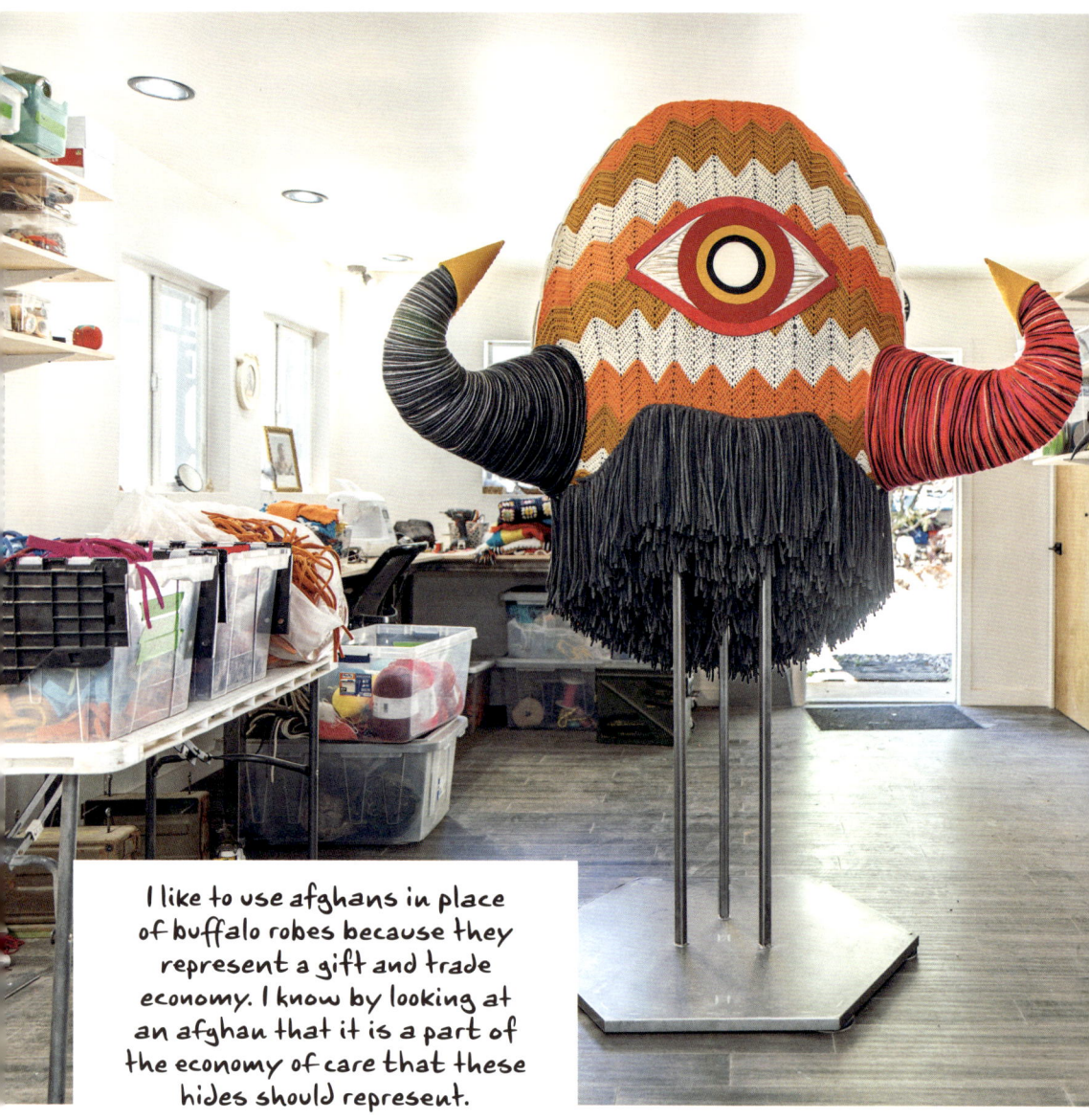

I like to use afghans in place of buffalo robes because they represent a gift and trade economy. I know by looking at an afghan that it is a part of the economy of care that these hides should represent.

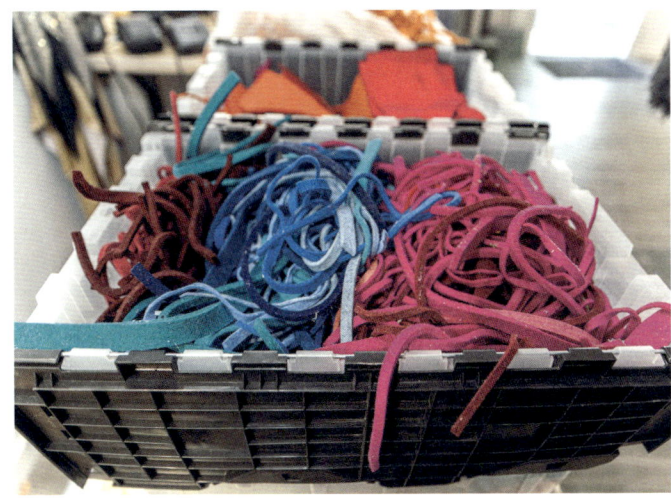

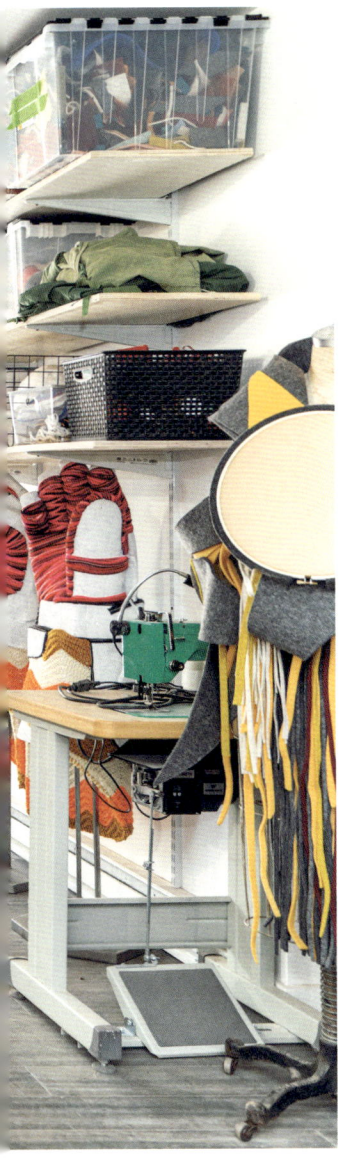

I want to maintain the customary practice of utilizing whatever materials were available to present a modern narrative—even more so, a future narrative of our survivance as Mandan and Hidatsa people.

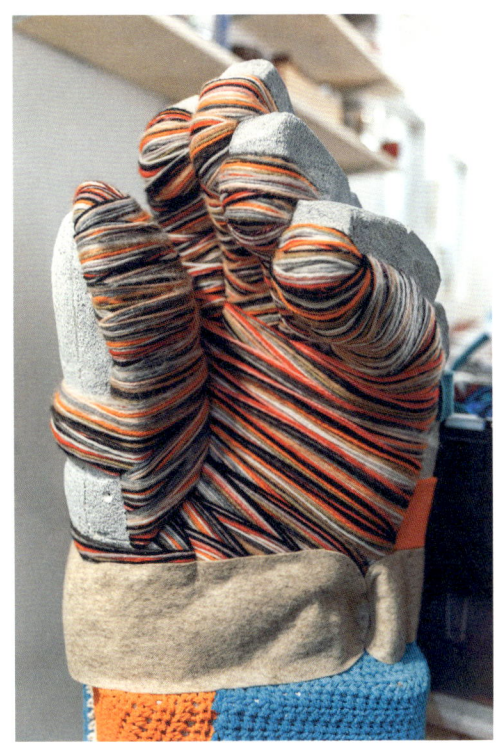

CANNUPA HANSKA LUGER

I wanted to play around with the idea of the impact of printmaking, the processes of taking real life and turning it into an illustration, turning that illustration into a lithograph, that lithograph into a print, that print into a book. What gets left out and what gets added in the practice of reproduction?

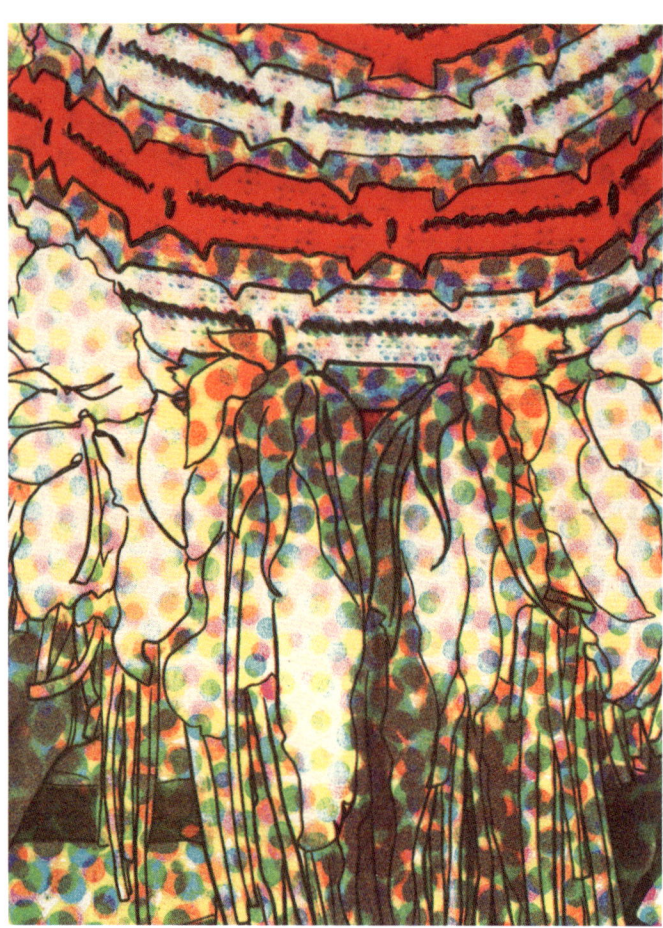

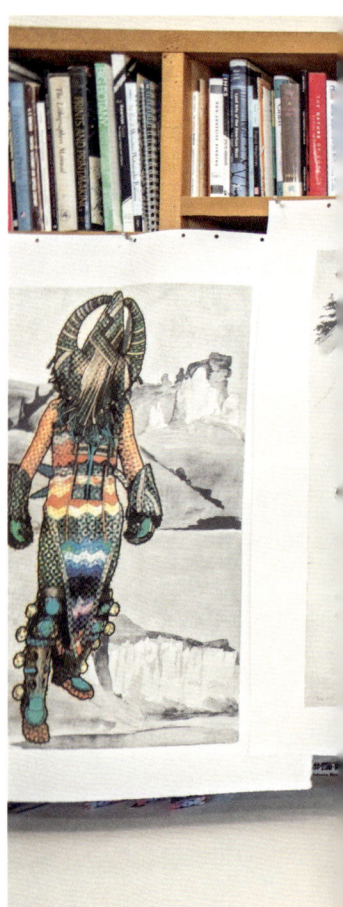

STUDIO NOTES

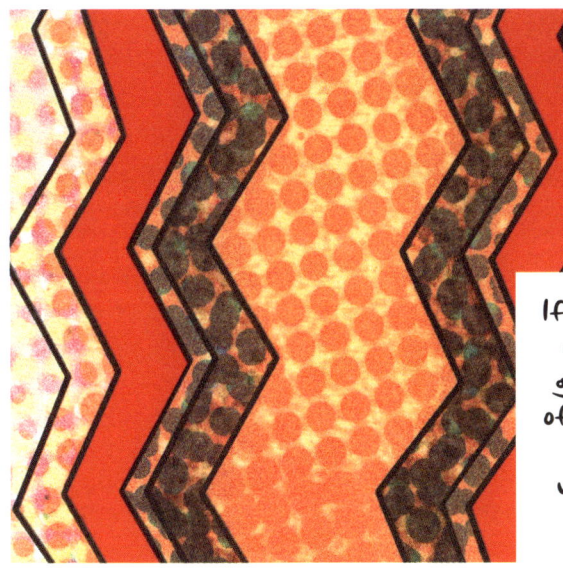

If I produce new regalia and present it in a future context, does that guarantee the future relationship of humans and buffalo? Can we call buffalo back to the land, and to a variety of lands? The *Midéegaadi* are a land-based performance piece—performed for the land— an extension of our more-than-human kinship with buffalo.

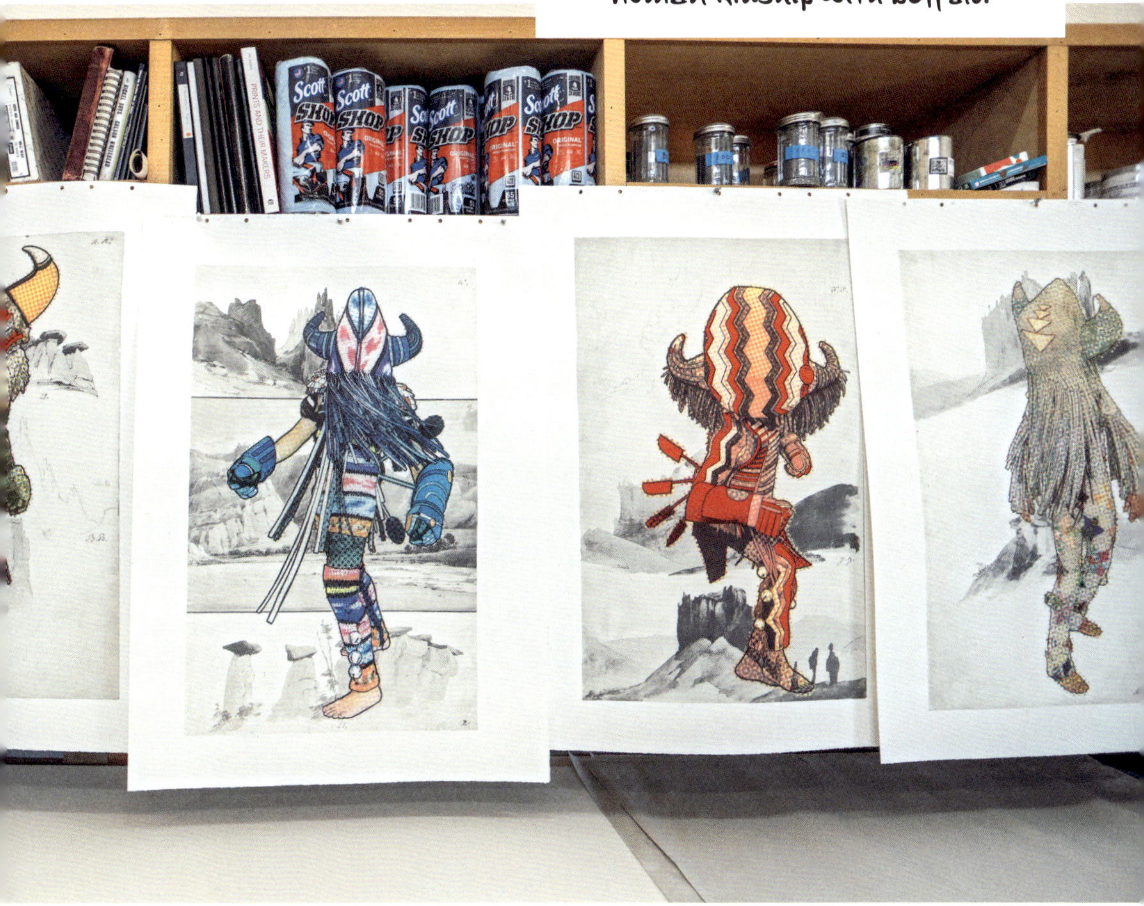

CANNUPA HANSKA LUGER

Scale, in *Northern Plains* traditions, is based on importance, not proximity. *A Nation* is about being big in a museum. It's a direct response to the small amount of space that's allotted for Indigenous populations and centuries of culture in museums. So, my idea of making this piece larger than life is to emphasize that we are too large to be held in these sorts of collections.

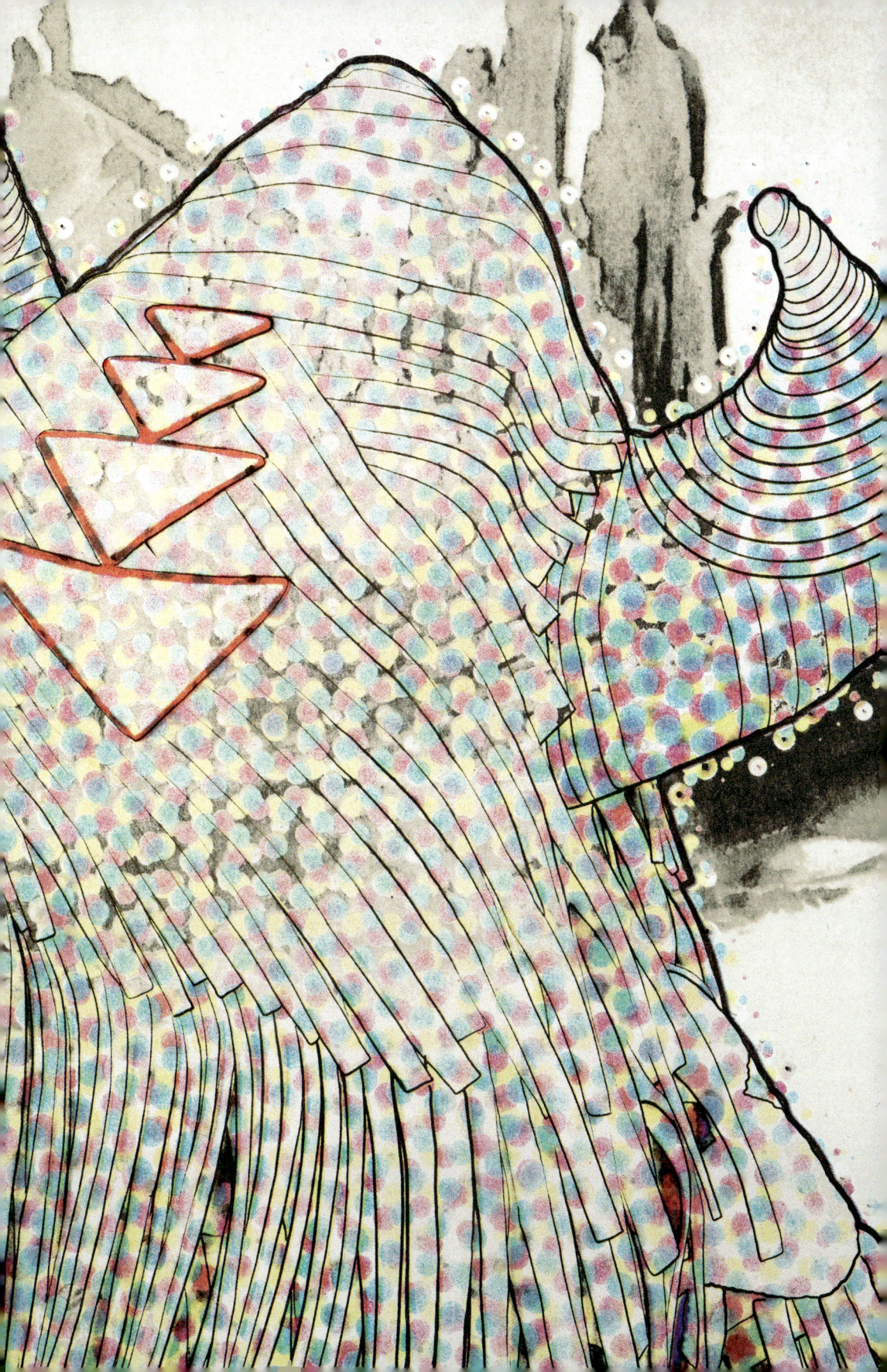

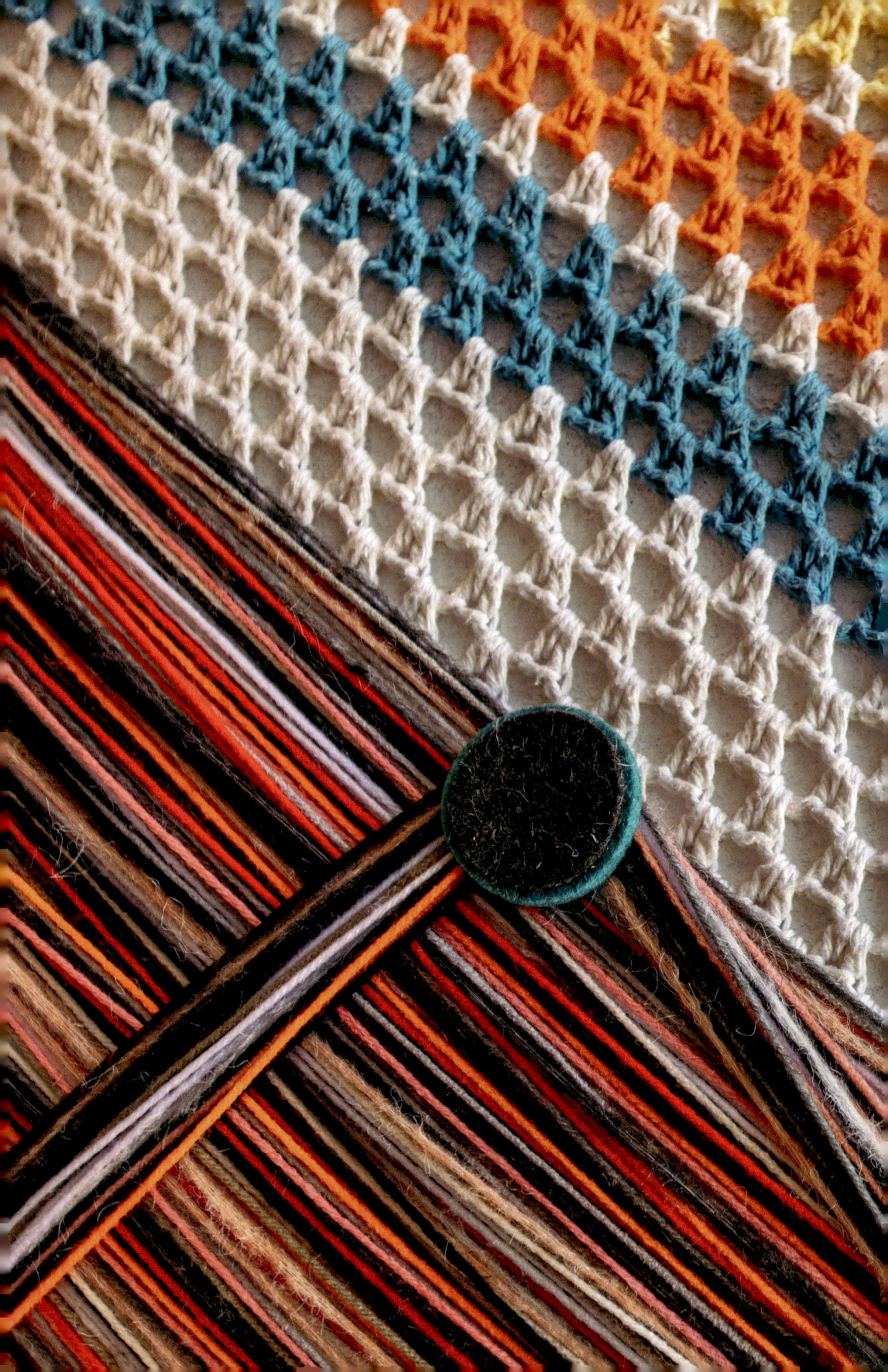

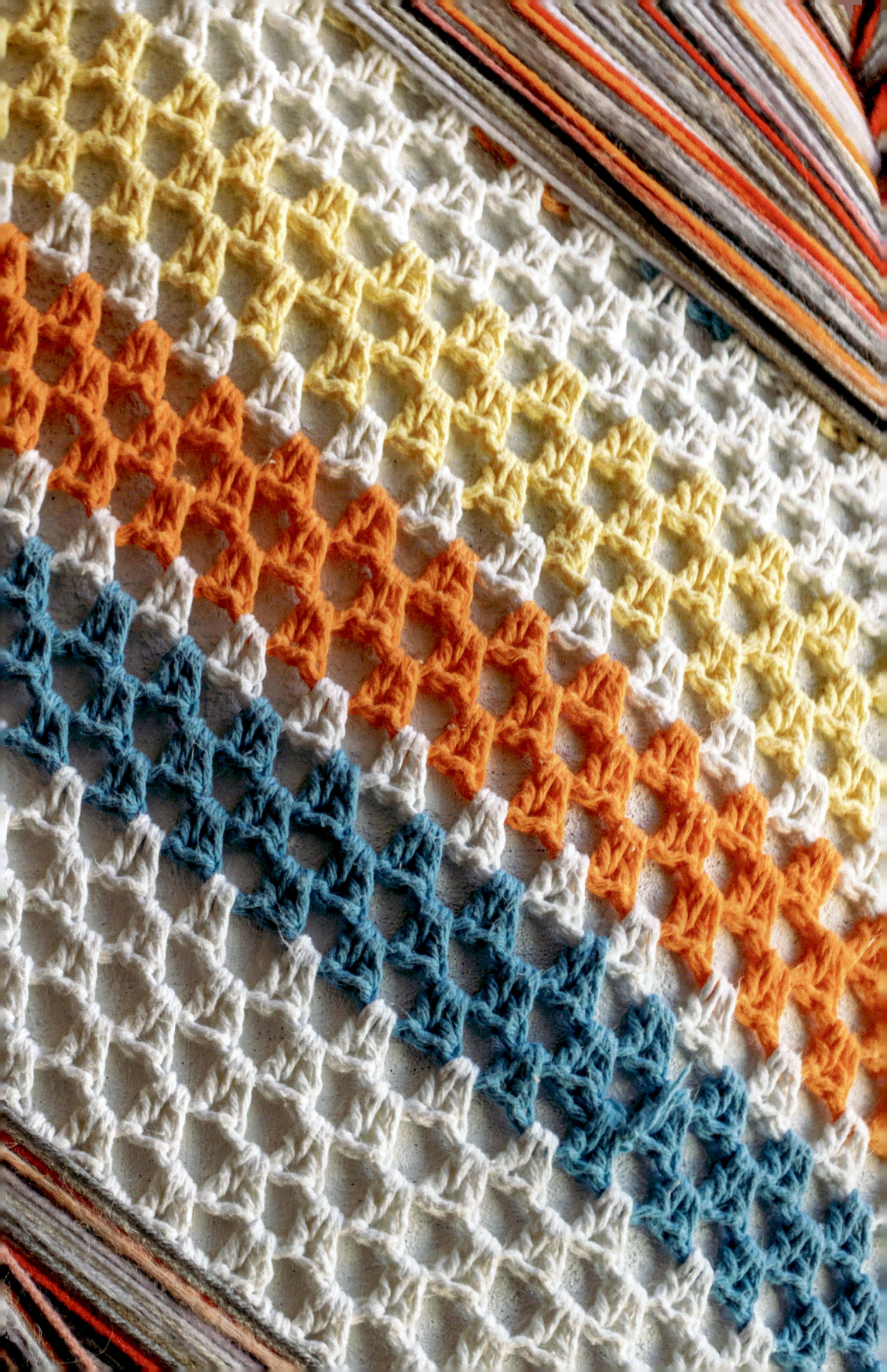

Fiber
Karin Campbell

Nestled in the hills outside Santa Fe, New Mexico, Luger's studio is a veritable cabinet of curiosities. Scraps of clay and wire, hunks of industrial-grade foam, and buckets of paint join less-expected materials: hockey gloves, shell casings, thick wool felt, and, most notably, brightly colored crocheted blankets. Metal shelves teem with these kaleidoscopic textiles, each awaiting a new life in the context of Luger's work (fig. 1). Commonly called afghans in an American context in deference to Afghanistan's rich textile traditions, the blankets feature exuberant palettes and geometric patterns and retain a decidedly handmade quality. Luger sources them from secondhand stores and estate sales for use as components in elaborate ensembles and garments he collectively calls *Midéegaadi*, which reference regalia customarily worn by Mandan Buffalo Bull Society members (p. 18). The artist acknowledges the irreverence in reimagining traditional regalia in wild colors and designs, and the visual punch the blankets carry is part of the point. The *Midéegaadi* are unabashed reminders that despite the generations of oppression Native people have endured, they will continue to not only survive but also thrive.

Repurposing fiber-based materials is not without precedent in the recent history of art. Sheila Hicks, who cites the universality of textile, has incorporated socks, bedsheets, and physicians' attire into tapestries and soft sculptures. Mike Kelley deployed doll clothing and baby blankets in his exploration of the complexities of childhood. Ann Hamilton's *indigo blue*, a commentary on invisible labor, includes fourteen thousand pounds of work shirts and pants, stacked neatly atop a steel base (fig. 2). Despite their varied approaches and motivations, these artists appreciate that discarded textiles hold specific histories. For Luger, crocheted blankets and other found fiber materials are living archives, offering the opportunity to locate a through line from past to present to future. "Someone's grandmother made these," the artist marveled while

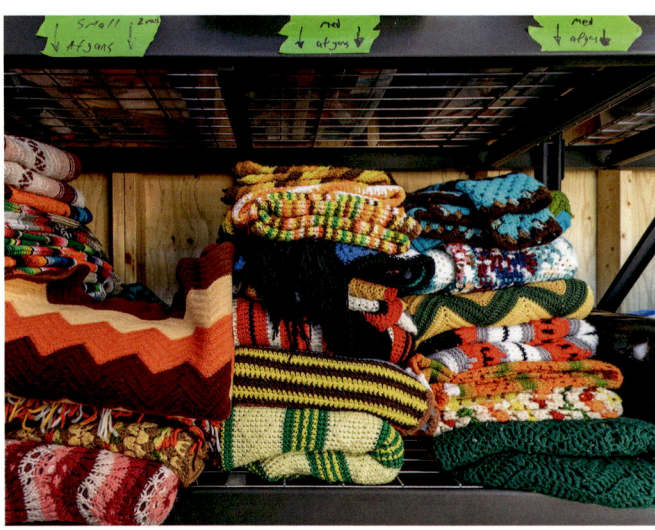

Fig. 1 Luger's collection of afghan blankets in his studio, 2025

surveying his afghan collection in late 2024.[1] Luger's matriarchal reference is intentional: Many crocheted blankets comprise dozens of so-called granny squares, small swatches resembling lace that, when pieced together, form the textiles' overall patterns. Luger honors the labor and time that the afghans' makers invested, casting the blankets as more than utilitarian household items or family heirlooms—they are also enduring symbols of care and kinship, values that resonate throughout his work.

Afghans almost become autonomous characters in Luger's filmed performances, during which he walks, dances, and engages in ritualistic acts. Staged in locations throughout the western United States, the performances propose that kinship extends beyond human bonds to encompass relationships among people, animals, and the earth. More than mere backdrops, landscapes guide the artist's movements: the prairie calls him to traverse its grassy hills, the desert invites him to kneel in its dunes, the mountains beckon him to wander their dusty paths (pp. 62–63). While the time he spends in these settings is finite, the natural world finds a lasting home in the yarn fibers of his clothing. During the performances, the afghans gather sand, seeds, and dirt, becoming repositories for new narratives born of Luger's dialogue with the landscape, while also preserving their origin stories. Such layering speaks to a concept at the core of Luger's broader project: that history is not a progression of events, but rather a continuum along which humans occasionally take a leading role. ✳

1. Cannupa Hanska Luger, conversation with the author, October 3, 2024.

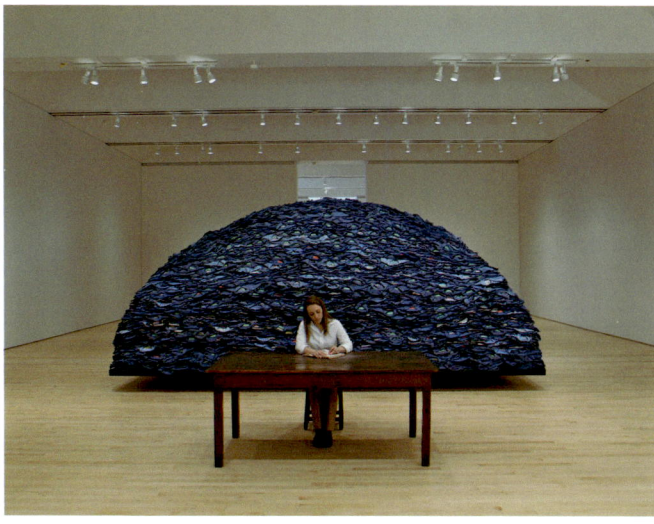

Fig. 2 Ann Hamilton, *indigo blue*, 1991/2007, cotton clothing, wood and steel platform, wood table and stool, book, and eraser, San Francisco Museum of Modern Art

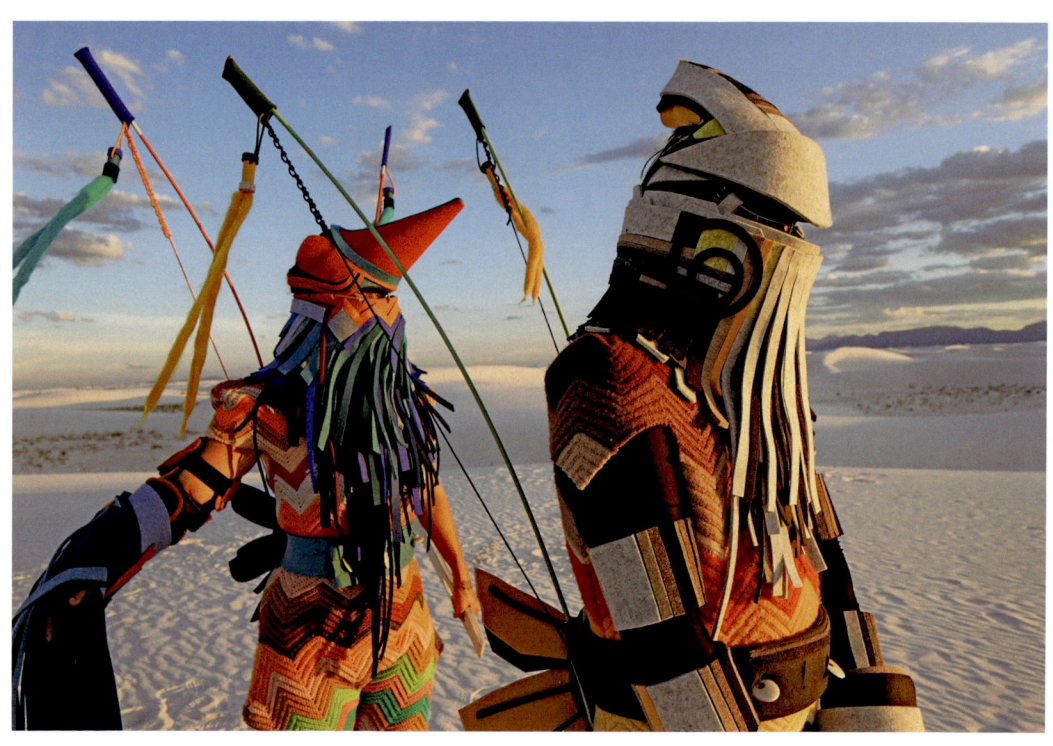

Stills from *New Myth*

2021, from the ongoing series
Future Ancestral Technologies,
2018–, single-channel video
with sound

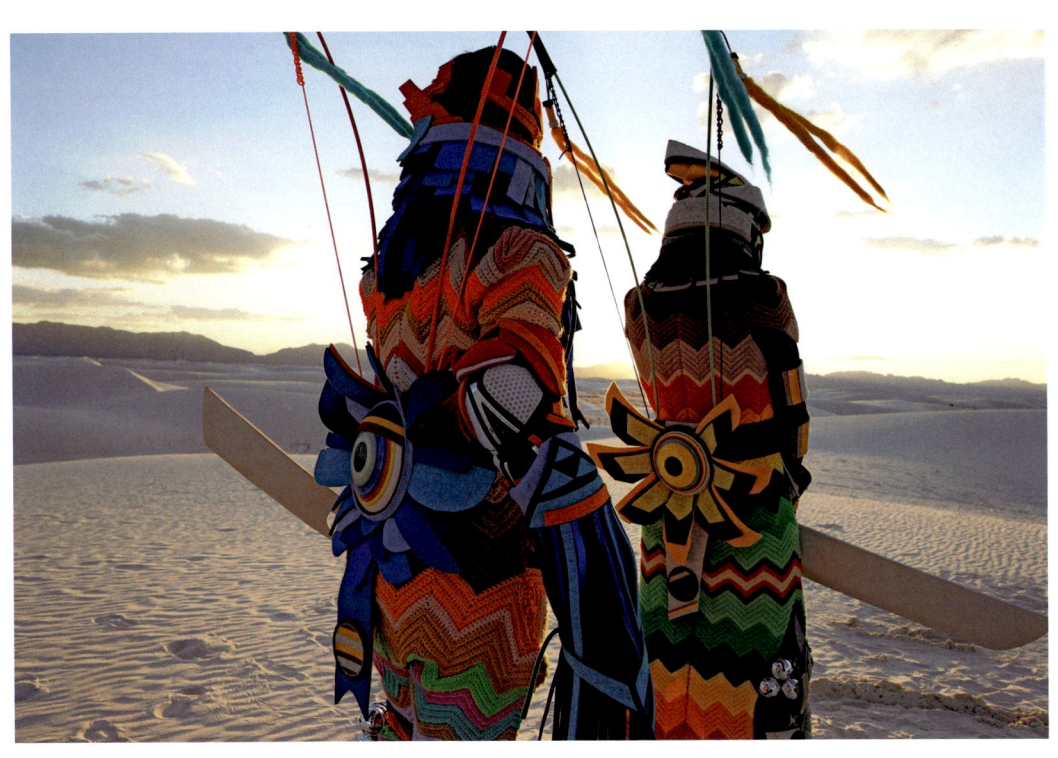

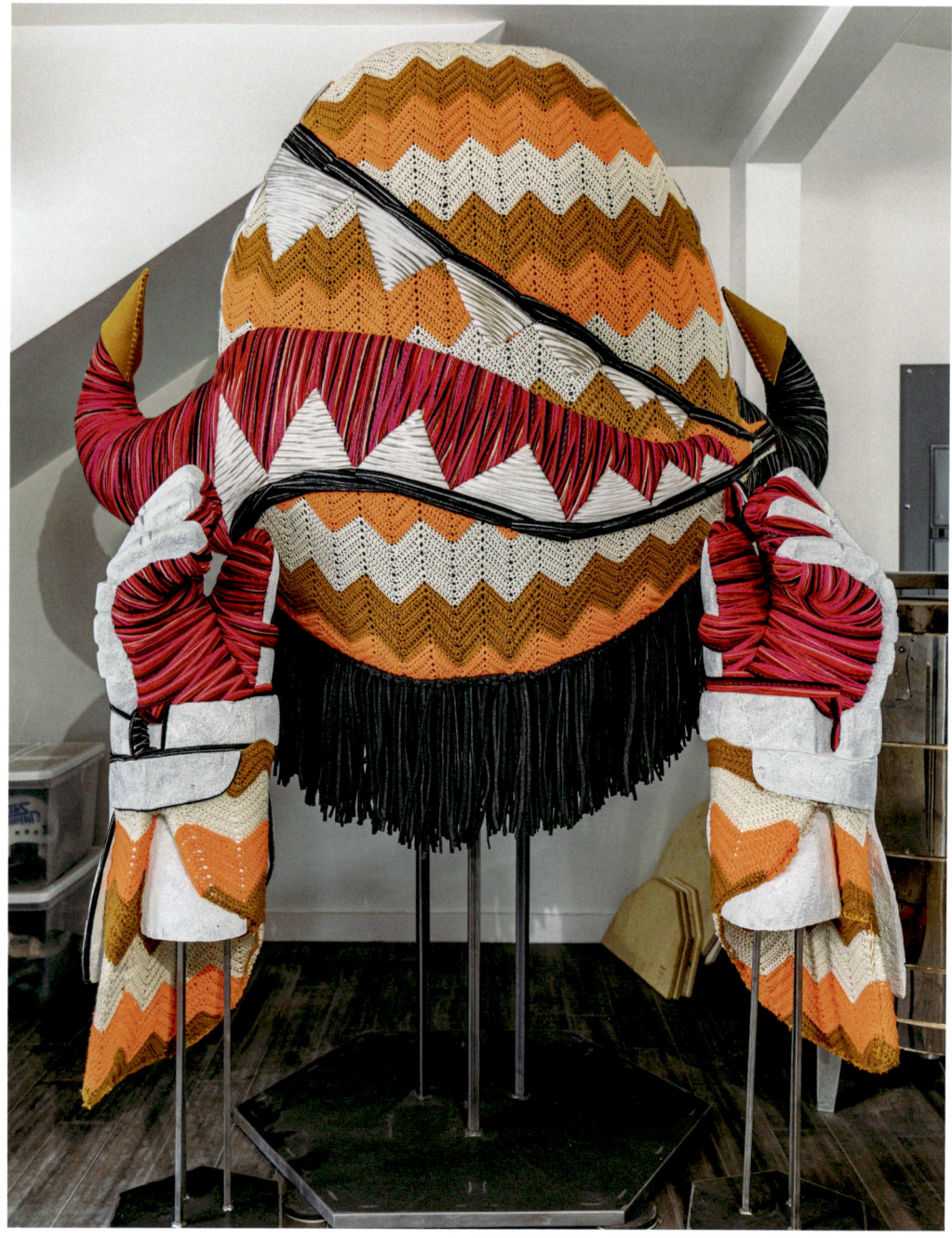

Nuxbaaga?ihdia: To Go Forth

2024–25, from the ongoing series *Future Ancestral Technologies*, 2018–, repurposed afghan blanket, industrial wool remnants, and yarn

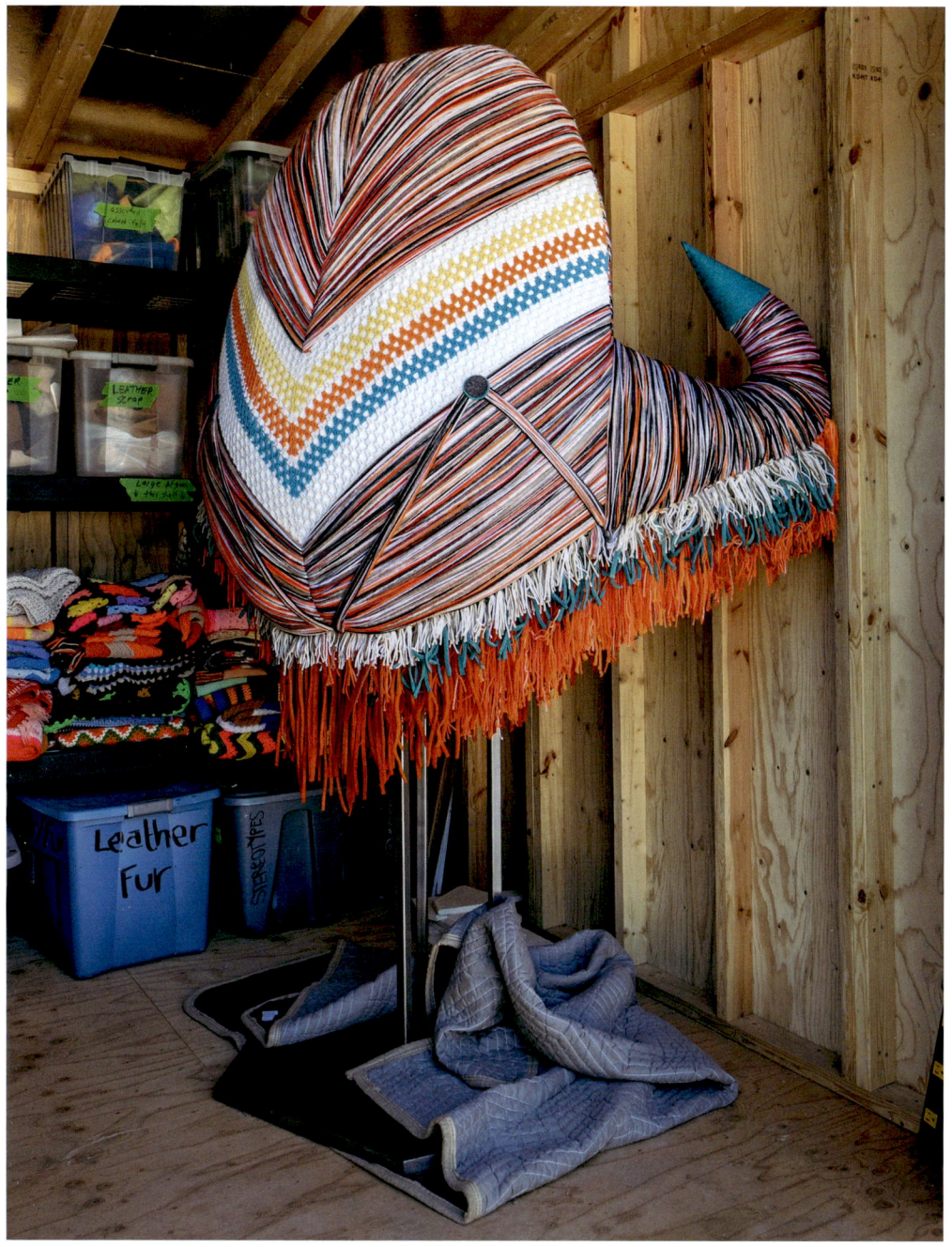

Nuxbaaga?ihdia: To Return

2024–25, from the ongoing series *Future Ancestral Technologies*, 2018–, repurposed afghan blanket, industrial wool remnants, and yarn

Midéegaadi – Bone

2021, from the ongoing series
Future Ancestral Technologies,
2018–, mixed-media bison regalia

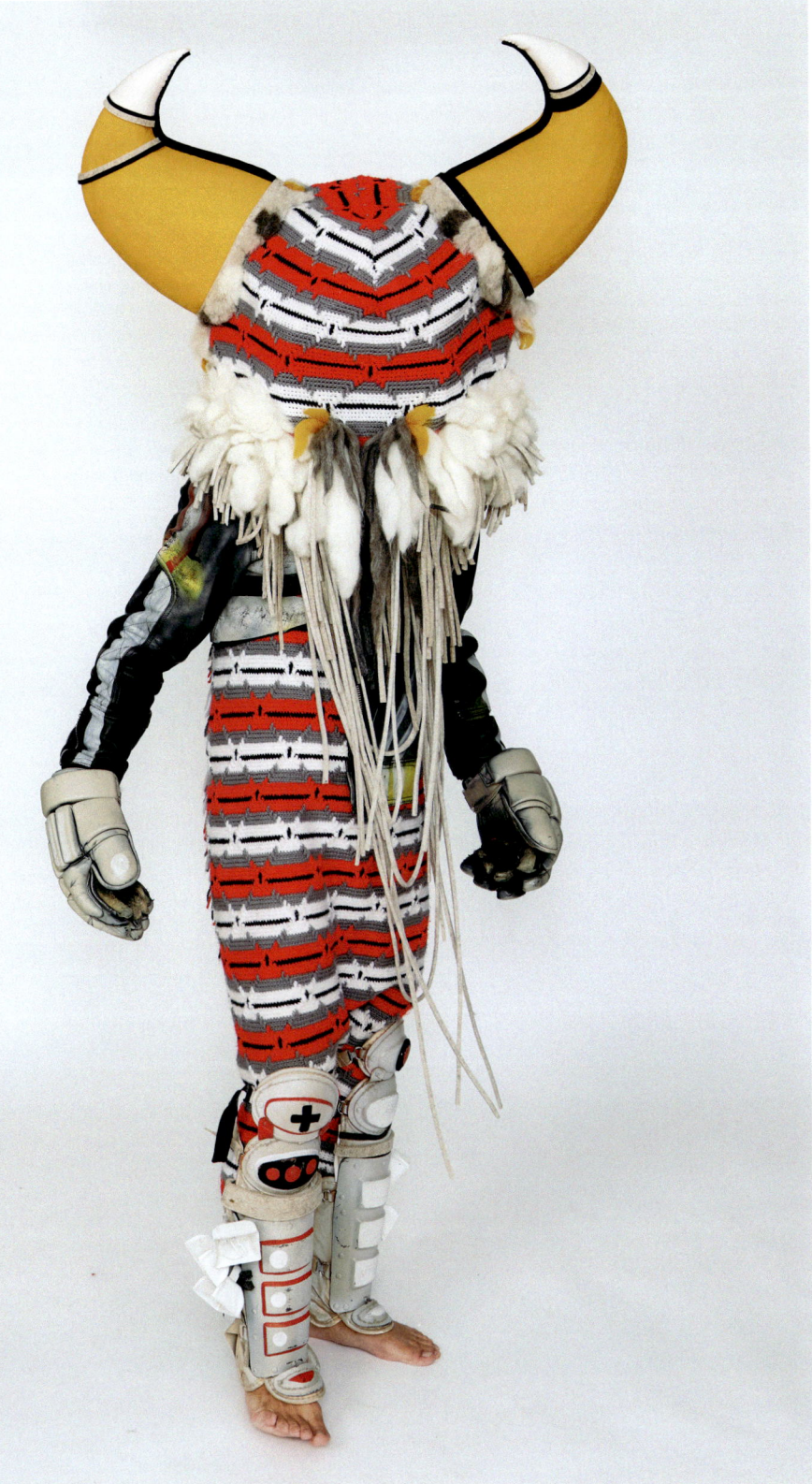

Midéegaadi – Muscle

2021, from the ongoing series
Future Ancestral Technologies,
2018–, mixed-media bison regalia

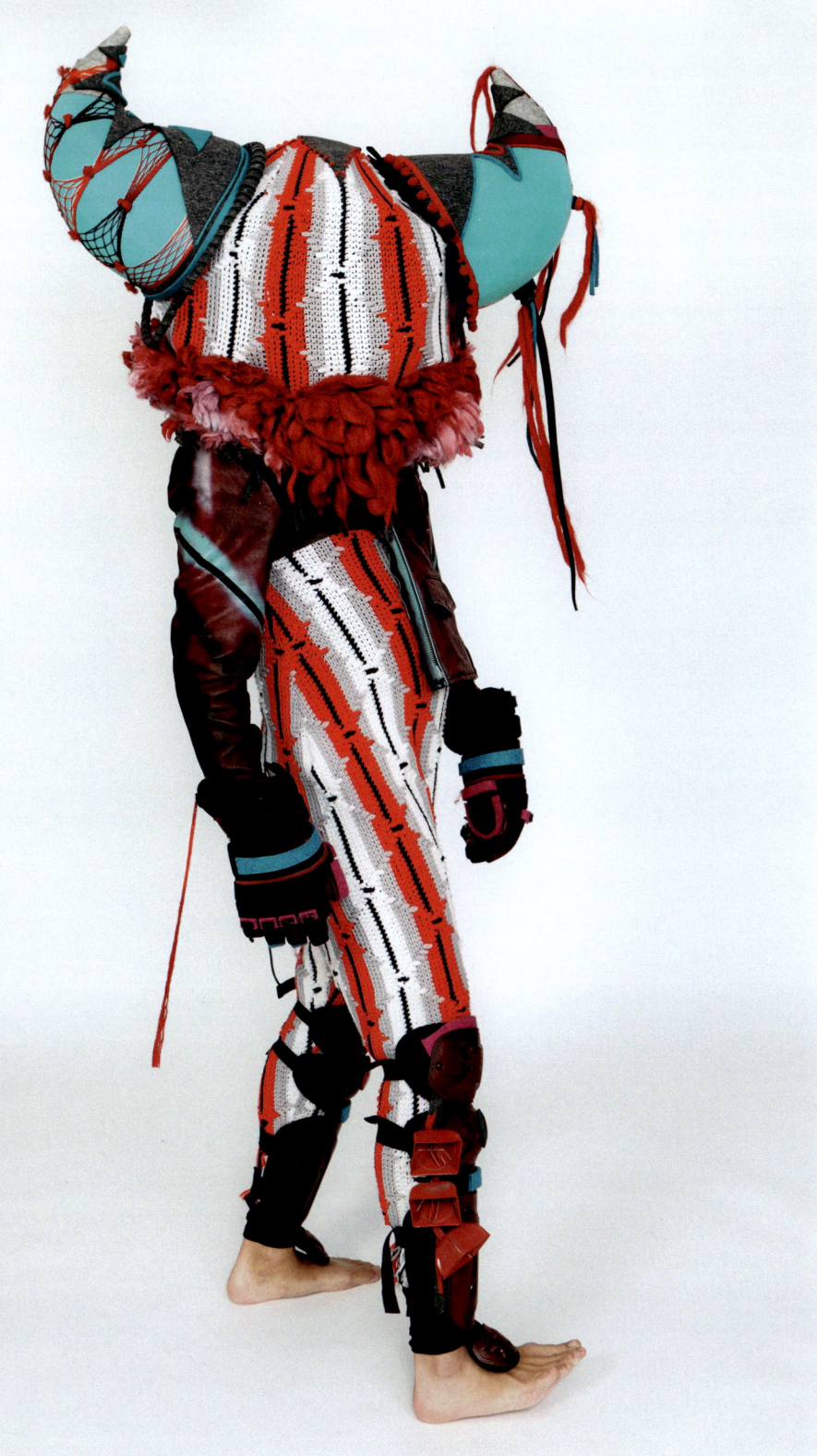

Midéegaadi – Light

2022, from the ongoing series
Future Ancestral Technologies,
2018–, mixed-media bison regalia

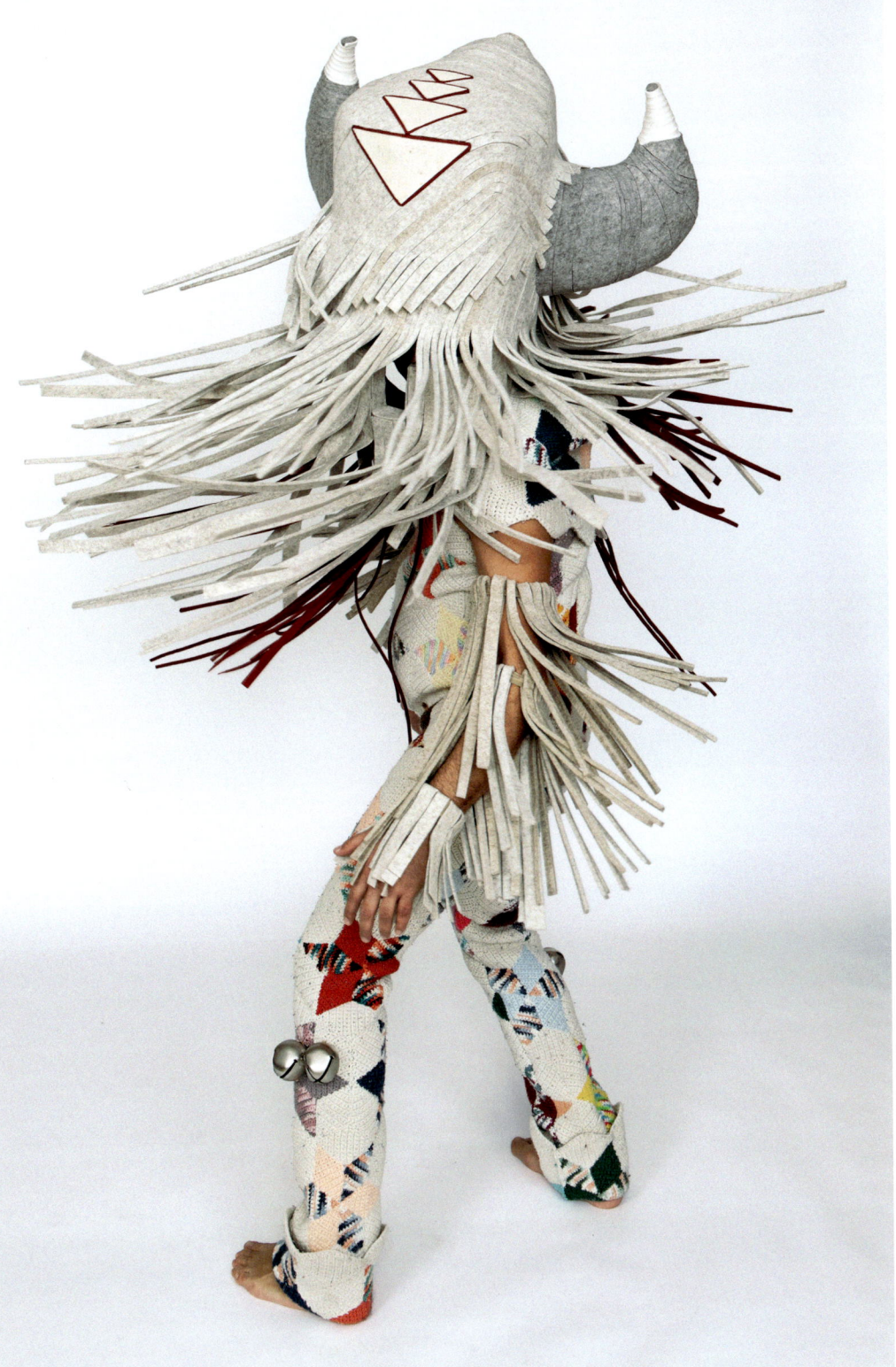

Midéegaadi – Fire

2022, from the ongoing series
Future Ancestral Technologies,
2018–, mixed-media bison regalia

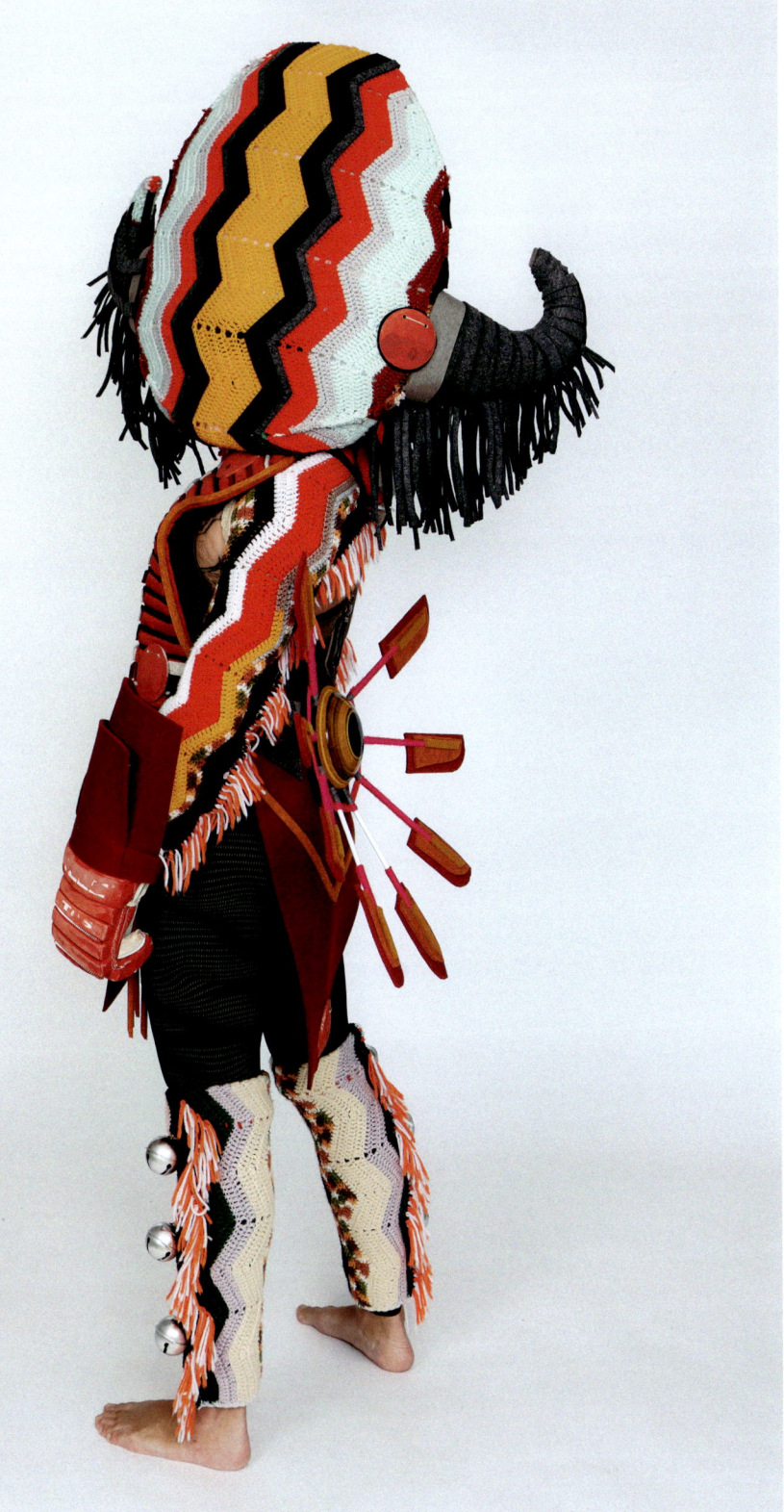

Midéegaadi – Water

2022, from the ongoing series
Future Ancestral Technologies,
2018–, mixed-media bison regalia

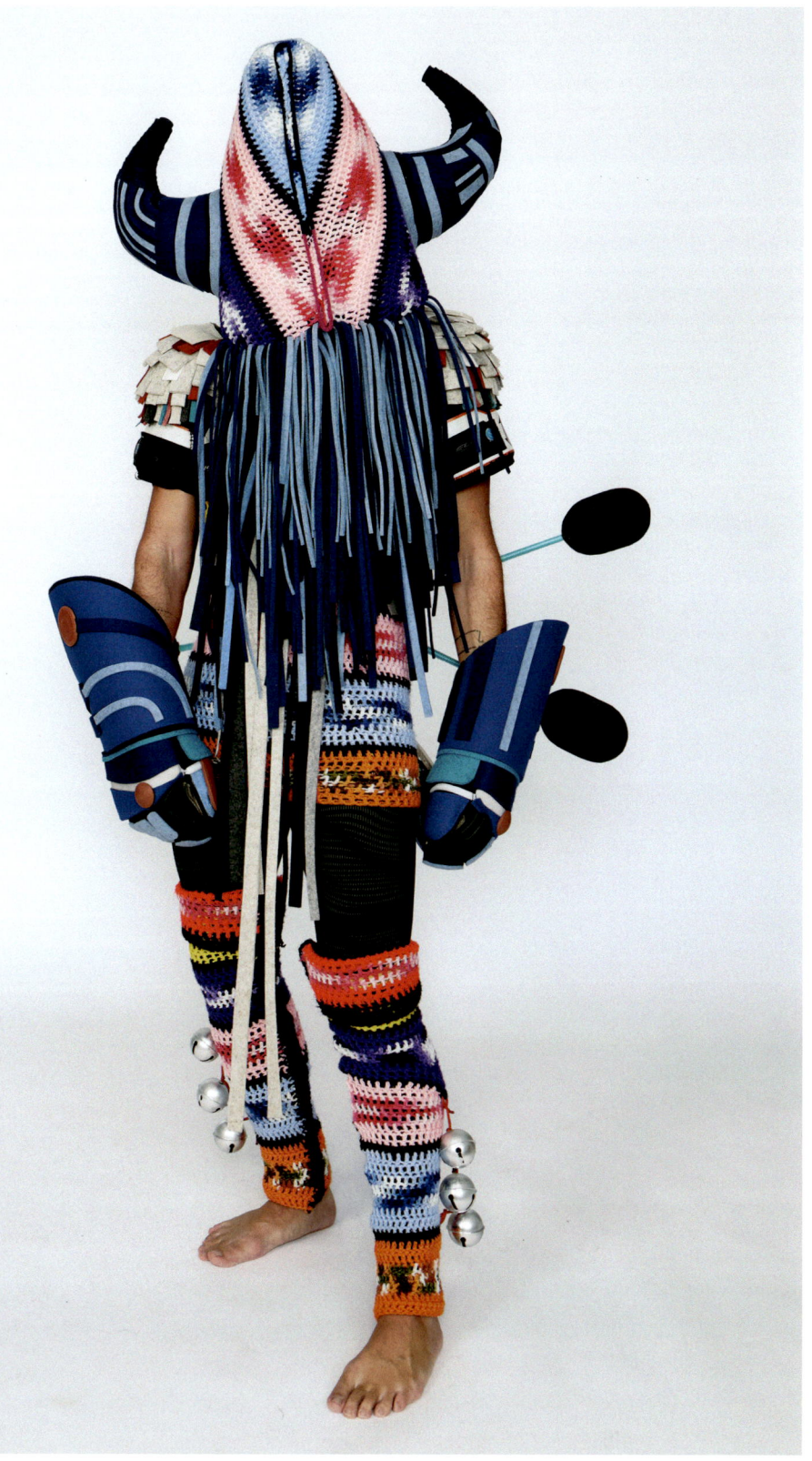

Midéegaadi – Thunder

2022, from the ongoing series
Future Ancestral Technologies,
2018–, mixed-media bison regalia

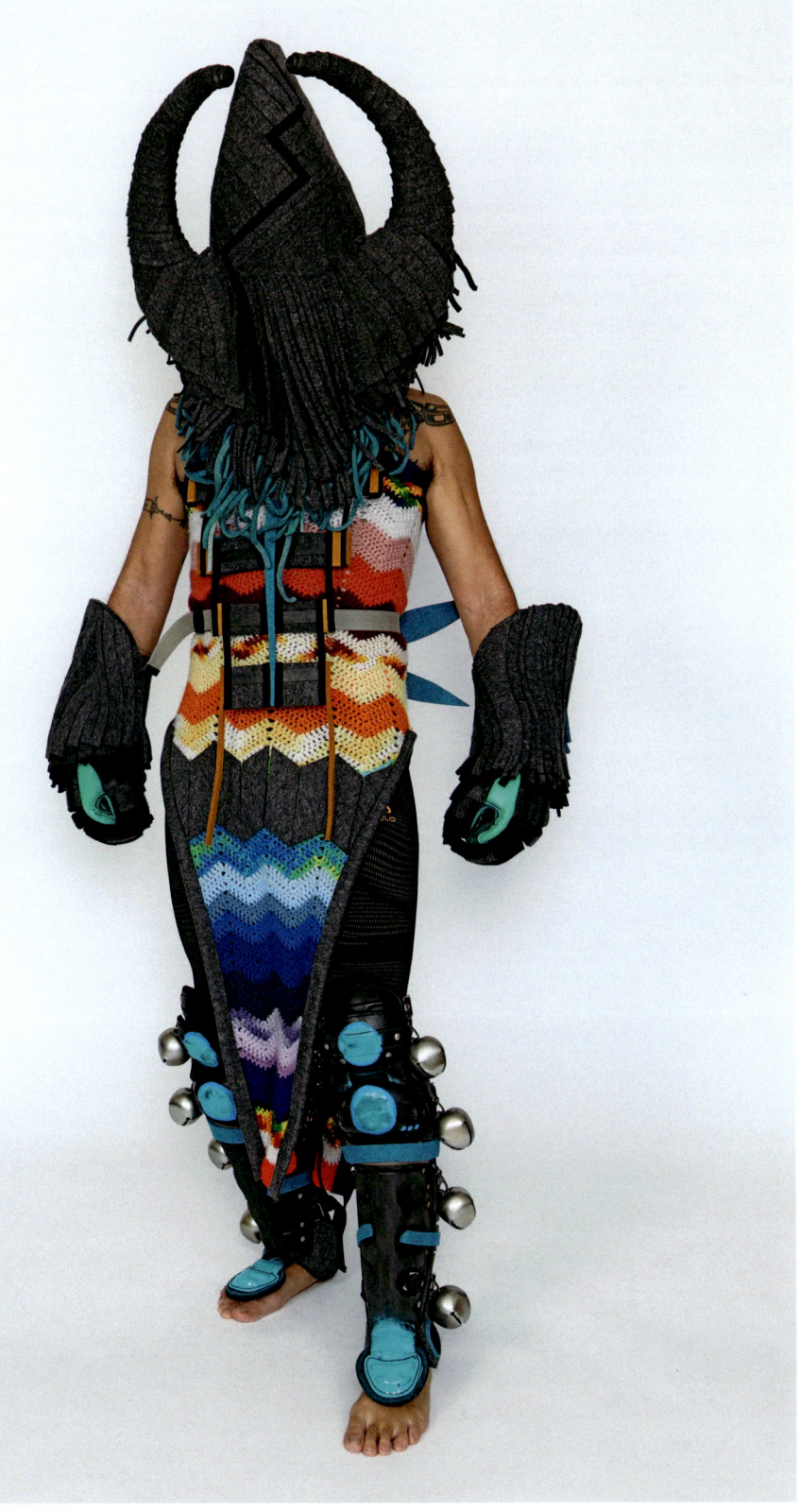

Midéegaadi – Lightning

2022, from the ongoing series
Future Ancestral Technologies,
2018–, mixed-media bison regalia

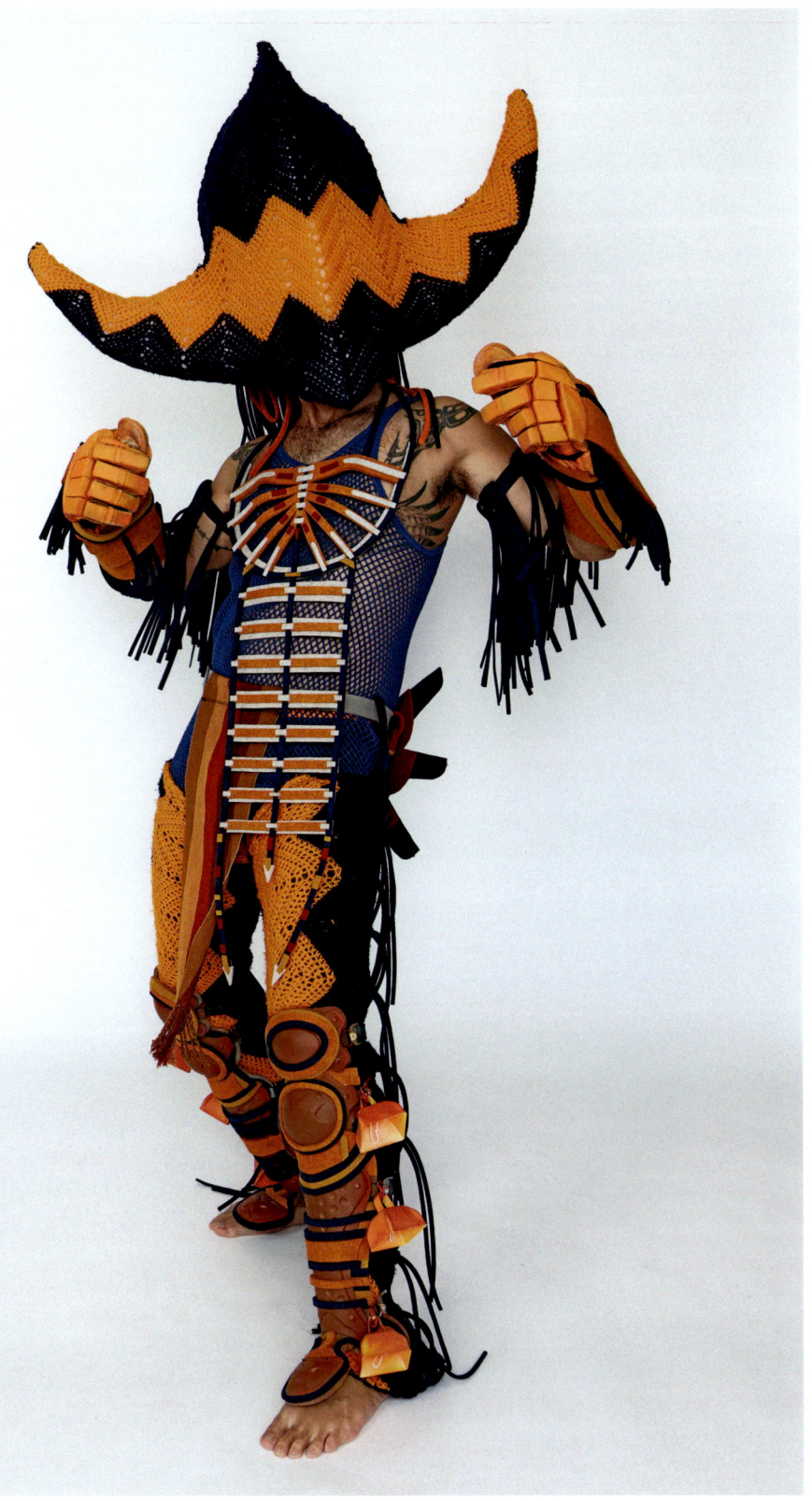

Practices of Place
The Monuments of Cannupa Hanska Luger
Paul Farber

The Lincoln Memorial, in Washington, DC, stands on the former riverbed of what we now call the Potomac. The name derives from the Patawomeke people who lived along its banks. In the late 1700s, the federal government undertook the transformation of this swampy tidal basin, which had previously accommodated the tobacco plantations of the nation's founders, to create the national monumental core. A giant marble representation of President Abraham Lincoln presides over the site, partitioned from the river that runs within view (fig. 1). Lincoln's record is entangled with abolition and conquest, the defense of the Union, and the simultaneity of the Civil War (1861–65) and the US-Dakota War of 1862, among other armed incursions into sovereign Indigenous lands. Today, visitors encounter the Lincoln Memorial within

a commemorative landscape that looms large in the American consciousness, with layered histories of protest, resistance, mourning, and mayhem throughout the twentieth and twenty-first centuries.

In *Dripping Earth*, Luger's *Midéegaadi* series (*midéegaadi* means "bison" or "buffalo" in Hidatsa) draws out the artist's relationships with monuments, kinship, and time. Luger grew up in the tradition of "winter counts," buffalo hide paintings made to mark and measure the progression of time across seasons, from thaw to freeze and back again. The winter was a time for story keeping and processing, and the counts tracked not linear histories but matters of significance. In *A Nation*, the giant figure, seated on a column fragment, wears buffalo regalia in a nod to the winter count's ties to ancestral pasts and

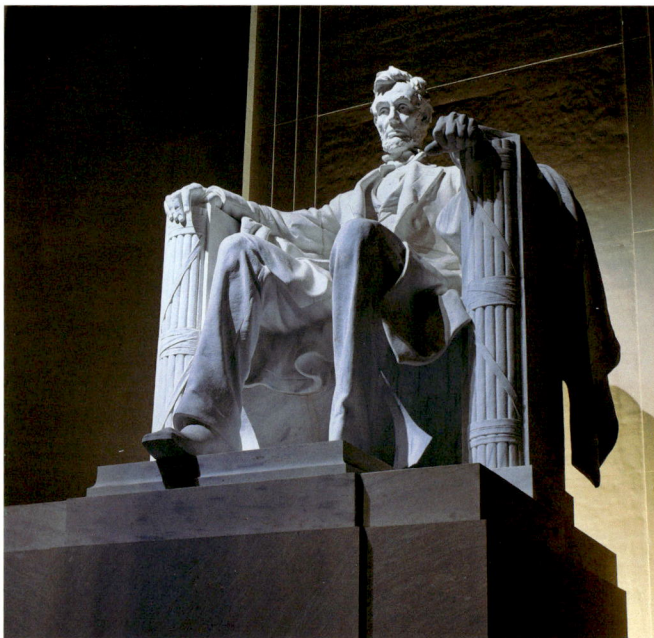

Fig. 1 Daniel Chester French, Statue of Abraham Lincoln for the Lincoln Memorial, Washington, DC, 1920–22

ripening futures (pp. 82–83). While the figure measures to the proportions of Michelangelo's *David* and borrows from the seated Abraham Lincoln's detached and distant gaze, the work does not celebrate human physiognomy or achievements; rather, it embodies Native conceptions of interrelation and time.

Early colonizers spotted buffalo herds along the waterways that now define the capital region. It may be hard to discern the ecosystems that preexisted such concretized locales as the National Mall or the capital as a whole, but there is power in seeking out other-than-human relatives, here and elsewhere, as a way of revisiting the linear narrative of the United States amid other intergenerational frameworks. Within the exhibition, the monument is both spectator and spectacle, subject and surveyor. We, as viewers, are invited to join in acts of witness and participation, implicated in a circular exchange that is far bigger than any one of us alone.

Such is the life force of Luger's artworks, which range from the sculptural to the digital and vary in scale, scope, and site. In each instance, the artist conjures the interrelationships between ancestral and future time; the personal and social dynamics of exchange; and the vital forces that contribute to human sustenance and survival. He brings out some of the most sublimated yet potent public presences of ancestors, both human and non-human, and the glorious entanglements of such relations, prompting us to see our inherited world anew. In widening the lens on monuments from individual to relational, Luger brings us into kinship with each other and the future. ✳

A Nation
(work in progress)

2025, from the ongoing series
Future Ancestral Technologies,
2018–, ceramic, steel, whitewash,
and detritus

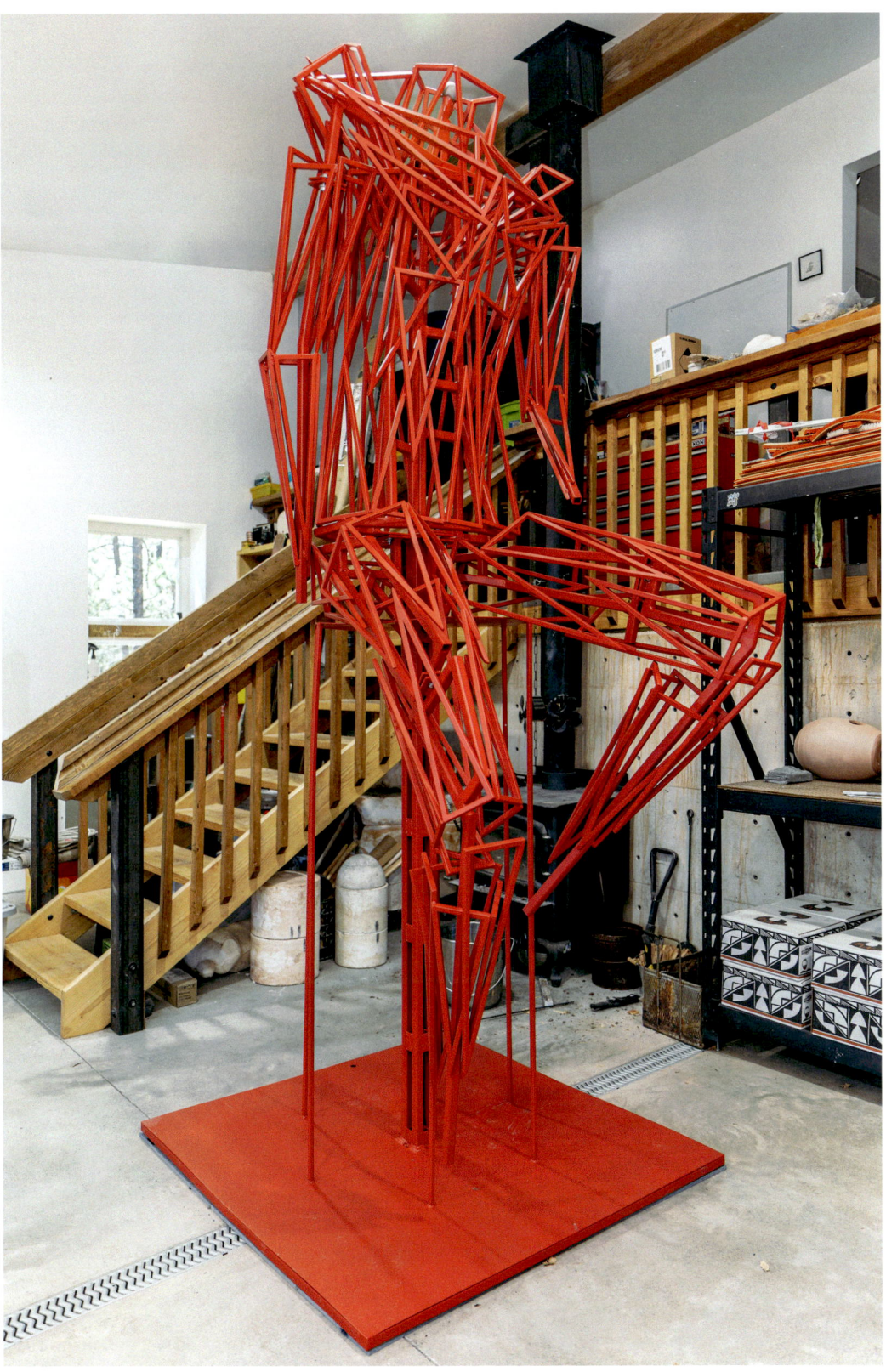

The Giant

Taylor J. Acosta

Part of Luger's ongoing series *Future Ancestral Technologies*, *A Nation* features an outsize incarnation of a *Midéegaadi* (pp. 82–83). The body, fabricated from powder-coated steel, assumes a confident, if relaxed, posture. The head, hands, and feet, sculpted in clay, convey both intention and strength (p. 56). This imposing figure rests on a base reminiscent of a classical column, comprising layers of whitewashed detritus. Luger's art historical citations are numerous, and gestures of reverence and critique are cannily deployed as he riffs on forms and styles. One can discern in his work a regard for classical ideals of scale, proportion, balance, and restraint, whether those principles are observed, inverted, or upended. Commanding in presence and sublime in aesthetic, *A Nation* comes to us from an Indigenous future Luger envisions and takes its place in a grand tradition of monumental figurative sculpture.

Sculpted figures have served a variety of functions in the history of art. In classical architecture, caryatids and atlantes take the place of columns to support entablatures. In the ancient world, figural sculptures embodied guardians, positioned to flank the entrances to temples. A mythological figure leaning on a pillar might be consecrated in a sanctuary or set within a garden to evoke an arcadian paradise. Although situated on an architectural base, Luger's giant is less tethered than any of these antecedents. Its purpose seems neither structural nor ornamental.

The pose and powerful physique depicted in *A Nation* recall the Hellenistic bronze statue *Boxer at Rest* (fig. 1).[1] The broad-shouldered pugilist sits atop a boulder, injured and exhausted after a match. While its iconography shares much with ancient statues of the Greek hero Herakles, the *Boxer* appears as a

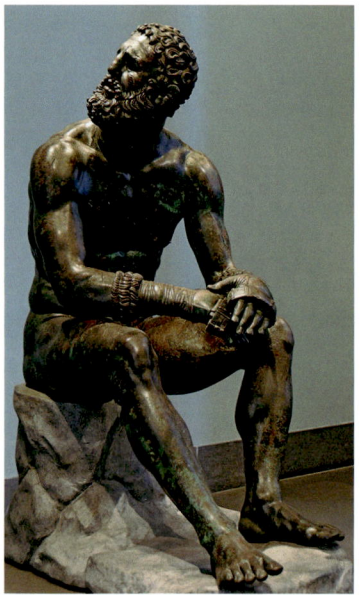

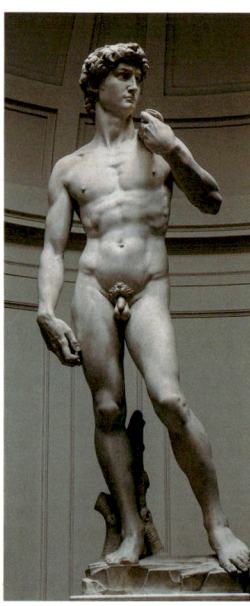

Fig. 1 *Boxer at Rest*, Greek, 3rd–2nd century BCE, bronze, Museo Nazionale Romano, Rome

Fig. 2 Michelangelo, *David*, c. 1501–4, marble, Galleria dell'Accademia, Florence

marked departure from classical renderings of athletic heroism. The unknown sculptor portrayed the subject with his forearms resting on his legs and his head upturned, a momentary pose rife with potential meaning. The boxer's massive form has an elemental quality. His gloved and battered hands are at once astounding and gentle. Luger's figure, too, is characterized by vulnerability and resilience. In stark contrast to the static portrayals of Native people in historical images and ethnological dioramas, Luger has created a momentary pose for his hero. *A Nation* has the aura of an ancient statue, but it is not a relic.

Affectionately called "the giant" from its conception, Luger's sculpture also resonates with Michelangelo's colossal *David*, which was described as a giant at its public installation (fig. 2). Enlisted to create a statue of the biblical hero David, the young Michelangelo was given a single block of marble, which he regarded as containing all the possibilities for a work of art.[2] The disproportionately large head, hands, and torso reflect the artist's careful consideration of viewing positions—the

exaggerated features would resolve when admired from below.[3] For Luger, the *David* offers a model for what scale can signify. The massive head and hands of *A Nation* embody the artist's conception of monumentality: "Scale, in Northern Plains traditions, is based on importance, not proximity," Luger has asserted.[4]

In *Dripping Earth*, Luger's giant casts its gaze over projected images from the artist's family archive. Installed within a gallery that can barely contain it, *A Nation* is placed in a dynamic and dialogic relationship with a particular kind of site—one that is social, political, and historiographic. Indeed, it is impossible to disregard the intersection of space and time at sites defined by perpetual and indefinite accumulation.[5] Museums are just these sorts of sites. Everywhere is here. Every time is now. The museum is thus a fitting stage for an encounter that forces us to reconsider power structures and historical narratives. If Luger is engaged in a kind of classicism, it is one predicated on revival, restoration, and synthesis, connecting his futurism with neoclassicisms throughout the ages. ✳

1. One of very few original bronze statues preserved from antiquity, the *Boxer at Rest* was excavated in 1885 in Rome, near the site of the ancient Baths of Constantine, where it is thought to have been displayed.

2. The block of marble had previously been worked and abandoned by two other artists.

Michelangelo was undeterred by imperfections in the marble's grain.

3. Originally commissioned for the roofline of the Opera del Duomo in Florence, the *David* was instead installed at the Palazzo Vecchio. It is now held in the collection of the Galleria dell'Accademia, Florence.

4. Luger, "Studio Notes," in this catalogue, 56.

5. As formulated by Michel Foucault and outlined in a frequently cited speech of 1967. Michel Foucault, "Of Other Spaces," *Diacritics* 16, no. 1 (Spring 1986): 26.

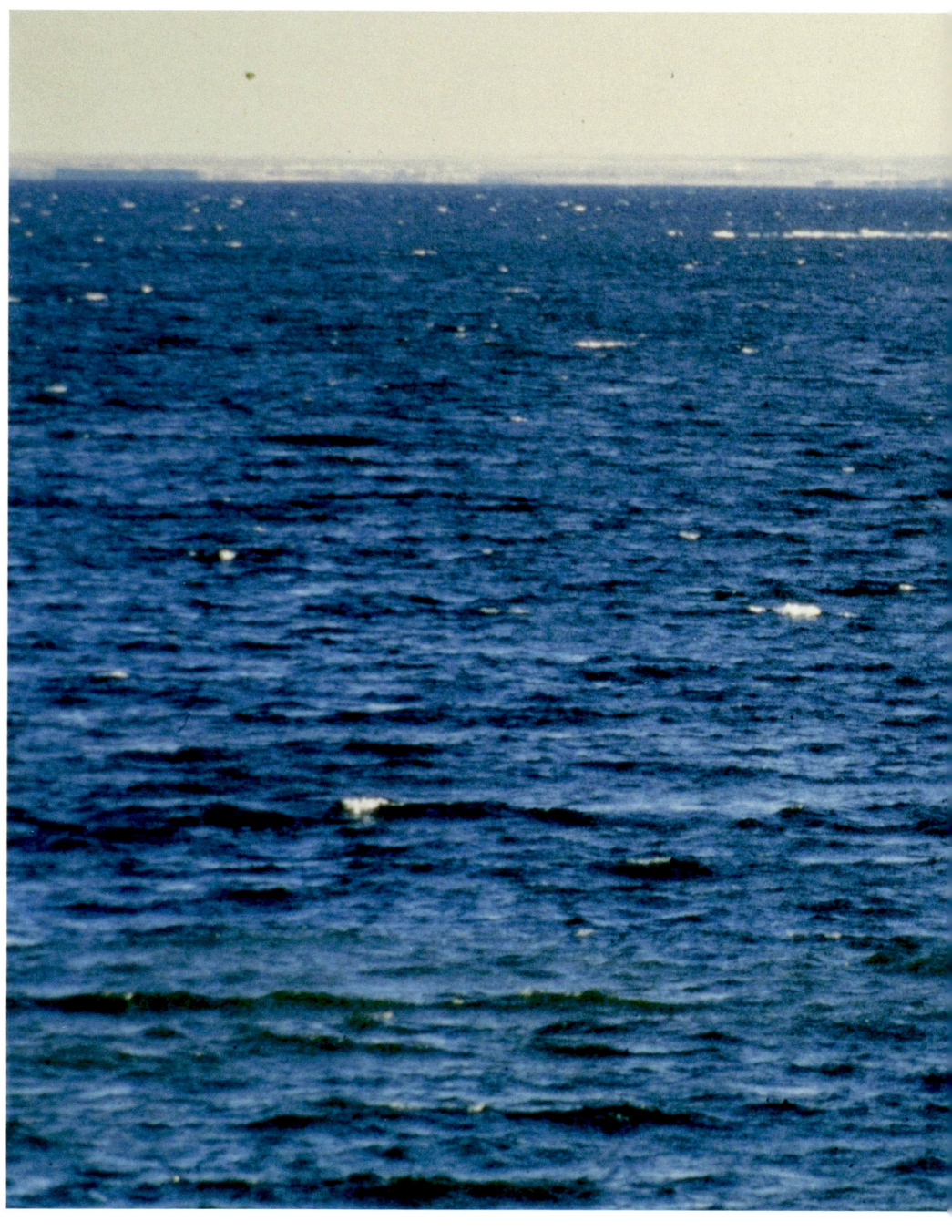

Still from *A/V Presentation:*
Past, Present + Future of FB Res,
2025, digitized slides and audio
from the Whitman Family
Archive and archival images.
Pictured: Lake Sakakawea
reservoir, date unknown

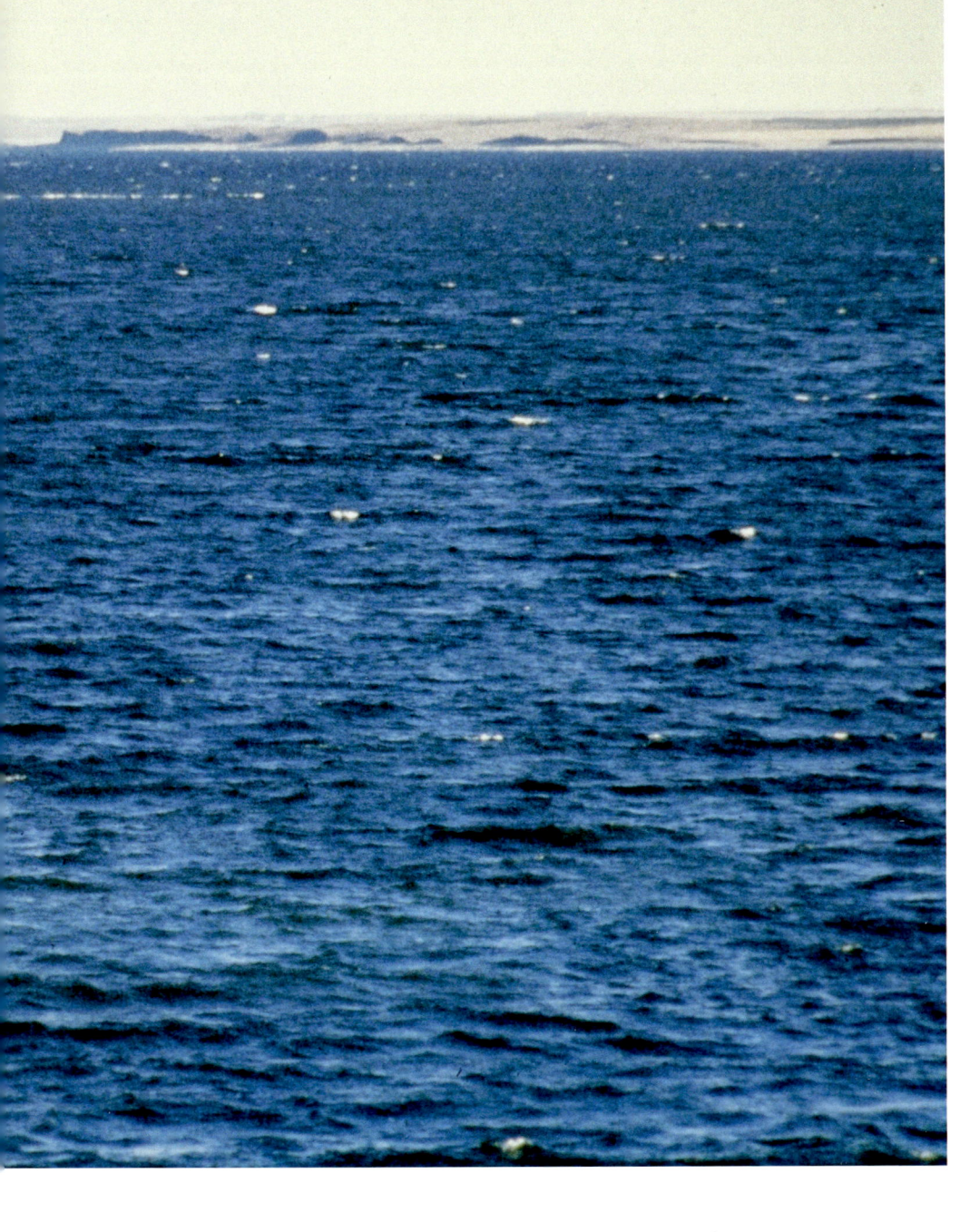

Elemental
Annika K. Johnson

Water is a central character in *Future Ancestral Technologies*, Luger's multimedia series that envisions a universe animated by elemental forces. In the sculptural installation *Máadiraxbi I* and *II*, life-size round boats made from willow branches float above the floor, submerging viewers in an otherworld (pp. 98–99). These Indigenous vessels conjure an imaginary high watermark on the wall, evoking water's capacity to measure time and reshape our relationship to the land.

Nowhere is water's enduring force more manifest than in the Badlands of present-day North Dakota, where dreamlike geological formations bear witness to the passage of deep time, the vast timescale of our planet's history. This landscape tells an epic story of ancient oceans, ice sheets, and meandering rivers. Swiss artist Karl Bodmer marveled at these landforms in the early nineteenth century, just as academics in the West were beginning to formulate the concept of geological time—earth's history recorded in stone and measured in eons. In addition to posing existential challenges, this colossal scale presented a dilemma of representation: how to convey not just what the human eye observes on the earth's surface but the immensity of time embedded in the land. As a ceramicist, Luger works with clay, a material shaped by deep time. In his poem "*Mįhą́pmąk*: A Way Home," he writes, "You are born of the weathering of mountains. / The child of water and rock" (p. 93). Clay, shaped by elemental forces, offers a way to grasp the existential questions that arise when confronting vast scales of time.

This ethos of clay extends beyond ceramics, informing Luger's work across media and underscoring the ongoing dialogue between land, time, and human experience. The *Midéegaadi* figures personify environmental and bodily elements: water, fire, light, thunder, lightning, bone, and muscle. Assembled in the gallery, these expressive figures assume active poses that could shake the floor, rattle light fixtures, and unleash the primordial energy of the Big Bang. They evoke a beginning. In *A Nation*, an eighth *Midéegaadi* figure sits alone atop a column made from the detritus of a consumerist society (pp. 82–83). The giant being watches a slideshow flicker across a screen in the shape of a tipi cover. Luger's grandfather Carl Whitman Jr. gathered the images to illustrate a lecture titled "The Past, Present and Futures of the Three Affiliated Tribes." Photographs of elders, traditional foods, log cabins, and great expanses of water chronicle the construction of the Garrison Dam, which flooded the bottom-lands community of Elbowoods. The giant absorbs testimony and archival imagery of the flood, bearing witness to millennia of ecological change compressed to human scale.

Future Ancestral Technologies builds upon the many futures Whitman imagined. Luger's speculative vision resonates with stories of colossal transformation in science fiction, like Kim Stanley Robinson's *Red Mars*, in which colonists struggle to terraform Mars's hostile, rocky terrain by reshaping an entire ecosphere. In N. K. Jemisin's *Broken Earth* trilogy, refugees of ecological collapse survive within an enormous underground geode powered by geological magic. Like these authors, Luger treats the elements as agents of change, collaborators in shaping futures grounded in ancestral knowledge and natural forces. He takes the long view, literally, extending a timeline in which humanity rediscovers itself in a land of extremes—drifting sand and rising waters—and making art out of the wreckage of catastrophe. ✱

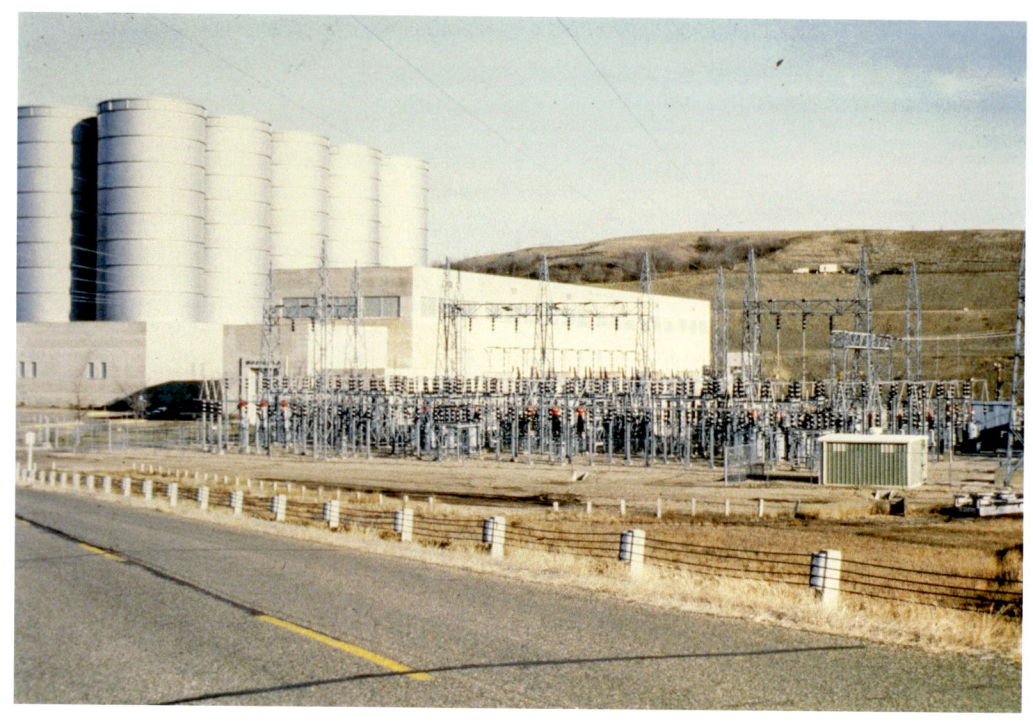

Stills from *A/V Presentation: Past, Present + Future of FB Res*

2025, digitized slides and audio from the Whitman Family Archive and archival images. Pictured, from left: The Garrison Dam and the old road to Elbowoods, dates unknown

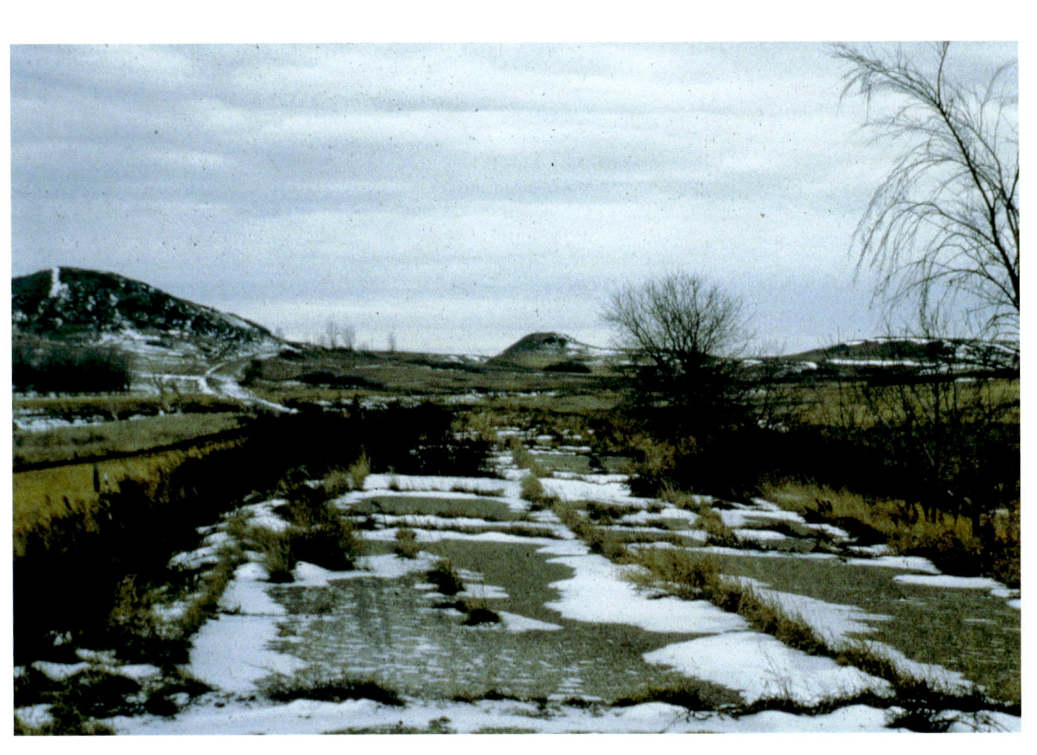

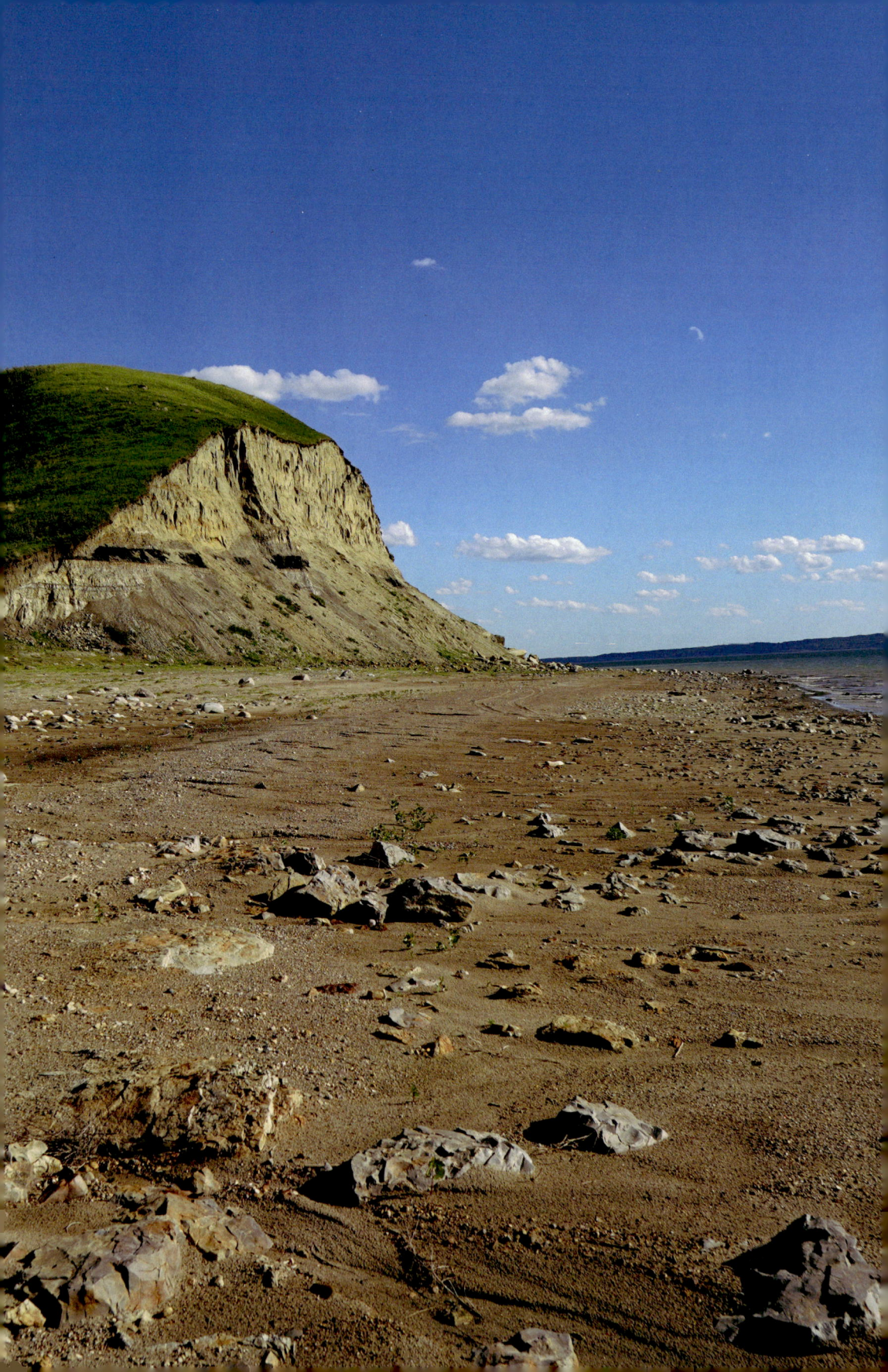

Mịhápmạk: A Way Home
Cannupa Hanska Luger

Stare across the cut banks and allow the eye to
be drawn to the deep black layer of coal.
Just below that, the sediment of ocean's rest.
You are born of the weathering of mountains.
You are the digestion of stone.
Your story is vessel to all stories.
Around the world the origin of humanity is
built of you.
You are memory.
The record of life is pressed into you.
Held by you.
You are archive.

You are in the foam of waves pulling the land
back to the sea.
Tumble in the water and become you.
Smooth pebbles smooth coral
smooth coastline.
You are churning.
You are the fermentation of liminal space.
You are the blur between opposites.
You are what is generated in the collision of
immovable objects and unstoppable forces.
You are forever possible.
Touch you and be touched
Press you and be impressed.

You are born of the weathering of mountains.
The child of water and rock.
You are the middle of soft and hard.
Cloud condensing to rain falling from great
heights kisses on the cliff face the gentle
abrasion is your birthday.
Puddle in the bedrock seeping between the
crystalline structure.
Gentle transformation.
You are time in memorial.

A caldron of mineral stirs beneath.
Without air it boils.
Earth expelled and turned to air.
Fire and smoke stoked in incomprehensible
depth breaches the surface and is transformed
in the violent eruption of worlds colliding.
Chaos to order in order for chaos.
Stability as an amorphous state.
Once so hot and now cool.
You are suspended in equilibrium.
Poised at the molecular edge of all that was
and all that will be.
You are the shape of water.
You are the shape of stone.
You are the shape of everything seen.
You are the shape of dream. *

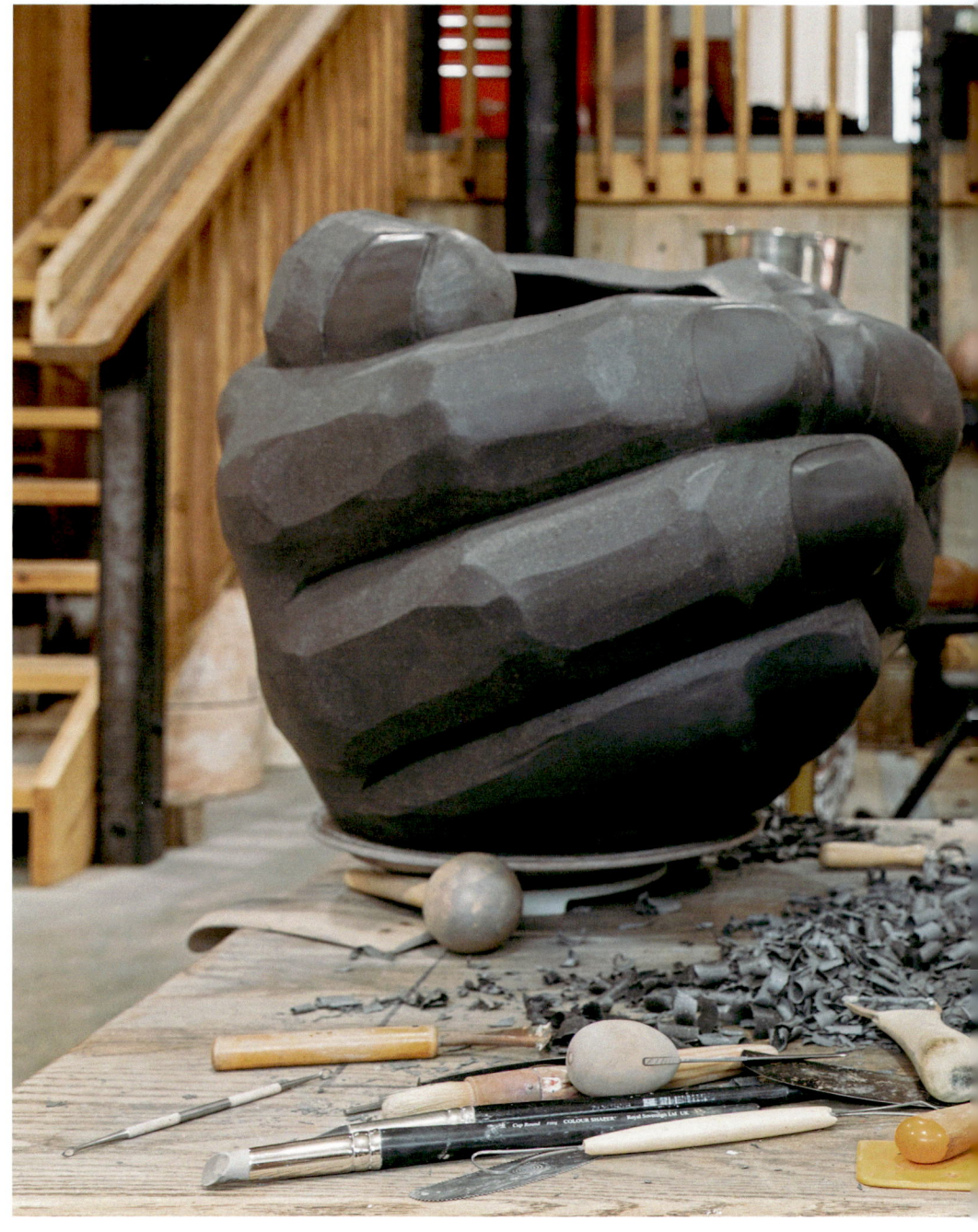

Irabágu (detail)

2025, ceramic

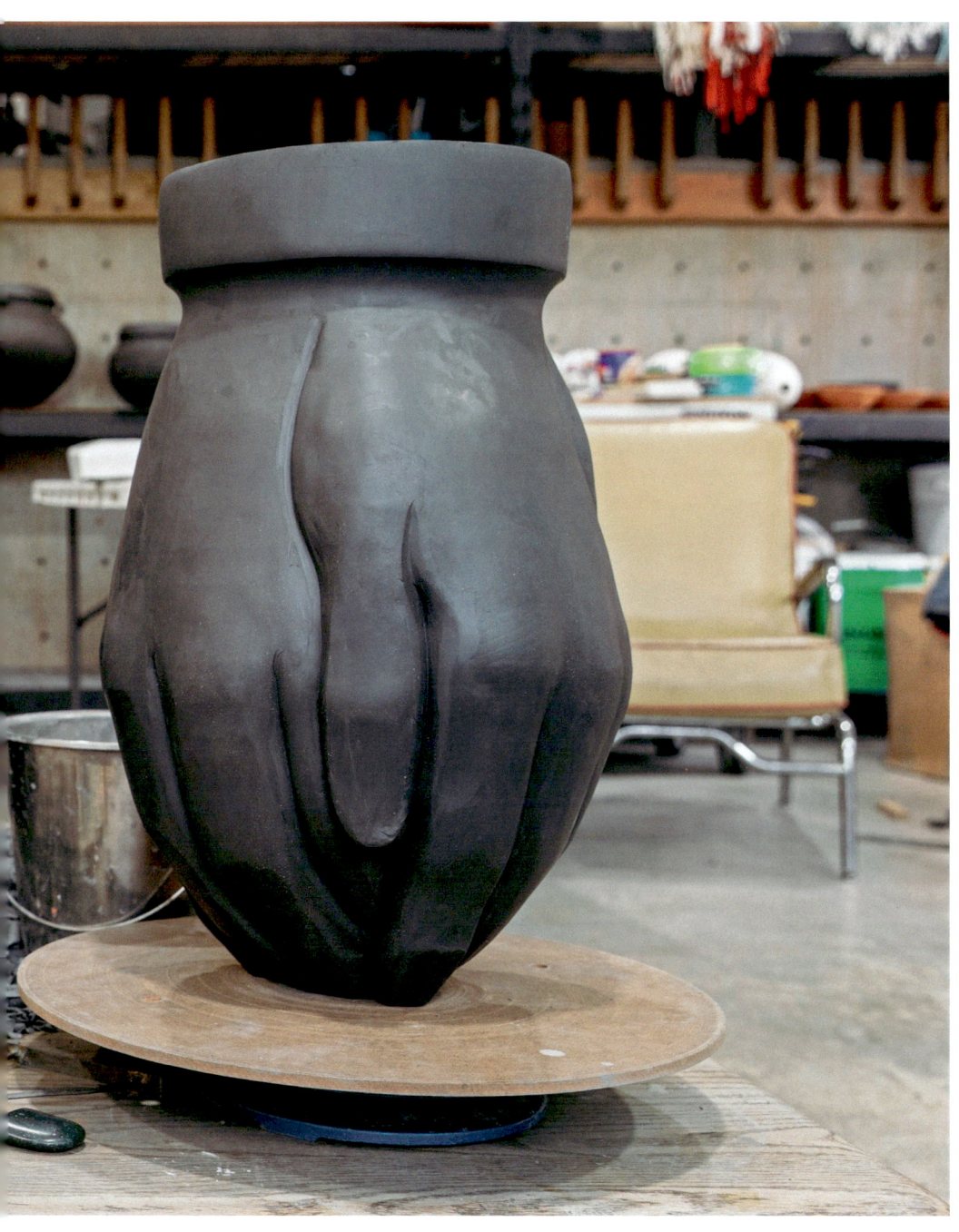

Living Landscapes
Alisha Deegan

The connection to place holds profound significance for all individuals, but for Indigenous peoples, it is steeped in thousands of years of ancestral ties. As a result, the landscape becomes an extension of our identity. From an Indigenous viewpoint, our relationship with the land is not merely one of caretaking; we see ourselves as partners in a living ecosystem. Our interconnectedness is woven into stories, the gathering and cultivation of food, and movement across rivers and terrains, all of which shape our connection to the land.

For the Mandan, Hidatsa, and Arikara (MHA) Nation, the Missouri River in North Dakota is the lifeblood of our living landscape, a sacred expanse we have inhabited and nurtured for centuries. This landscape is dotted with numerous villages and significant sites that tell our story. The Knife River Indian Villages National Historic Site, which includes three Hidatsa villages and two Mandan villages collectively known as Awadi Gixhuush (Five Villages), testifies to our enduring presence. Renowned historical figures including Sacagawea (Eagle Woman), Meriwether Lewis, William Clark, Prince Maximilian of Wied, and the artist Karl Bodmer walked here.

Bodmer's paintings serve as historical records, capturing the landscapes, people, and artifacts he encountered during his journey with Prince Maximilian (fig. 1). In making *Máadiraxbi I* and *II*, Luger drew inspiration from Bodmer's watercolors, intertwining thousands of years of history with contemporary narratives (pp. 98–99). Across his practice, Luger invites viewers to engage with these living landscapes and explore narratives that challenge conventional understandings of our existence.

However, some of the landscapes depicted in Bodmer's works are not as they once were.

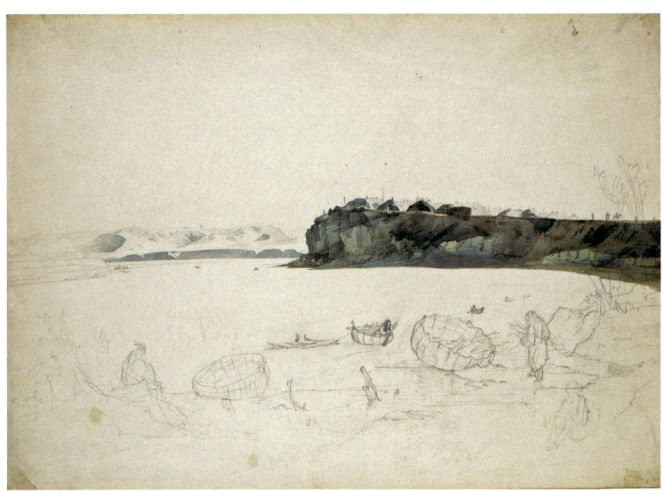

Fig. 1 Karl Bodmer, *Mih-Tutta-Hangkusch, Mandan Village*, 1833, watercolor and graphite on paper, Joslyn Art Museum, Omaha, Nebraska, Gift of the Enron Art Foundation, 1986.49.166

Many have been irrevocably altered or destroyed, particularly due to the flooding of the Missouri River that created Lake Sakakawea as part of the Garrison Dam diversion. The loss of our bottomlands is the result of policies imposed upon us with lasting repercussions and represents a painful chapter in our history. In the 1940s, when construction of the Garrison Dam began, my grandparents Edward Hall Jr. and Delphine Young Bird Hall, along with the entire MHA Nation, faced the unimaginable reality of their birthplace and sacred sites being submerged under twenty to fifty feet of water. My grandfather was tasked with the heart-wrenching responsibility of hiring young boys to relocate cemeteries, exhuming the remains of their ancestors to be moved to higher ground.

The grief and loss associated with these displacements are still deeply felt within our communities. For families on the Fort Berthold Reservation, the lake now serves as a constant reminder of separation. Yet when we return to the site of Awadi Gixhuush, we find that our villages remain. The bends of the river and the rolling hills still carry the same names, and we can walk upon them, reclaiming our connection to the land.

While Bodmer offers us a glimpse into our past, Luger illuminates the paths of our present and future. His work serves as a powerful reminder that Indigenous peoples are still here, thriving, and our existence is a beautiful testament to resilience and continuity. In this way, we honor our ancestors and the landscapes that have shaped us, reaffirming our place within this world. ✳

Wire maquette for
Máadiraxbi I and *II*

2025, wood, including willow
collected in present-day
North Dakota

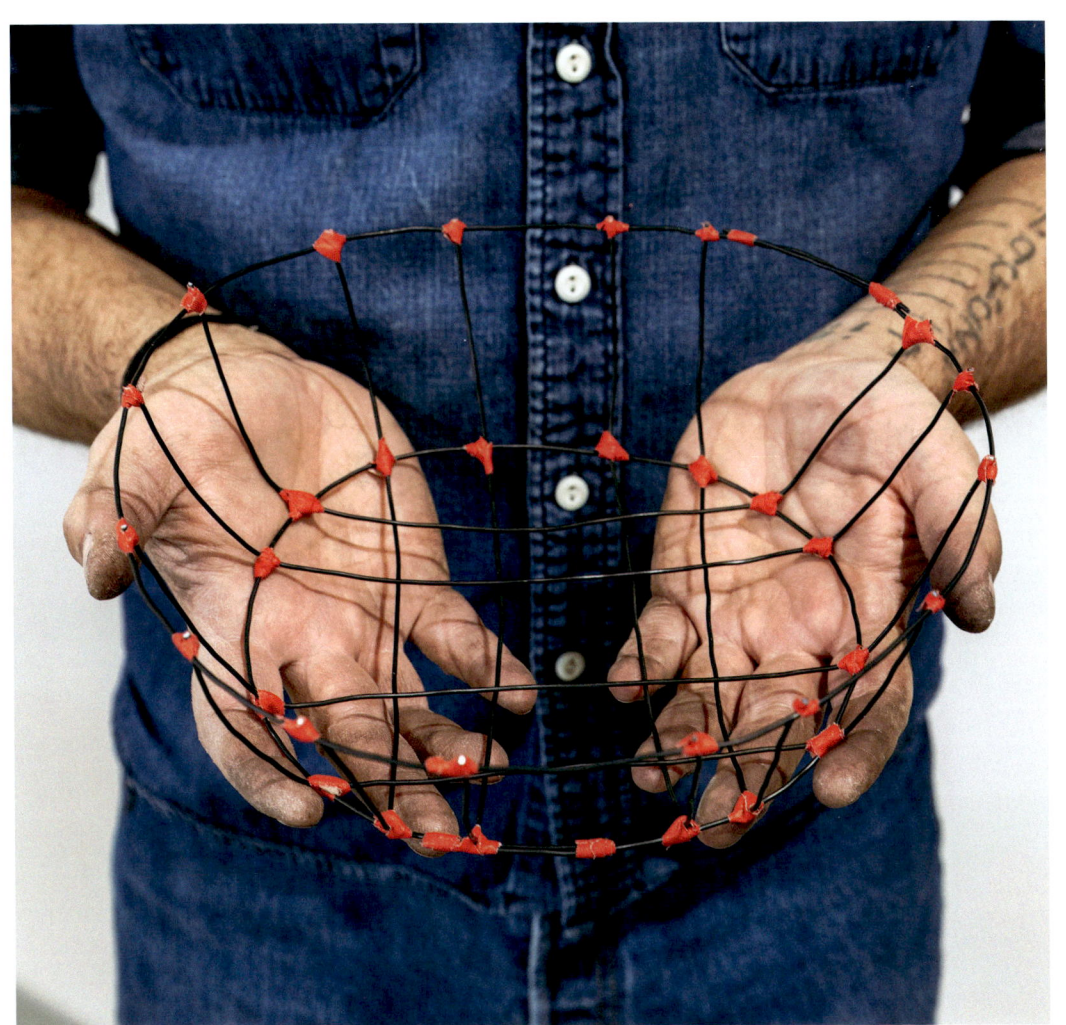

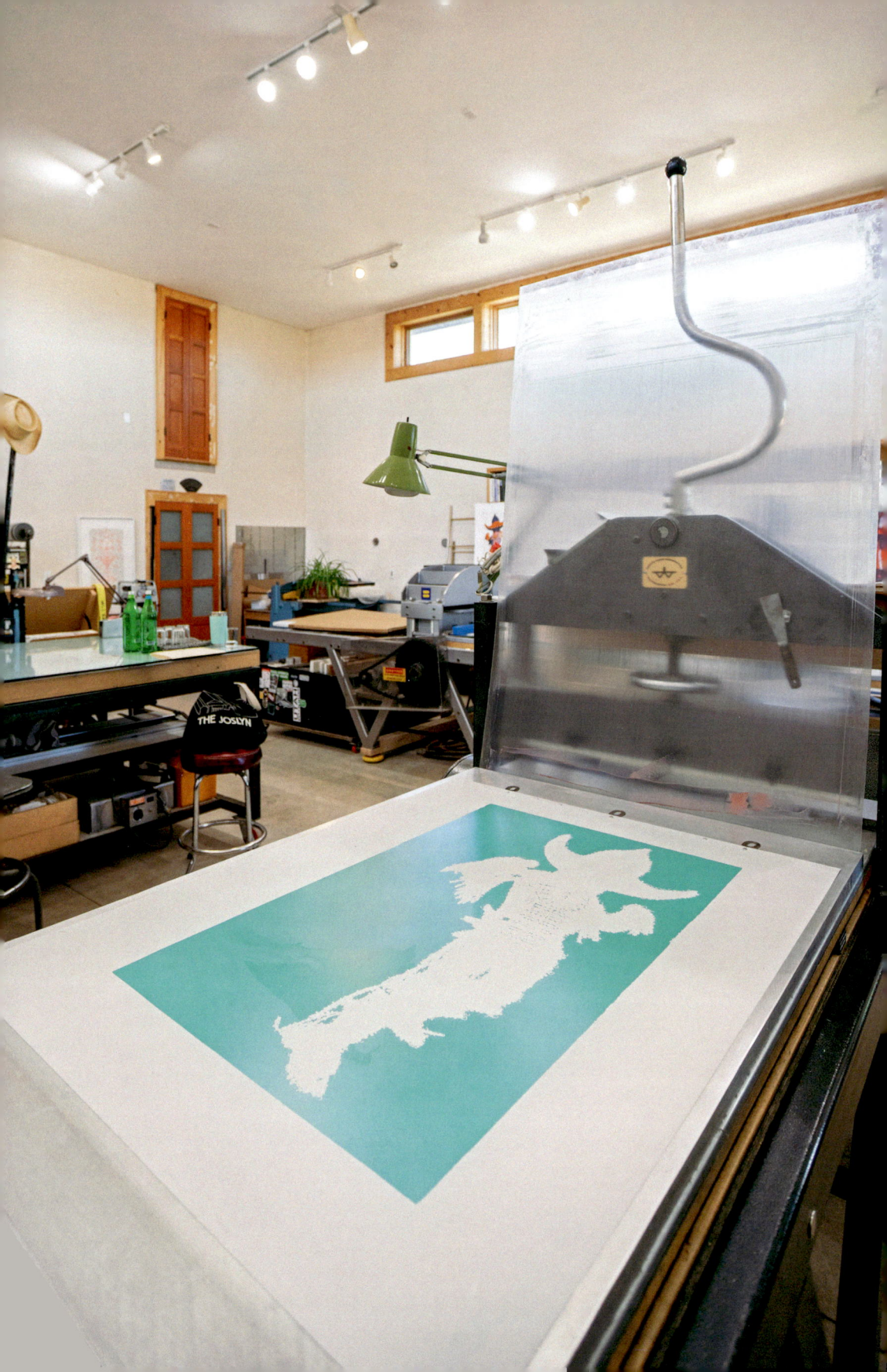

Midéegaadi
A Future Ancestral Transmission

Josie Lopez

The figures of Midéegaadi exist throughout time, maintaining a pledge of accountability to the land and waters that have sustained the Buffalo Nation and, in turn, human beings.

—Cannupa Hanska Luger

Luger's ongoing series *Future Ancestral Technologies* simultaneously traverses the past, present, and future, seeking to reveal and disrupt the damaging legacies of colonial power that decimated the buffalo and led to the misperception of disappearing Indigenous peoples, land, and knowledge systems. Engaging with futurism and science fiction, the works in this series embody transport systems, storytellers, protectors, and Indigenous technologies that have always persisted. Through a stunning range of materials, from earth to fiber to film, Luger is not reclaiming but rather making future narratives. The most recent installment in *Future Ancestral Technologies* is a suite of seven lithographs made in collaboration with master printmaker Mitchell Marti (pp. 104–17). The portfolio constitutes a foray into a medium that shaped the European imaginary of the lands and people of the so-called New World.

Luger looks to Karl Bodmer's watercolor sketches and drawings created during his travels through the Missouri River region from 1832 to 1834. These renderings were and are often considered to be foundational documentary representations of the Upper Missouri River Basin and the tribes that lived there, including Luger's Mandan and Hidatsa ancestors. According to art historian Stanton L. Catlin, traveler-reporter artists were most active in the Americas from 1810 to 1860, during which time they captured four primary types of images: scientific, ecological, topological, and social. Regardless of the artists' intentions, these acts of picturing and categorizing land and people were also a means of advancing colonization.[1]

Bodmer's renderings of the Missouri River landscape and its Indigenous inhabitants reflect more than mere observation—they constitute acts of translation, filtering a world of complex relationships through the European gaze. As such, they can also be seen as forms of speculation. Prince Maximilian of Wied reproduced Bodmer's works as prints and ultimately disseminated them in scientific and travel publications. The process of translating the drawings and watercolors into prints created another layer of interpretation and resulted in alterations to some of Bodmer's original works.[2] Moreover, some of the landscapes Bodmer depicted are unknowable today, either submerged by rising waters due to the construction of dams and reservoirs or drastically changed.[3] Consequently, Bodmer's images of the land and people not only informed European views of the Americas but also became source material for Indigenous self-perception. In engaging with his renderings and their print reproductions, Luger considers the significance of slippages while asking a key question: "What is missing?"[4]

With the *Remarkable Landscape* lithographs, printmaking becomes a form of resistance, a means of reprogramming history while telegraphing a new way of seeing the land. Through the visible layering of land formations and Luger's *Midéegaadi* figures, the artist collapses time and transforms Bodmer's compositions into palimpsests. He disrupts and questions these visual legacies by centering the dancing *Midéegaadi* figures, who exist outside of linear time. These beings have survived extinction-level colonial violence and emerged as something larger than history itself, a convergence of human, land, and cosmic forces. Clad in buffalo regalia, the figures expand to the scale of the land, dissolving the boundaries between portraiture, history, and landscape to construct a new genre and a new ethos.

Typically rendered as a symbol of the "disappearing frontier," the buffalo embodies an ancestor in Luger's prints, traveling through time with Indigenous knowledge and memory of entire ecosystems and homelands. In this way, it functions as an archive, encoded with knowledge systems often absent from Western historical narratives.[5] Depictions of rituals and ceremonies, such as Bodmer's 1834 sketch of buffalo dancers (p. 32), became part of the enduring visual lexicon of images claiming to capture a moment in time. They spawned many reproductions, ultimately resulting in a proliferation of homogeneous depictions of Indigenous peoples.[6]

The *Remarkable Landscape* prints call attention to Luger's act of looking at his own history through Bodmer's renderings and subsequent reproductions. Luger does not simply mourn the losses experienced by Indigenous peoples—he summons them. Created from a process of finely layered inks and carefully rendered halftones intentionally made visible through dot matrices, his lithographs fracture space and time, pulling these narratives, rituals, and drowned landscapes into the picture plane. As such, they represent a physical and geological act of remembering while simultaneously looking to the future. The buffalo resurfaces as part of the fabric of land-human relationships, not just in these prints but also in the other works that make up *Future Ancestral Technologies.* These works are not nostalgic, they are prefigurative. Together, they compose a world where lost landscapes and beings persist.

As sites for imagining an alternate reality, the *Remarkable Landscape* prints are rooted in concepts of futurism. They break colonial timelines and refuse the myth of disappearance.[7] The buffalo endures. Indigenous cosmologies, erased from mainstream history, persist. The Missouri River, despite being dammed and altered, remembers. The *Remarkable Landscape* project functions as a transmission from the future, through which Luger invites us to step into a world where Indigenous survival is not an anomaly but a testament to the survivance of living systems, more-than-human kinships, and time itself. ✳

1. Stanton L. Catlin, "Traveler-Reporter Artists and the Empirical Tradition in Post-Independence Latin American Art," in *Art in Latin America: The Modern Era, 1820–1980*, ed. Dawn Ades (New Haven: Yale University Press, 1989), 48. See also Mary Louise Pratt, *Imperial Eyes: Travel Writing and Transculturation* (London: Routledge, 1992).

2. Kristine K. Ronan, "Paint and Print in Motion: Karl Bodmer's Atlas," in *Faces from the Interior: The North American Portraits of Karl Bodmer*, ed. Toby Jurovics (Omaha, NE: Joslyn Art Museum, 2021), 206.

3. Cannupa Hanska Luger, conversation with the author, January 20, 2025. See also Toby Jurovics, ed., "Missouri River Notes," in *Faces from the Interior*, 11.

4. Luger, conversation with the author.

5. Luger, conversation with the author.

6. Luger, conversation with the author.

7. Grace L. Dillon, ed., *Walking the Clouds: An Anthology of Indigenous Science Fiction* (Tucson: University of Arizona Press, 2012).

Bone as
Remarkable
Landscape

————————

2025, from the ongoing series
Future Ancestral Technologies,
2018–, eight-color lithograph

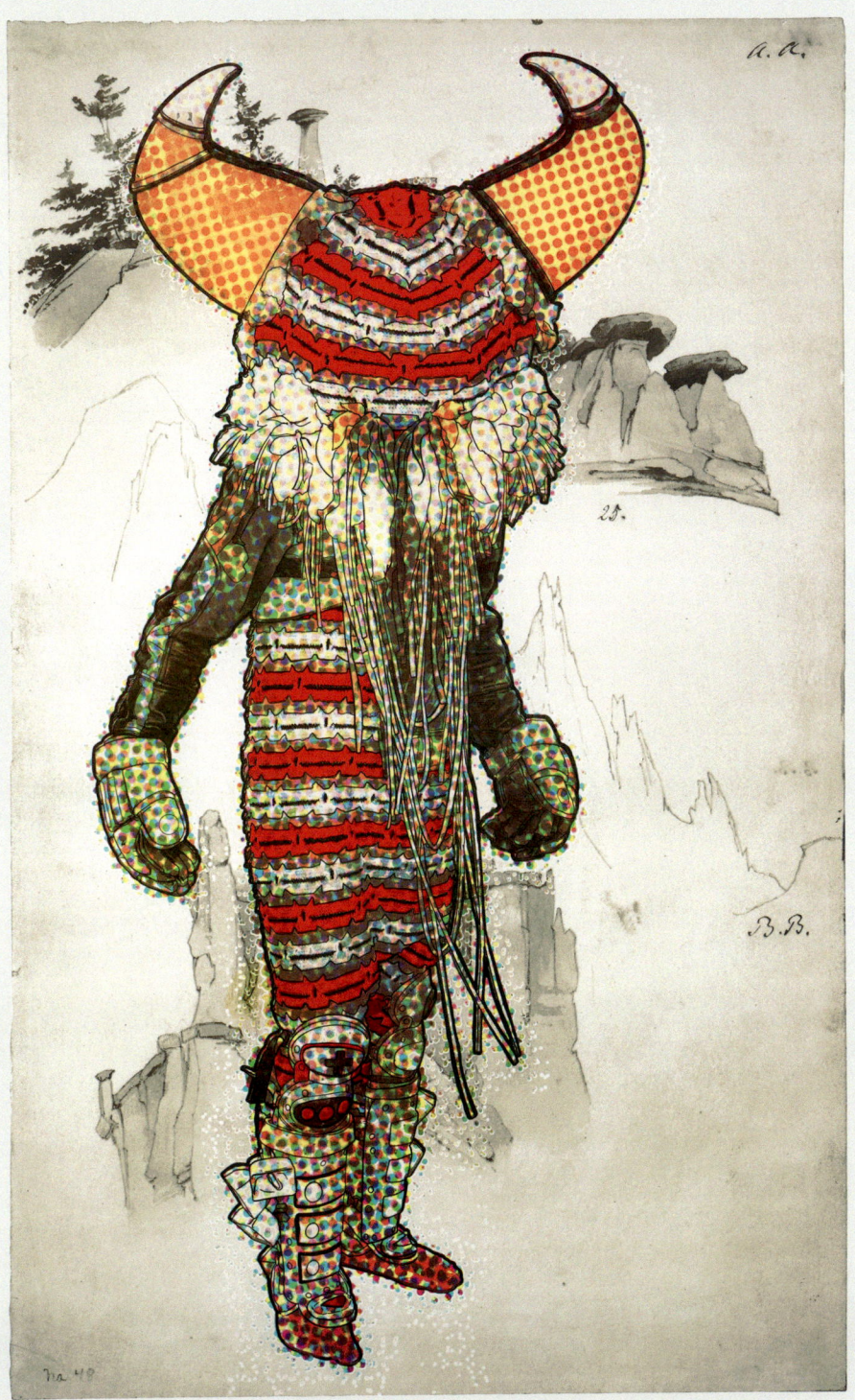

Muscle as Remarkable Landscape

2025, from the ongoing series
Future Ancestral Technologies,
2018–, eight-color lithograph

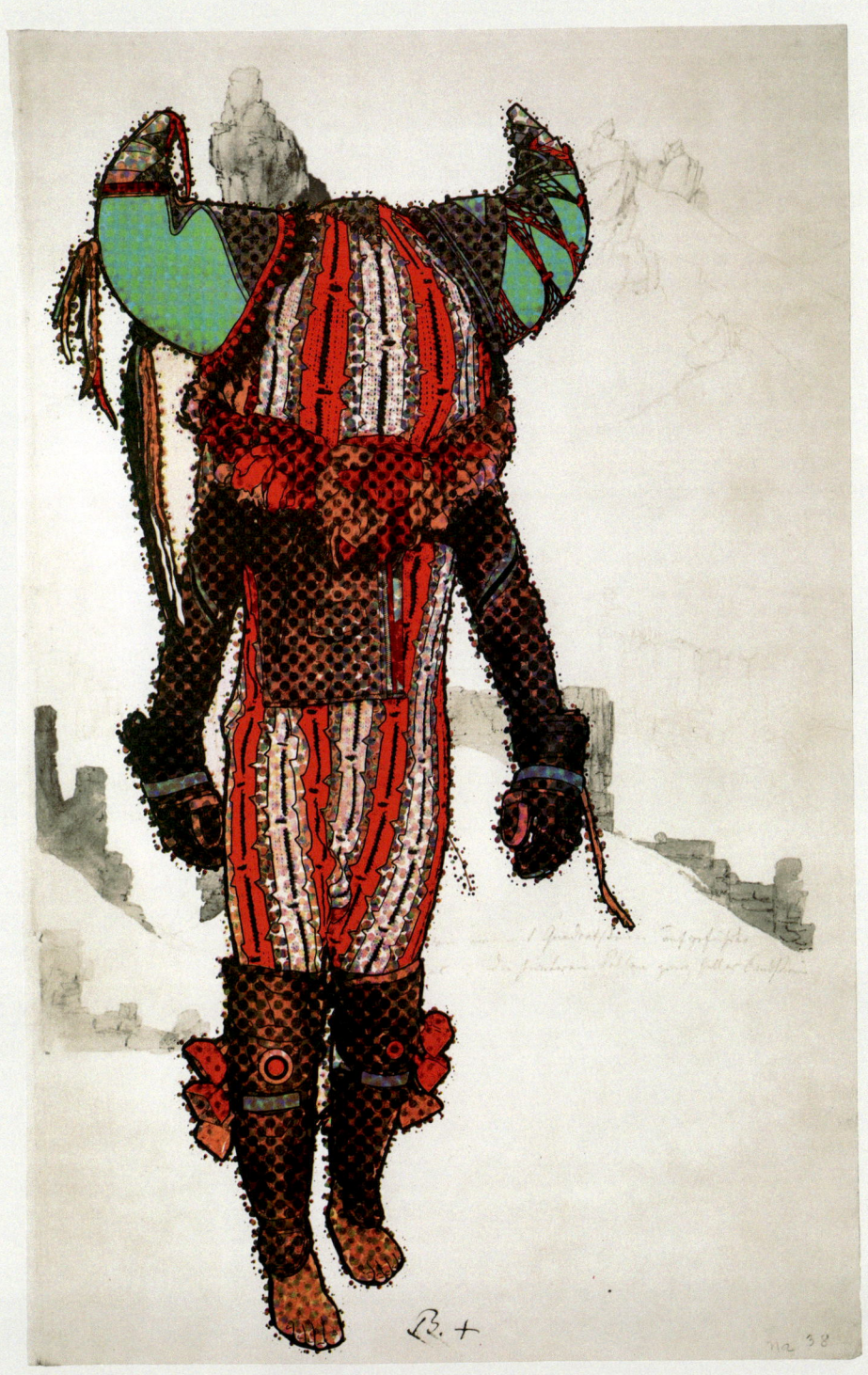

Light as Remarkable Landscape

2025, from the ongoing series
Future Ancestral Technologies,
2018–, eight-color lithograph

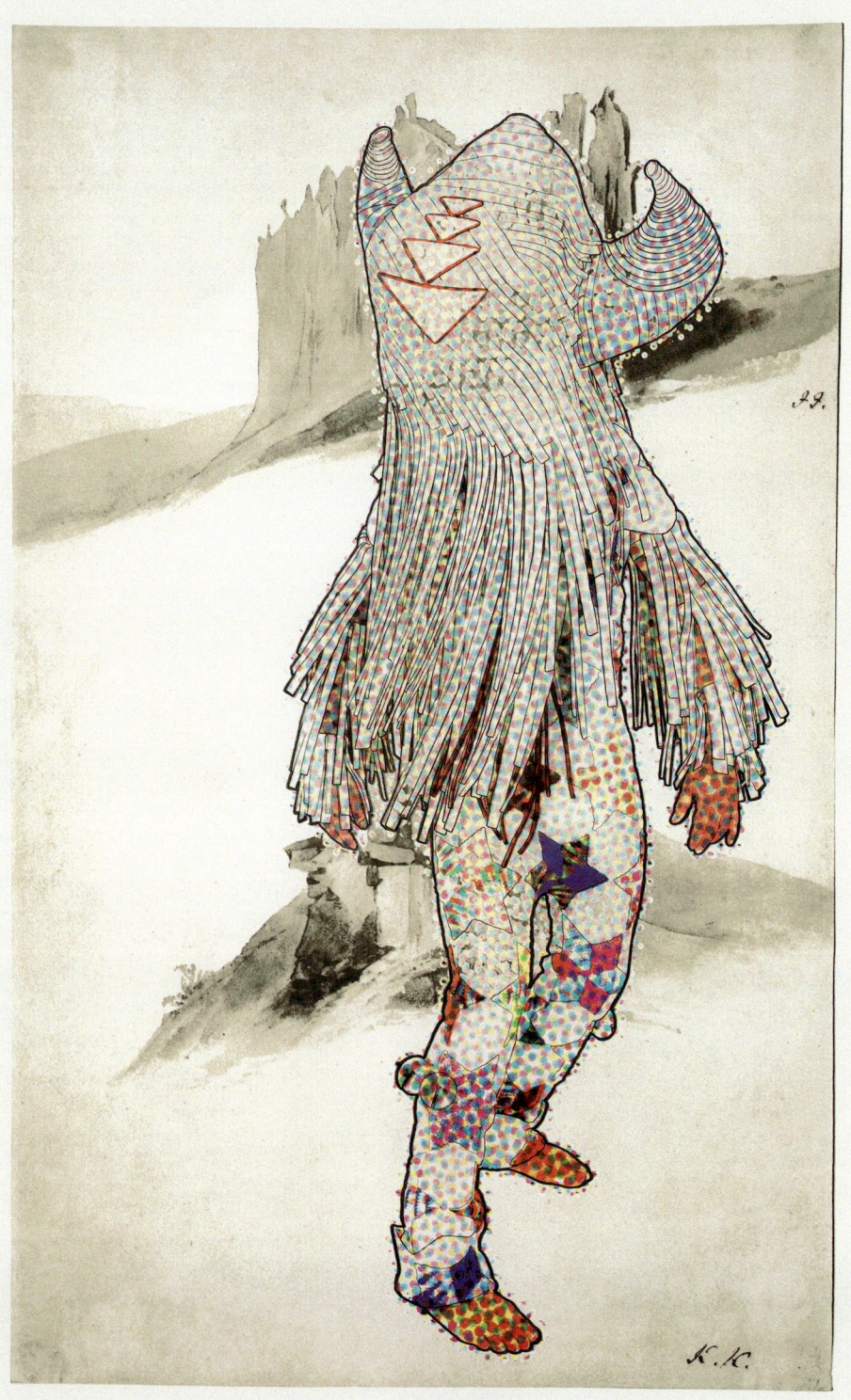

Fire as Remarkable Landscape

2025, from the ongoing series
Future Ancestral Technologies,
2018–, eight-color lithograph

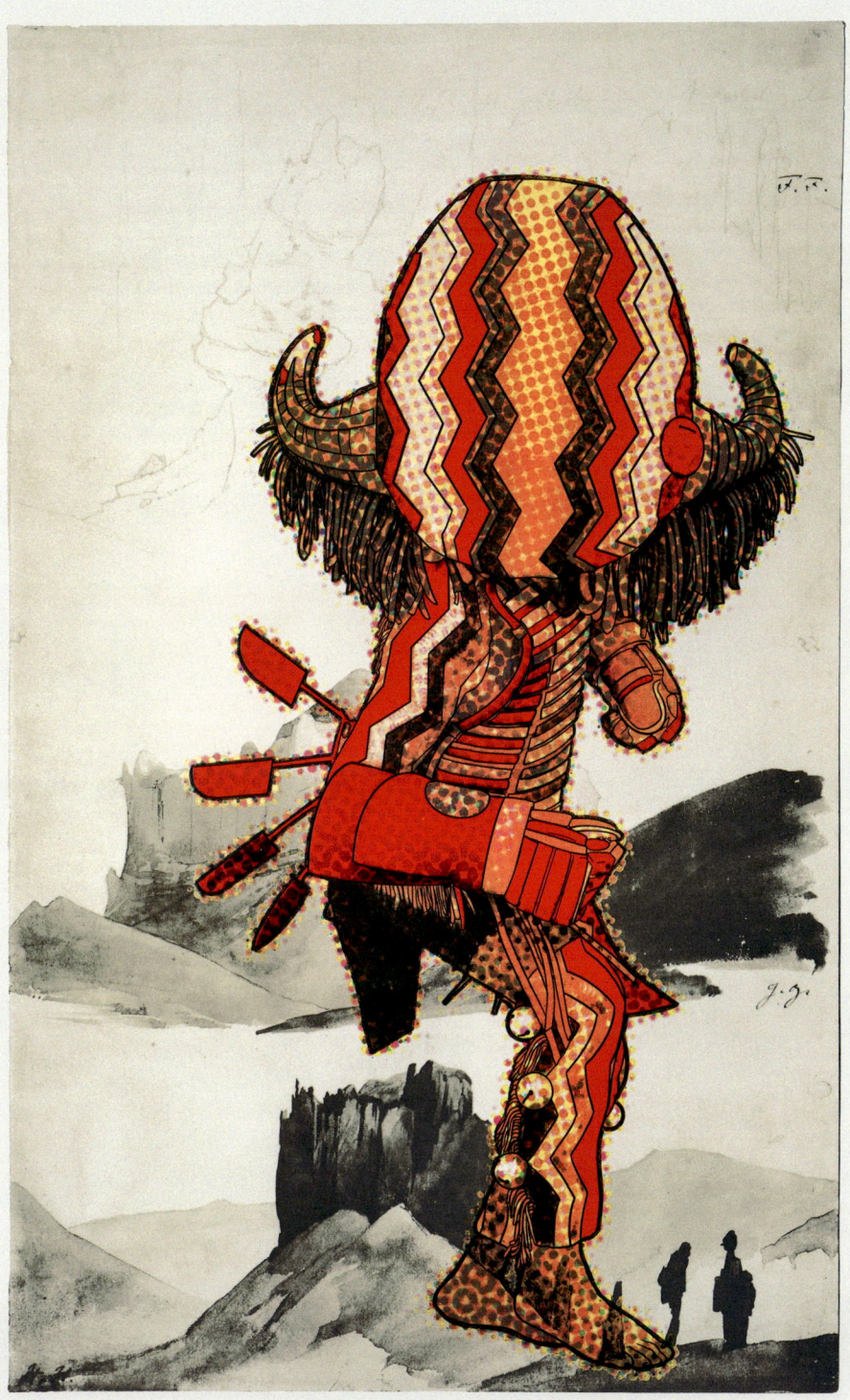

Water as Remarkable Landscape

2025, from the ongoing series
Future Ancestral Technologies,
2018–, eight-color lithograph

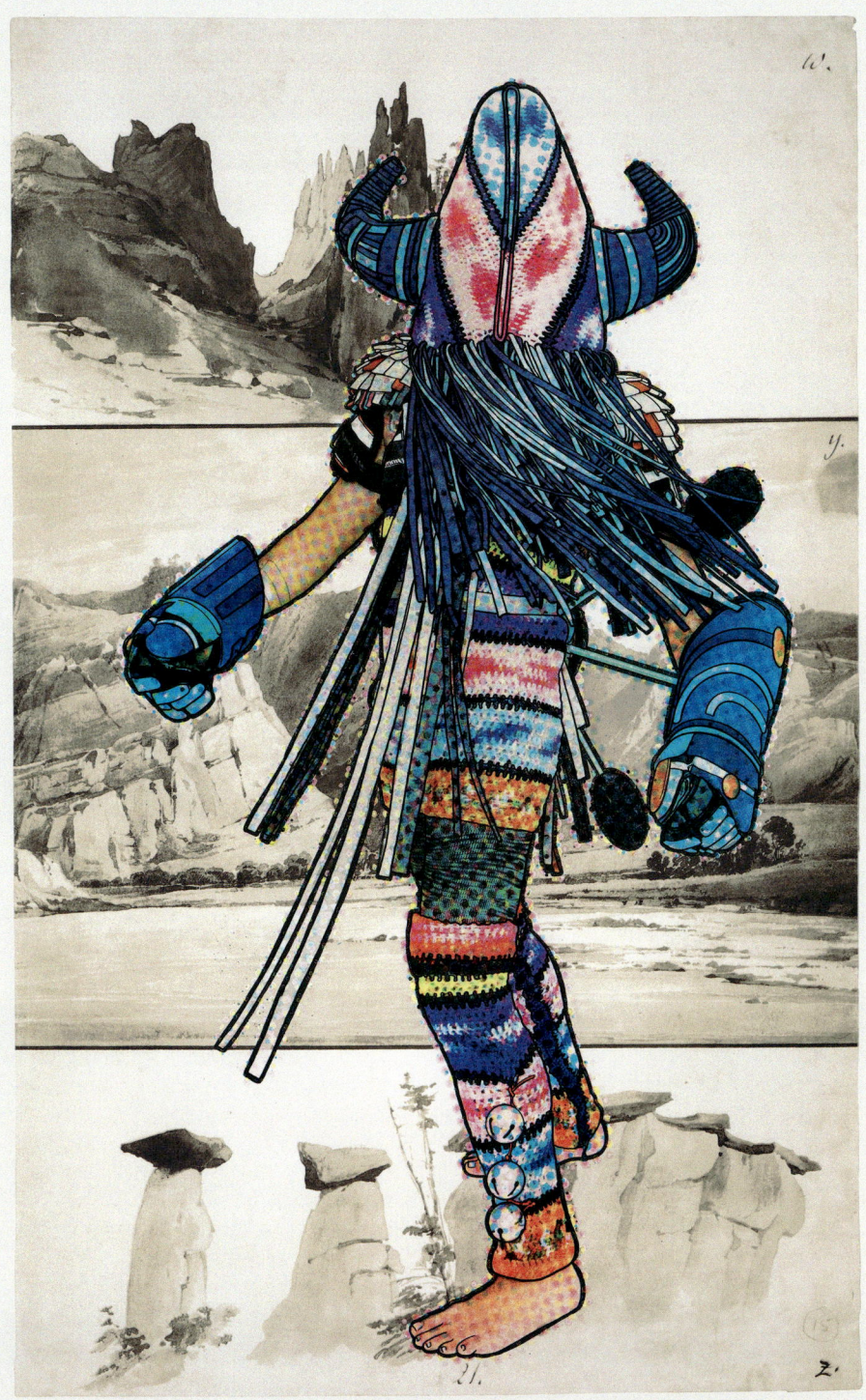

Thunder as Remarkable Landscape

2025, from the ongoing series
Future Ancestral Technologies,
2018–, eight-color lithograph

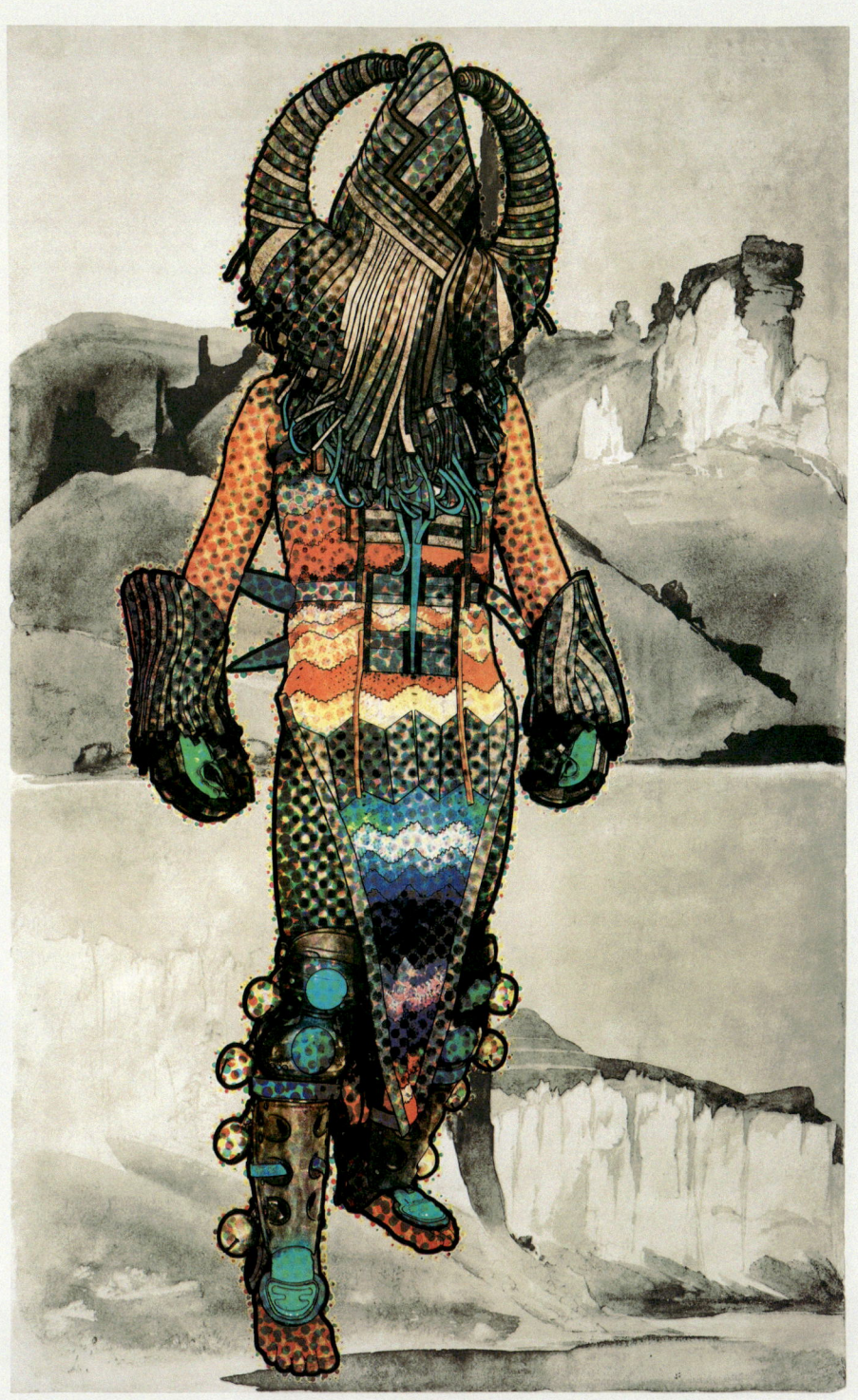

Lightning as Remarkable Landscape

2025, from the ongoing series
Future Ancestral Technologies,
2018–, eight-color lithograph

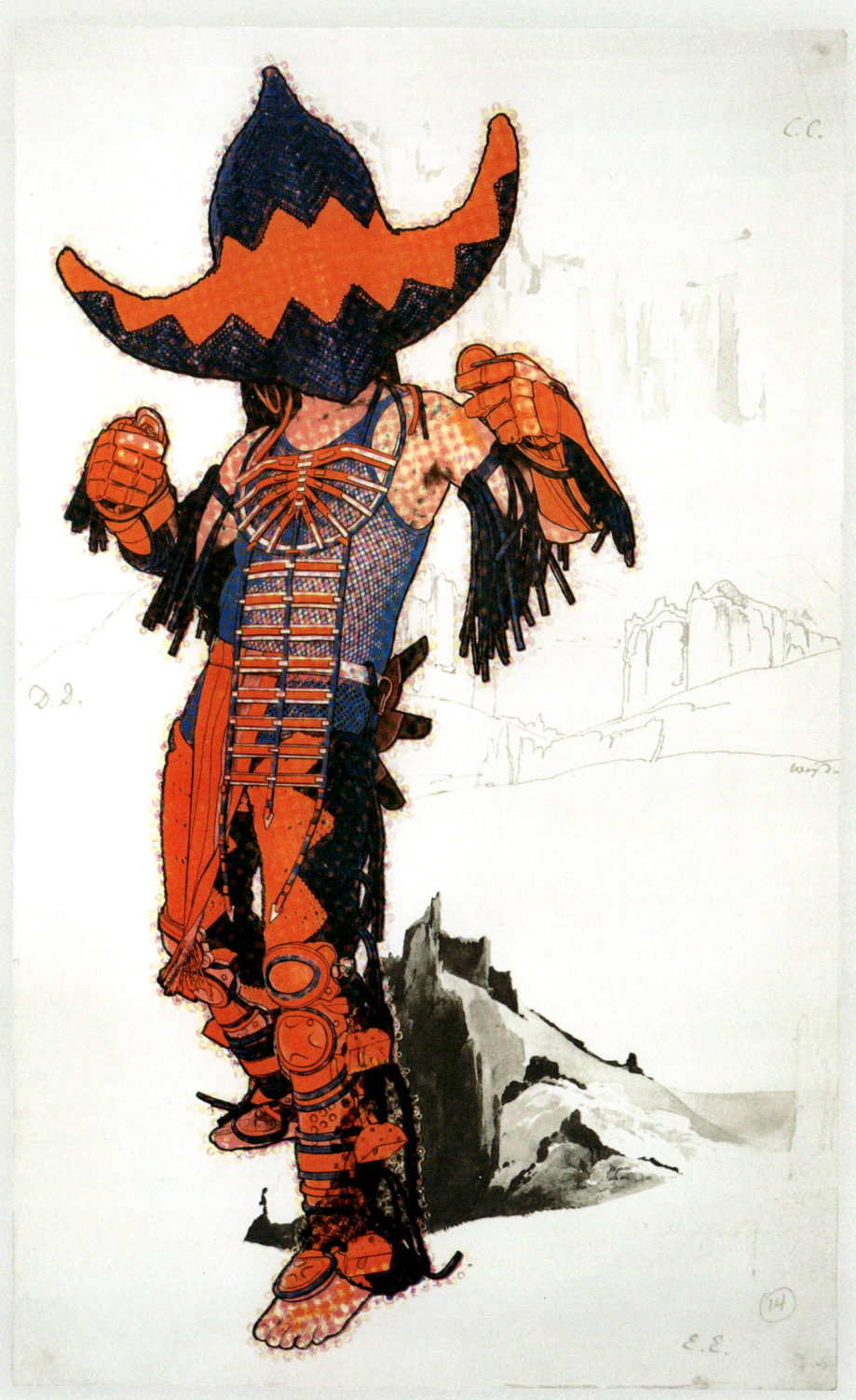

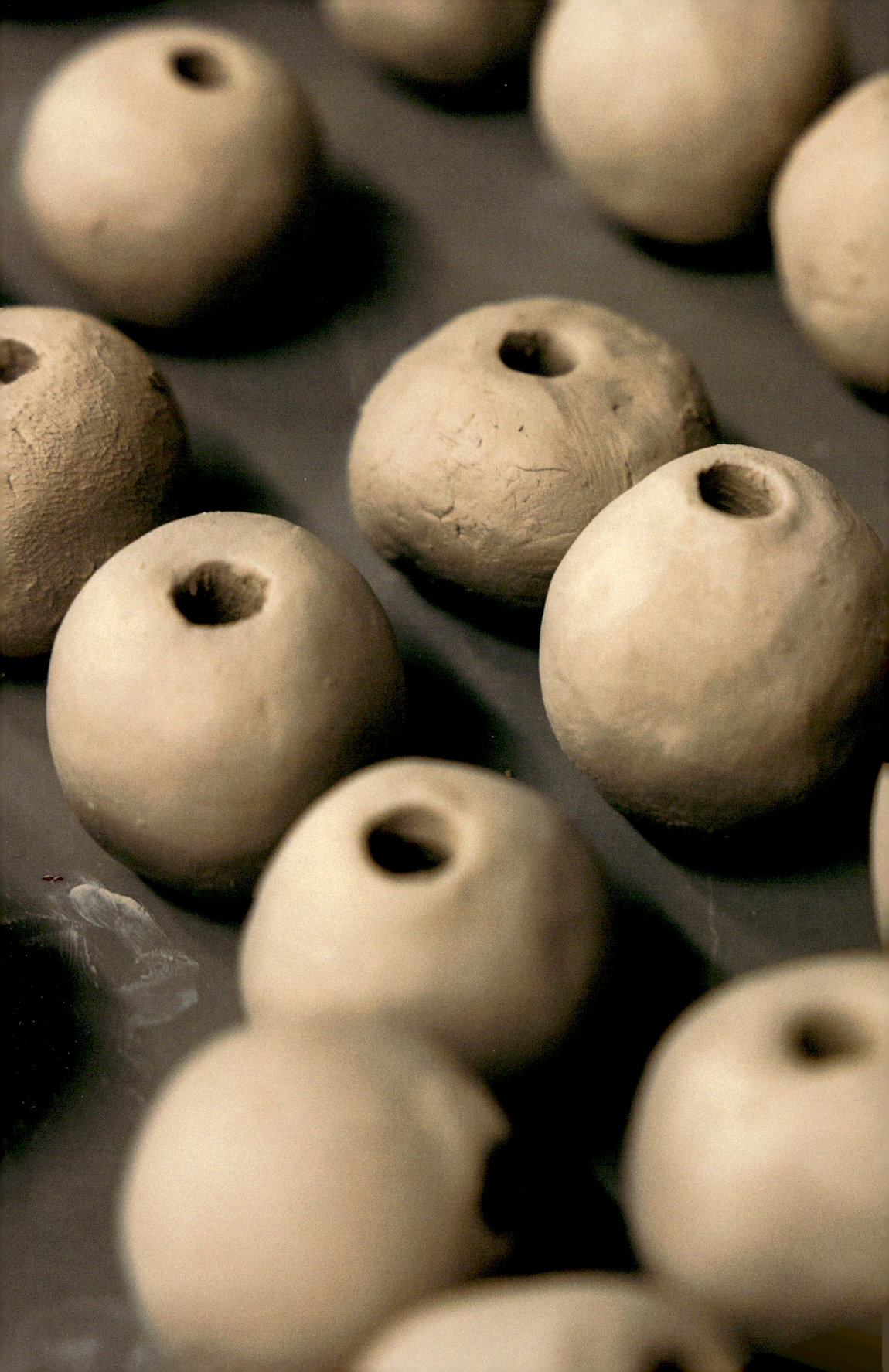

Of the Beings That Roam the Earth
Steve Tamayo

The buffalo, *tatanka*, is great in size and great in stature.[1] It is also great in its status among all other beings. The buffalo nation is a leader among the four-legged and the winged nations. Long ago, Buffalo agreed to be a sacrifice so that mankind could thrive on the earth. In exchange, the people must be the caretakers of Unci Mah'ka, Grandmother Earth, with responsibility for the land, the buffalo nation, and all other beings that roam the earth.

This agreement took place in the sacred Black Hills (He Sapa). All of the nations were there to take part in the Great Race. It was the winged nation, called upon by Man, that helped set the plan into motion, for Man was slower than any among the four-legged nation. He asked Magpie, Meadowlark, Hawk, and Hummingbird to fly on his behalf should he fall behind. Hummingbird dropped out first—his wings were far too small for the long journey. Next was Meadowlark, who landed with exhaustion. Then Hawk swooped in to pass Buffalo but didn't have the stamina. Finally, Magpie caught up to Buffalo and whispered into her ear, "Let me win, Ta. Then Man will be in our debt and provide all that we need."

Magpie and Buffalo were neck and neck as they neared the end of the race. Buffalo complied with Magpie's plan and conceded. Man kept his promise to care for all the beings of the earth. From time immemorial, the people of Turtle Island held their stewardship of the land and all who relied on it as one of their most treasured values.[2] The buffalo population grew and thrived enough to provide everything for mankind, and the nations thrived in turn. At its largest, the buffalo nation was millions strong.

But not all of mankind honored the agreement to care for the buffalo nation. Colonization and exploration led to its rapid decline.

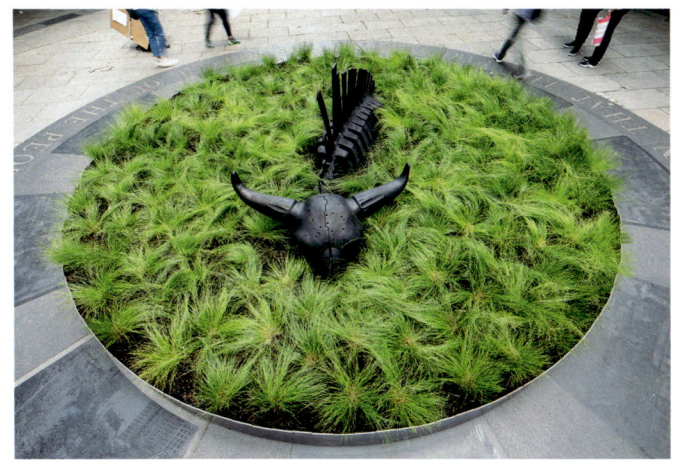

Fig. 1 *Attrition*, 2024, cast steel

By 1889, there were only a few hundred buffalo to be found throughout the plains of North America.[3] The Native tribes' fate seems to parallel that of the buffalo nation. It has been estimated that before European invasion, up to twelve million Indigenous people lived on Turtle Island.[4] Through the hardships that have befallen our people, there were just over 237,000 by 1900.[5] The perils of colonization—disease, famine, and warfare—caused a population decline of over 95 percent. Through hunting, sport, and blatant disregard for mankind's role as stewards, the buffalo have suffered along with our tribal nations (fig. 1).

Ours is a story of resilience. Today, we represent 1 percent of the US population, with 3.3 million Americans identifying primarily as Native Americans in the 2020 census. Through conservation efforts, the American bison now number over five hundred thousand, including commercial herds. Native nations hold approximately twenty thousand bison on tribal lands (fig. 2).[6] ✳

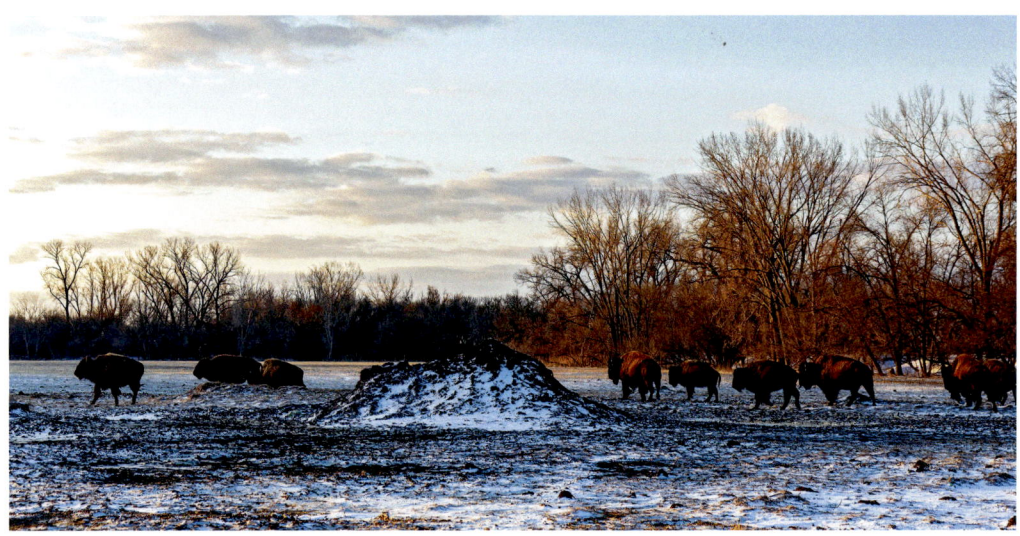

Fig. 2 The Omaha Tribe of Nebraska's bison herd at Big Elk Park, Macy, Nebraska, 2024

1. *Ta* means "buffalo," and *tanka* means "large."

2. "Turtle Island," a name for North America, originates from various Indigenous creation stories that describe a time when the world was covered in water, and land first took shape on a turtle's back. Used today by many Native people, the term affirms Indigenous identity and sovereignty.

3. "Plains Bison," US Fish and Wildlife Service, accessed February 5, 2025, https://www.fws.gov /species/plains-bison-bison -bison-bison.

4. David E. Stannard, *American Holocaust: The Conquest of the New World* (New York: Oxford University Press, 1992), 11.

5. US Bureau of the Census, "Indian Population of the United States and Alaska," 1910 (Washington, DC: US Government Printing Office, 1915), 10, https:// www.census.gov/library /publications/1915/dec/aian .html.

6. "Plains Bison," US Fish and Wildlife Service.

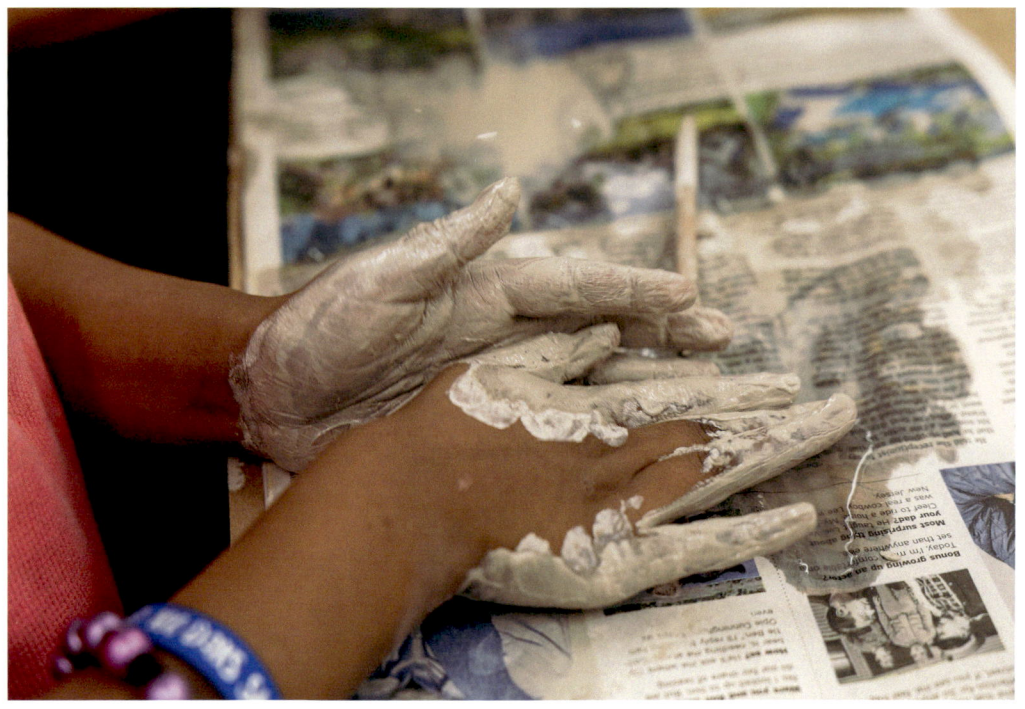

Bison Bead Project workshop
held at the Joslyn Art Museum,
Omaha, Nebraska, February 6,
2025

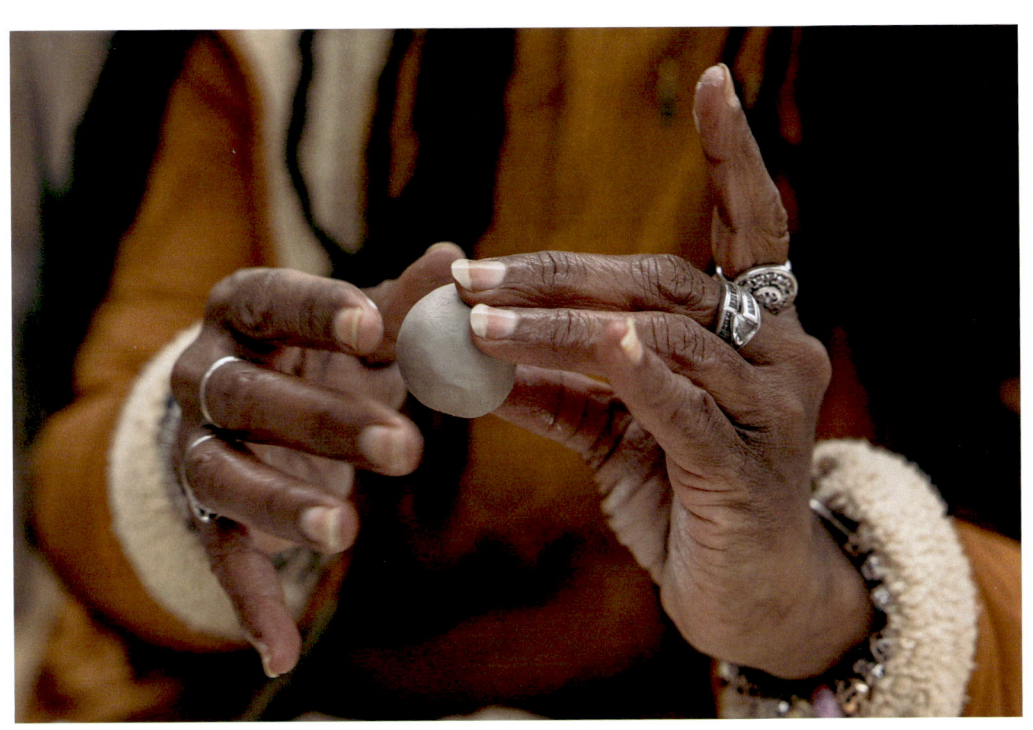

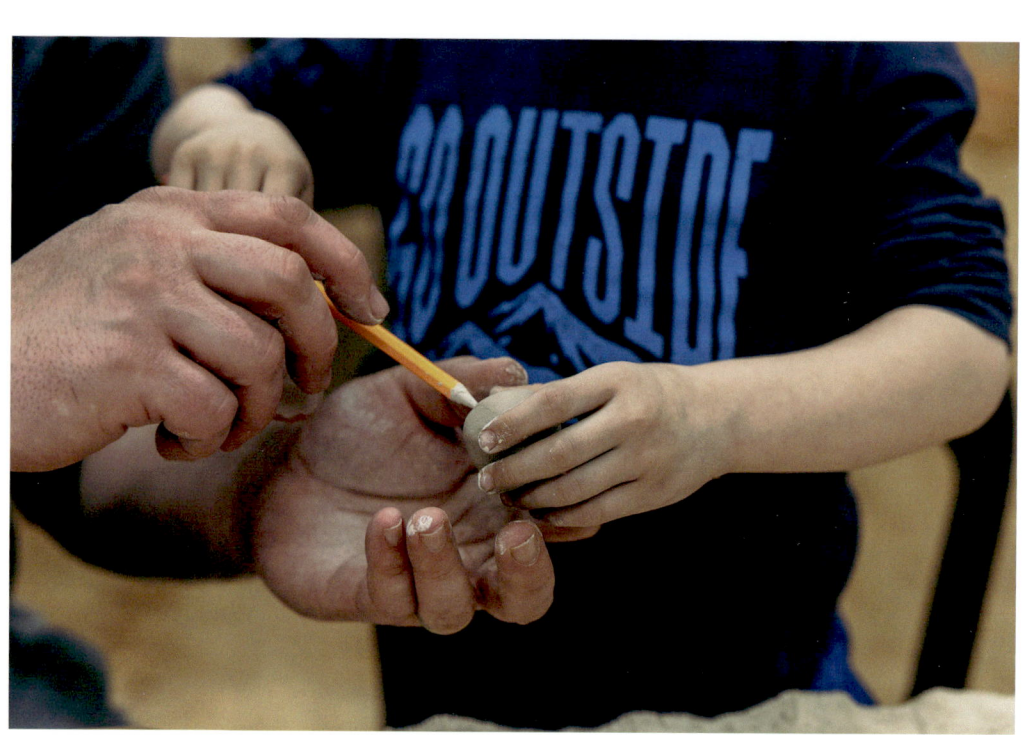

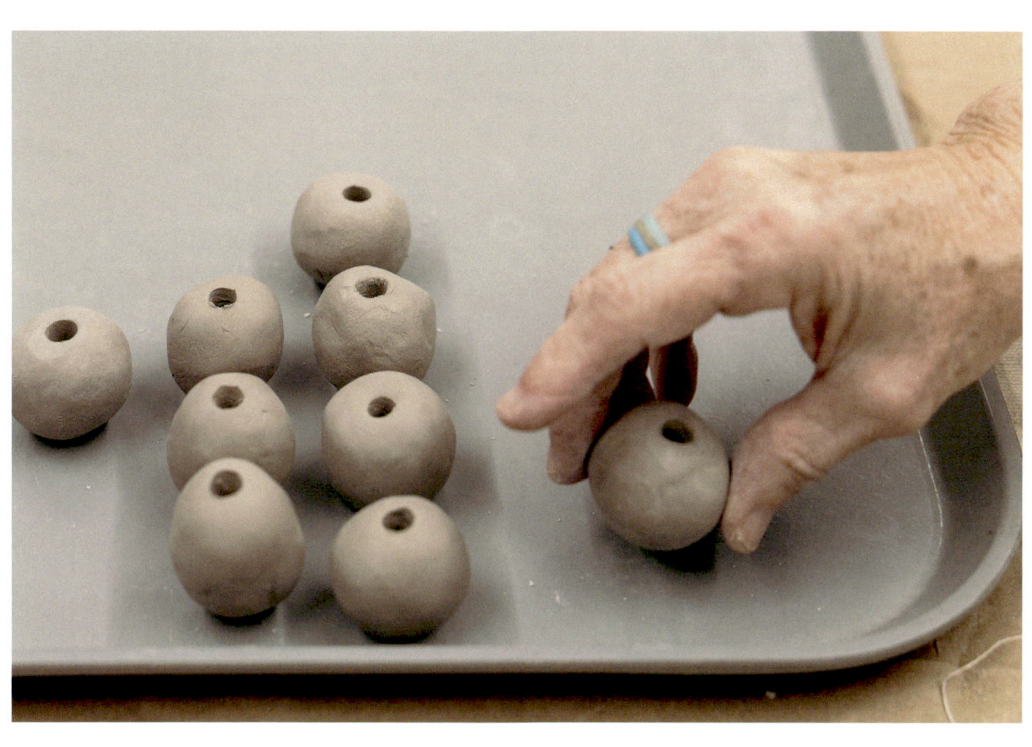

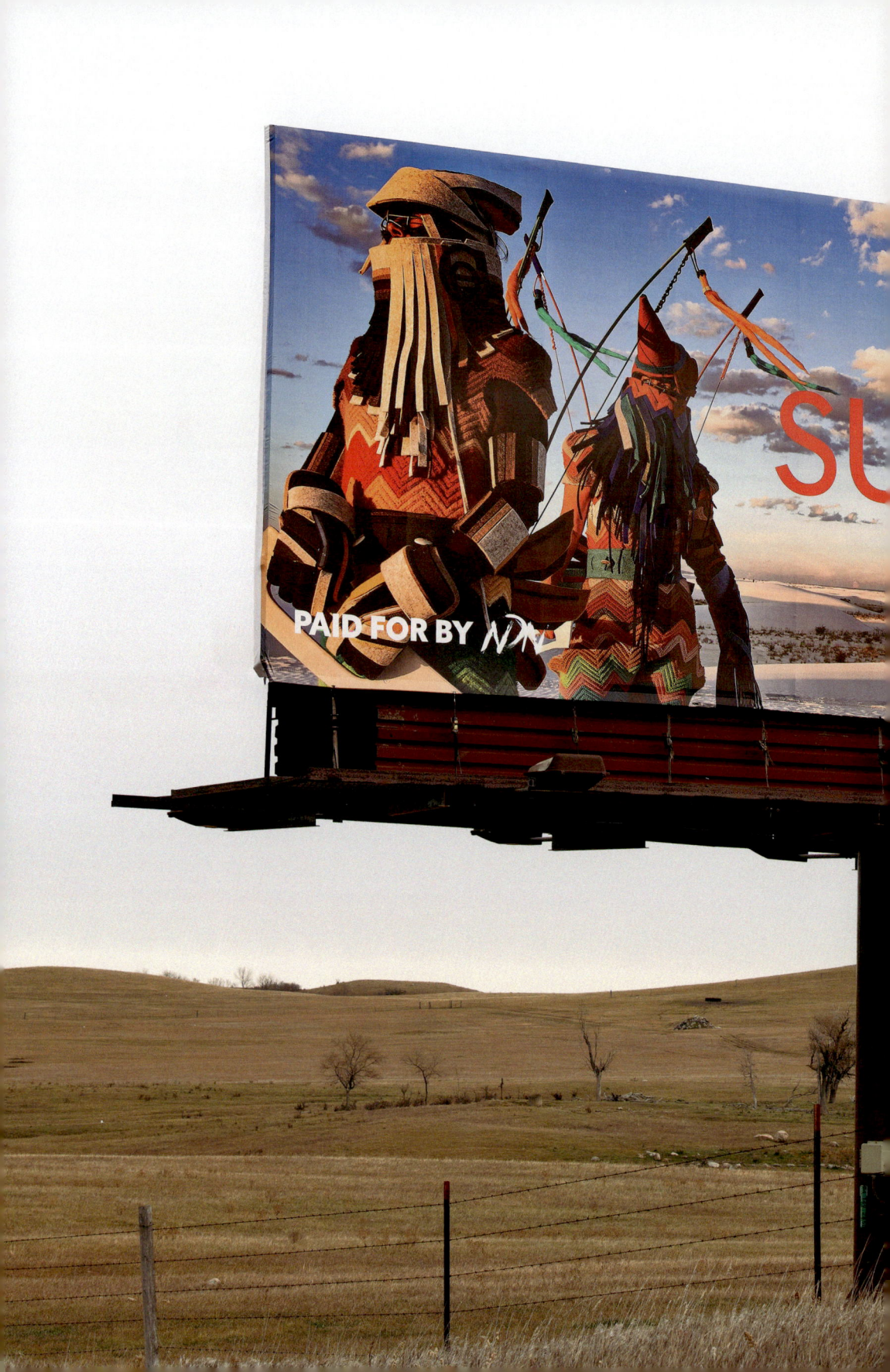

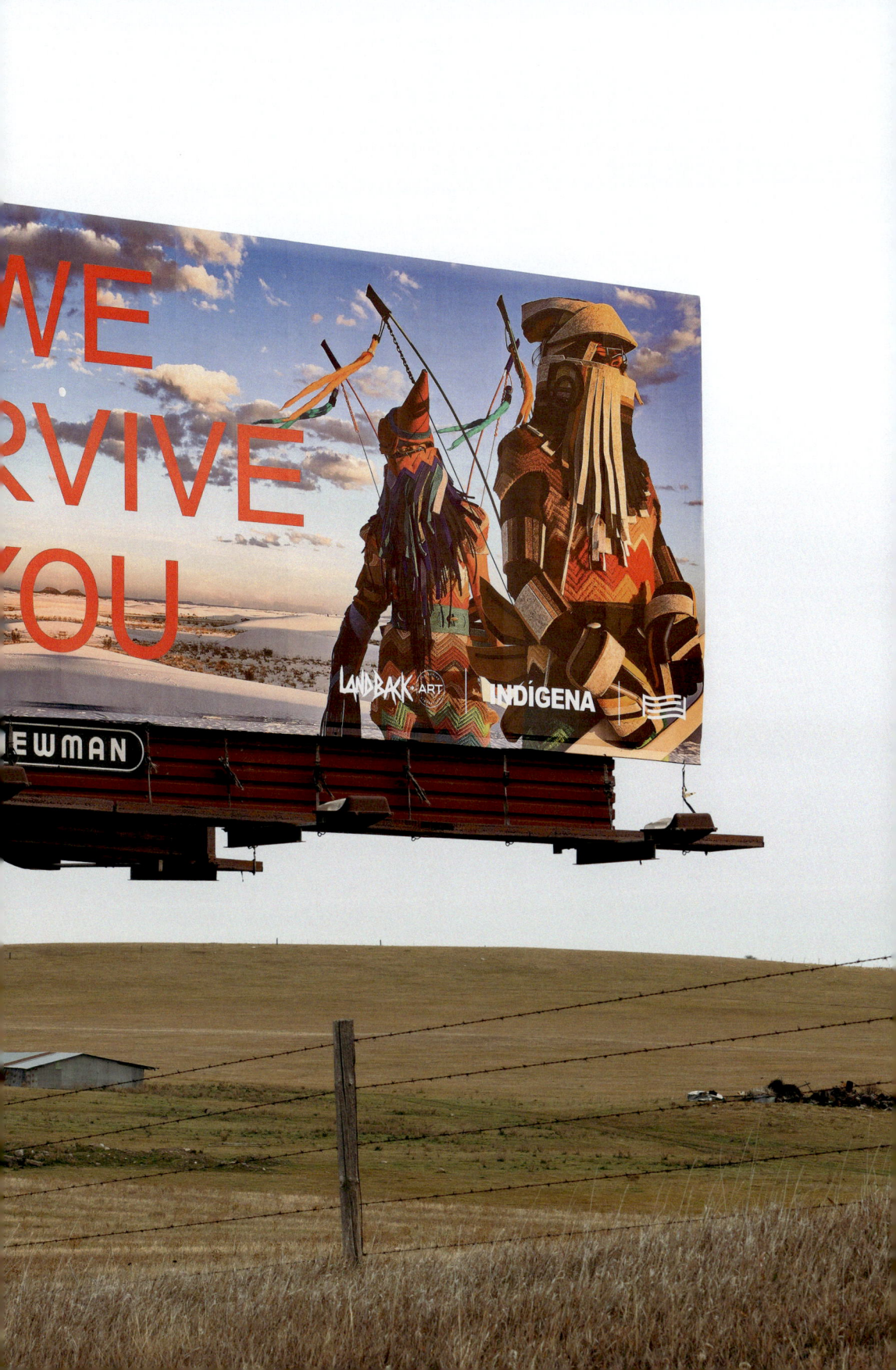

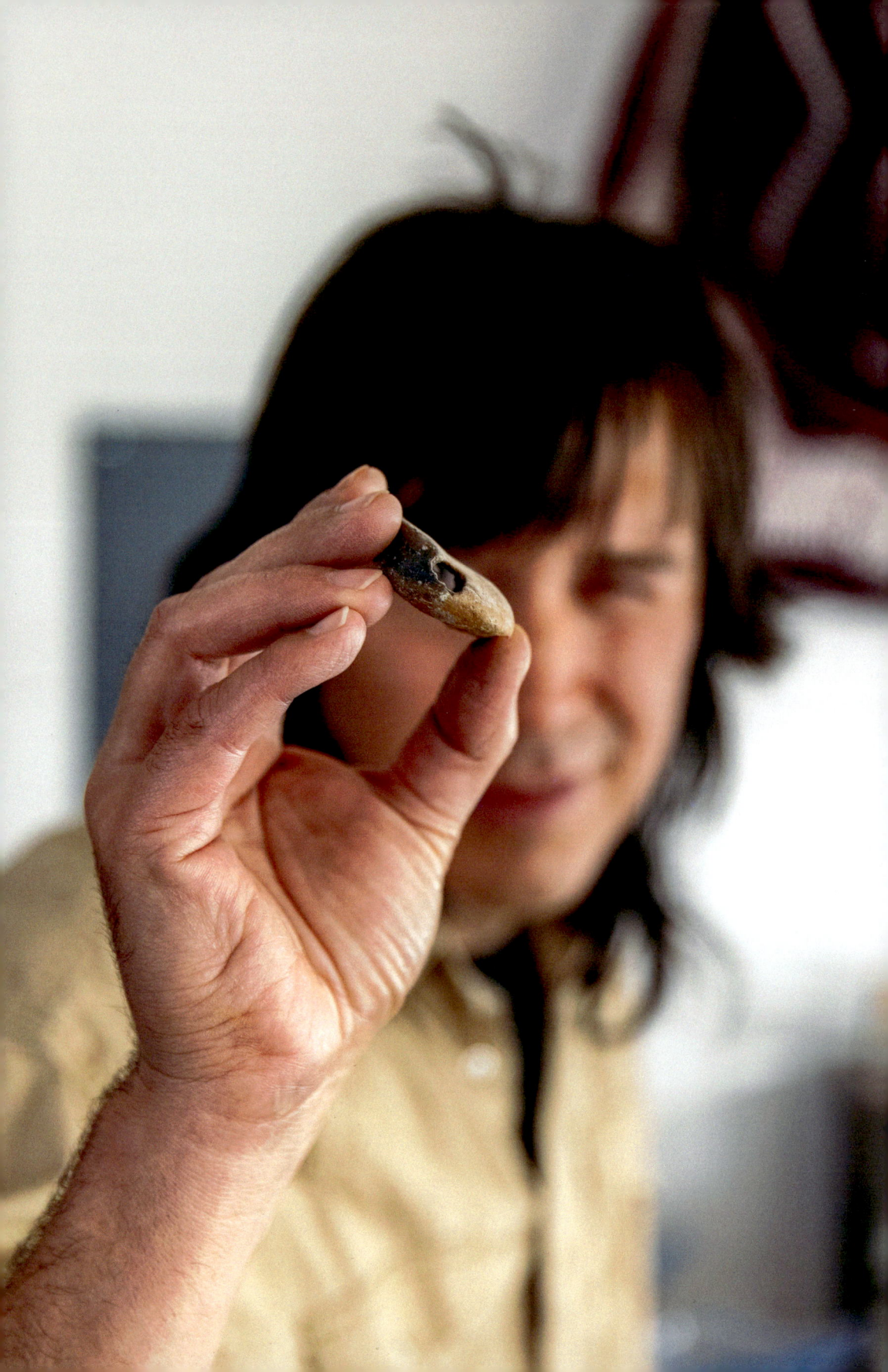

Awa xee
Cannupa Hanska Luger and Michael Barthelemy Jr. in Conversation

Michael Barthelemy Jr. is Cannupa Hanska Luger's grandfather in the Hidatsa way—a connection we discovered after proposing to include their transcribed conversation in the *Dripping Earth* catalogue. This revelation was serendipitous. For both Barthelemy, a historian, and Luger, an artist, kinship is central: Ties to extended family, clans, and the nonhuman world shape their work and guide their responsibilities to community.

Their conversation took place over Zoom on November 22, 2024. Earlier that day, Barthelemy and a coalition of conservation organizations had urged President Joe Biden to designate the Maah Daah Hey National Monument, seeking protections for nearly 140,000 acres of the Badlands in present-day North Dakota. The monument's name, meaning "grandfather, long-lasting," reflects the region's enduring cultural significance—a place of prayer, eagle trapping, and gathering medicines.[1] Two centuries ago, this landscape's otherworldly banded buttes captivated Karl Bodmer and Prince Maximilian of Wied during their North American travels. Both Barthelemy and Luger engage with this historical encounter in their work, centering Mandan and Hidatsa relationships to land. In the discussion that follows, they reflect on the powerful connection between storytelling and culturally significant places and how introspection and adaptation can strengthen bonds across time, space, and peoples.

Karin Campbell
Annika K. Johnson

1. "Proposal: Creation of the Maah Daah Hey National Monument," Protect Maah Daah Hey, 2024, https://www.protectmdh.com/proposal.

This conversation has been condensed and edited for clarity.

2. Born near Elbowoods on the Fort Berthold Reservation, North Dakota, Luger's grandfather Carl Whitman Jr. (1913–1995) chaired the Three Affiliated Tribes tribal government from 1948 to 1950 and again in 1956, in addition to holding various other tribal government and state advisory positions in the mid-twentieth century. A 1984 recording of Whitman accompanies Luger's film *Transmission Fluid 2042* (2019). In the recording, Whitman is heard saying, "We can decide a better future; it can be done. However, it will require effort from everyone."

Michael Barthelemy I love your perspective on static versus fluid culture, because I think that in Indian Country as a whole, we embrace some of the negative elements of static culture, and we get caught up on things like traditionalism. But, you know, your grandpa [Carl Whitman Jr.] was really of that mind. He was ahead of his time in that way.[2] There's a really good recording, and he's reflecting on the dam era, because, of course, he was leader during the dam era, and a lot of his ideas that he brings forth are incredibly innovative. He really had these notions of fluid culture [fig. 1].

Cannupa Hanska Luger He used to talk about how he tried everything the white way. Cut his hair, put the pomade in, wore the suit, went to Washington, did everything he could, and it still didn't work. He was like, "Okay, let's look at the customary parts of our culture, and then how do we adapt those?" Because we *always* have. That's the imposition of us being part of the historical record, and embedded in a nineteenth- and, at maximum, twentieth-century [context], but not a contemporary [one]. A lot of that has to do with us holding on to things as tradition, but forgetting why, and the practical aspects of it. I experienced that quite a bit, just in talking to some of my elders, and asking, "Why was it like this?" And about 60 percent of the time they're like, "We don't ask that question." But that's not true, because the other 40 percent of the time, they tell me [the answer]. And I'm [thinking], *You* didn't ask that question. How do we have those recollections? How do we have that memory? And how do we move forward? How do we adapt to what we have? Because if there is something traditional about us, it's that we have always been incredibly innovative and adaptable to our landscapes and our environments [figs. 2, 3].

MB When I worked on the cultural landscape report for Knife River Indian Villages for the National Park Service, I worked with some incredibly smart people who were PhDs and landscape architects and historians. I had to get them to move outside of this understanding that we lived within the park boundary. We're people of movement. It speaks to historical narratives and the idea that the nature of discovery is something only mashíis do—when in reality, if you look at any of

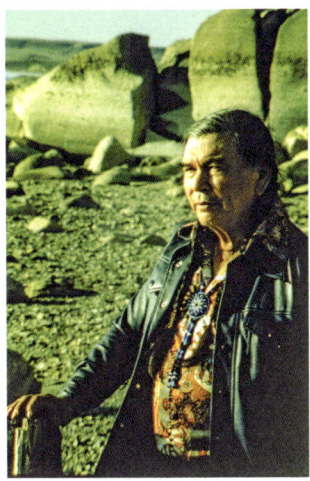

Fig. 1 Portrait of Carl Whitman Jr., date unknown, still from *A/V Presentation: Past, Present + Future of FB Res*, 2025, digitized slides and audio from the Whitman Family Archive and archival images

3. *Mashii* means "white man" in the Hidatsa language.

4. Edward Sheriff Curtis (1868–1952) is widely recognized for his portraits of Native American people published in *The North American Indian* between 1907 and 1930. His photographs, though celebrated, reinforced the myth of the "vanishing Indian."

our Mandan and Hidatsa stories, we're people who traverse space.³ We're people who are curious. That's such an embedded human quality. To think, Who's over that hill? What do they live like? What are their customs? And then the big Mandan question is always, What do those guys eat?

This was something that a lot of the early explorers, traders, trappers highlighted: meeting with people at the cultural and trade epicenter, and understanding who all the neighbors were in the vicinity. I think because of the label anthropologists placed on us of "semisedentary," it leaves us in a place where we're fixed. Mandan and Hidatsa, they're semisedentary, so they stay here, and they don't go anywhere. And then you have the Lakota, who are "nomadic." They have no place. They just move about haphazardly, wherever the buffalo will go. And it's such a strange thing, because they're migratory, they're people of nodal travel. You ask a Hidatsa at any point within the season, "Where are the Hunkpapa?" and it's like, well, they're over there, because that's where the camps are. That's where they would have the tipi rings. And they've done those camps for how long?

CHL Right.

MB This is something that I always see in your art. I know that artists are striving to send messages and impart ideas. I know we [historians] strive for objectivity, but we're always basing it off our own experiences and ideas. I see that within your own work, these elements of cultural fluidity in survivance. It's pretty incredible that our people have appropriated so much from the colonial era, from things that are imposed. Like, Edward Curtis really imposes this idea of the mugshot Indian and the stoic brave.⁴

CHL That's the technology, right? Like, the photograph could not capture the image, and even the language of photography: "capture," "shoot!" It's all really weird. But, because the camera could not receive the image quick enough, you had to be static. Then that gets embedded in our cultural context, because it's the only [point of reference for] the whole Western part of the world. And it's like, Why so stoic? Why so serious? Whoever got photographed in that time was like [*holds pose; laughter*].

CANNUPA HANSKA LUGER AND MICHAEL BARTHELEMY JR.

Fig. 2 Loading a house onto
a trailer, Elbowoods, North
Dakota, July 1953, State Historical
Society of North Dakota,
11517-00123

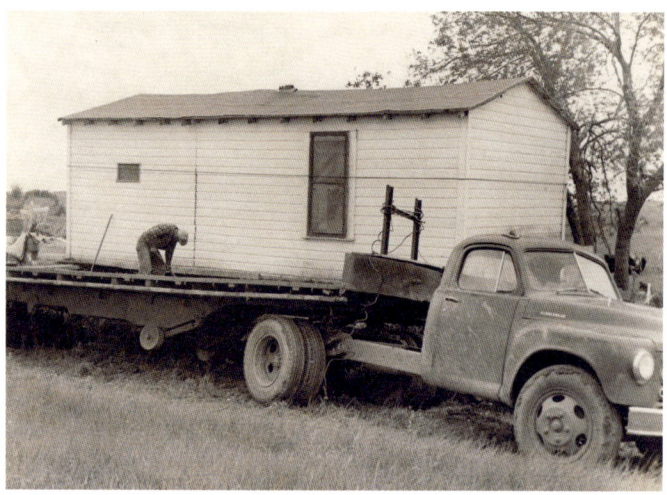

MB Also, it's the structured portraiture. What's being inter-
jected into the image? Curtis was one that was really trying
to impart this idea of traditionalism and the Indian caught
in time. If you look at any of Curtis's work, and at his background, and who he was working with as informants—a lot
of times they wanted to add things into the shot that were of
that time. They were like, "Hey, this is some new thing that I
got that I want to showcase."

CHL Look at this clock. Look! I traded for this clock. [*laughter*]

MB As a historian, I'm thinking about the era of Americanization
and acculturation. And you have this concerted effort by the
federal government toward cultural erasure. And then, when
we do come to a time where we have the ability to do cultural
revitalization and retention, we're appropriating ideas and
myths that were placed upon us in the late nineteenth century and early twentieth century. I see it all the time working in community, the notion of "this is the traditional way
of doing this." When you understand the history, when you
understand the fluid movement of people, then you get a
better understanding that there isn't this fixed point. Everything is always fluid. Everything is always changing. People
who take my course are always shocked when they look at the
plethora of earth lodge villages that were in the Heart River
and Knife River complex prior to contact. And they're like,
"Oh, my God! We're all over." Why wouldn't we be? There's no
reason why we would stay in one spot.

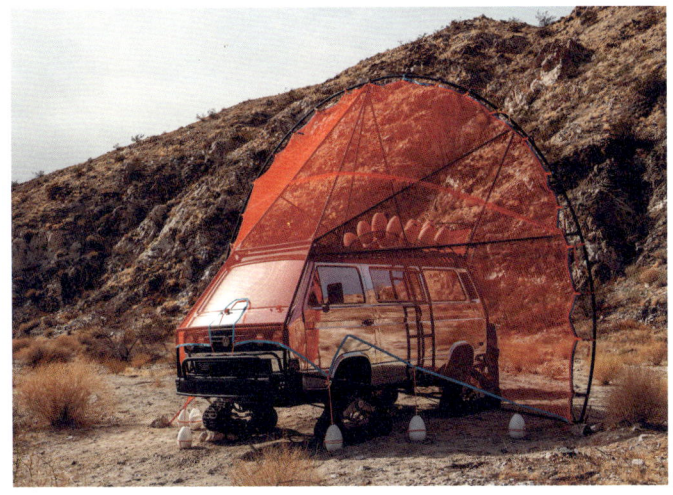

Fig. 3 Installation view of Desert X 2025, Coachella Valley, California, March 8–May 11, 2025. Pictured: *G.H.O.S.T. Ride (Generative Habitation Operating System Technology)*, 2025, from the ongoing series *Future Ancestral Technologies*, 2018–, nomadic land installation and video documentation

<u>CHL</u> The resource extraction and all of those Western narratives… how is it possible to sustain a population in one location? We were savvy enough not to exhaust the spaces, and [instead] to let [them] heal. That, oftentimes, was the purpose of seasonal movement.

<u>MB</u> Even at the rare points that we did exhaust the environment, that we caused ecological collapse, there are really intense stories about it. This is what we did and there are stories that are repeated within a yearly cycle. Every winter, you're hearing those stories of the Old Woman Who Never Dies, and she's imparting these lessons that were learned at places like Eagle Nose Village, which got too big too quick, right?[5] They exhausted the timber supply and eventually they collapsed. And it was a lesson about our hubris. By thinking, "Well, the cash pits are deep and we've cultivated enough," we placed ourselves in a position of individualism: We're fine, we don't have to live in this symbiotic relationship with the river or the environment. Because of it, there were droughts and floods, and everything else. We paid for it to the degree that they had to break that corn up and give it to all the head men and say, "All right, we can't live here anymore, we have to spread out into different directions." Our sacred stories are expressions of those lessons and those things that we witness when we do things wrong and we learn from those mistakes.

5. The Old Woman Who Never Dies figures into Mandan and Hidatsa stories and customs related to agriculture.

<u>CHL</u> Failure is a great teacher.

CANNUPA HANSKA LUGER AND MICHAEL BARTHELEMY JR.

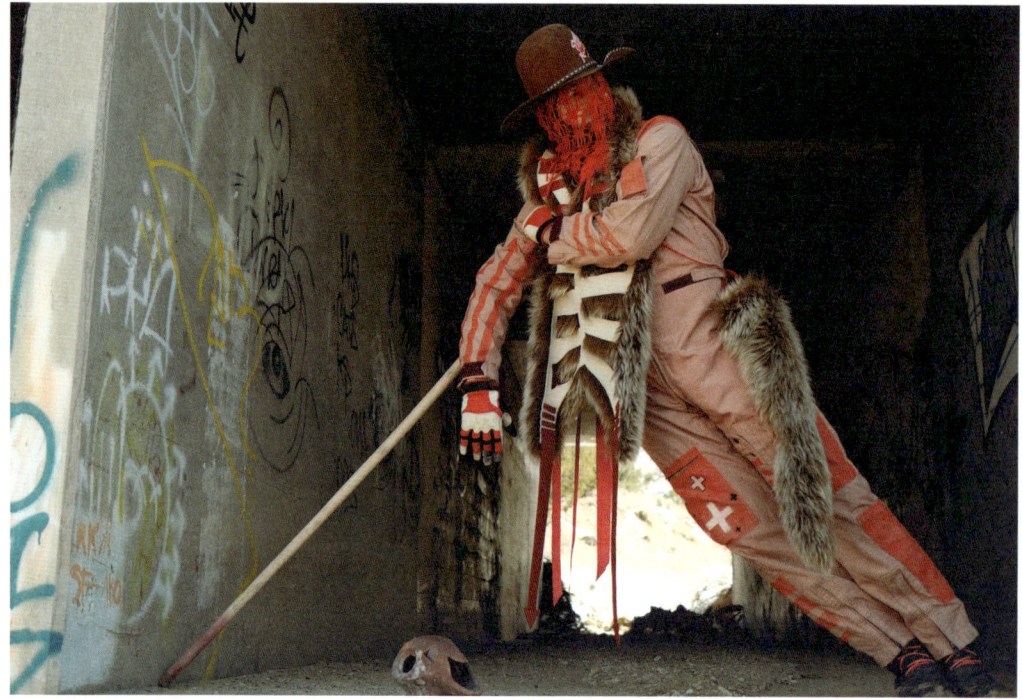

Fig. 4 *Wathéča*, 2023, from the ongoing series *Future Ancestral Technologies*, 2018–, single-channel video with sound, 8 min. 16 sec.

MB It's kind of like the sacred quality of Iicihgaa Waa Hirish. Everybody has a tendency to be dismissive of Coyote Chief, but he's really holy and sacred in the sense that he's the biggest lesson. He's such a fool. He's so embarrassing and is showcasing the behavior that you don't want to be associated with. I think we find points in our own life—at least, I have found points in my own life, where I look back, and I'm like, "Gee! I was really like Iicihgaa Waa Hirish. I was really foolish, and I really thought something of myself." That's part of that quality where he's incredibly important. Through these trials, through these faults, there's a lot to be learned in such a humorous way.

CHL Totally. And as a model, consider teaching your children your own personal failures, but not carrying the burden of your own ignorance. You get to maintain your own shine in the eyes of your children by telling them your own failures as Coyote. I've been thinking a lot about how we need to rebuild these stories because there's new things, new ways that we've screwed up. How do we add to the lineage and history of Coyote tales [fig. 4]?

AWA XEE

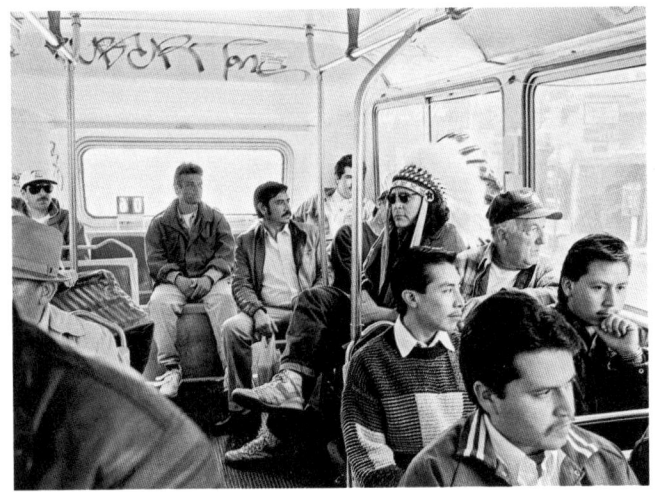

Fig. 5 Zig Jackson, *Indian Man on the Bus*, 1994 (printed 1997), from the series *Indian Man in San Francisco*, 1994, gelatin silver print, Joslyn Art Museum, Omaha, Nebraska, Museum purchase with funds provided by Richard and Audrey Kauders, 1997.17.2

MB And then we have those individuals in our lives that are supposed to play that role where they tell stories that are incredibly embarrassing, and it's the role of a grandfather. For example, my grandpa [artist] Zig Jackson used to come and visit us at the house, and he would tell the most embarrassing stories about himself and just make us so upset as kids [fig. 5]. He'd be like, "Oh, I was just, gee, I was in love with this nun." "Gee, I went to the side of that road, and I just *cried*." It's in a similar vein in which we learn these lessons and we think about these things from the positionality of Coyote Chief. [Zig] very much played that kinship role for us and told us those foolish episodes of his life. It was really functional in that he was also showcasing, "I don't think a lot of myself." In the white Western culture, they're always perplexed why we're so self-deprecating, and why we make fun of ourselves all the time. It's such a good cultural quality. It really expresses and echoes that idea of humility.

CHL As an artist, I have the luxury of supporting myself through make-believe, and that's a unique gift, and when it's hard and I'm struggling to finish and catch up on a deadline, I have to step back and look at what I'm creating. I think that that's probably true for all of us: that the power of storytelling, the power of making a really secular, normal, everyday story into myth and magic—like we were talking about with Coyote Chief—is one of those powers in which you can hold and carry a story and guarantee that it's going to move through generations.

CANNUPA HANSKA LUGER AND MICHAEL BARTHELEMY JR.

You're familiar with The Joslyn and Karl Bodmer cruising through [the Plains], and all of the painting and things like that. I remember hearing stories about [Mandan people] having a blue glass bead from before contact. But Western culture was like, "You didn't have the technology to make glass, that was not available." And I'm like, "Yeah, but I've heard tales of us having this sort of thing as a technique," or even embedded in a ceremony or a rite to produce it. But over time, I got into working with clay, and I didn't have anybody from our community or culture teaching me how to create clay work. I'm down here in New Mexico, [and the Native communities here have] these deep generational relationships to clay [that are very prominent]. It always kind of stung that there wasn't somebody [from my community that] I could go to and continue that cultural relationship with the material. I just started working with clay because I liked it. I liked its plasticity. I also didn't know anything about it. And when I went to school at IAIA [Institute of American Indian Arts], I thought of knowing nothing as a great way to start. I just felt like clay remembered this old relationship, you know? I took to it in a way that felt like it was awakening something, in the epigenetic space.

So, I'm working with clay and I remember hearing about this blue glass bead from when I was young. And then I'm traveling around, and I come across faience, which is also known as Egyptian paste [fig. 6]. It's a clay body that is copper rich. It's somewhere between a clay and a glaze, so when you fire it, the copper oxidizes to the surface and produces this beautiful blue. I wondered if we had a faience recipe. It would make sense because of our clay knowledge and our trade routes, and being in relationship and proximity to the Great Lakes and copper-rich areas. Maybe we somehow maintained an old recipe [to make faience]. I'm looking at Karl Bodmer's paintings, and I'm like, "Look at the amount of blue on these Mandan folks" [fig. 7]! You go through all the pictures of everybody and Maximilian's journey up the Missouri River, and once you get to Mandans, the blue on their regalia, it's just out of control! I feel that reinforces our customary narrative. I know there was already trade and they were receiving glass beads and stuff like that at this point. But if you have a visual language that's recirculating, and blue is prominent in the regalia, then it's probably a really old relationship to that blue, you know?

When I started looking at Bodmer's watercolors [at The Joslyn], I started to see all these really interesting parallels

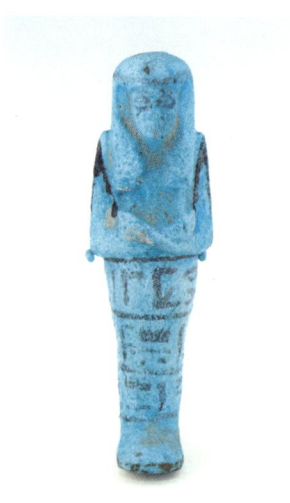

Fig. 6 Ushebti, 1075–656 BCE, faience, Joslyn Art Museum, Omaha, Nebraska, Gift of Mrs. A.F. Jonas, 1936.330

AWA XEE

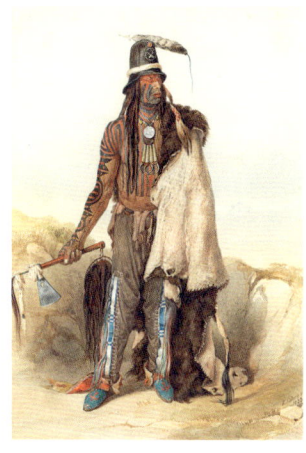

Fig. 7 Karl Bodmer, *Addih-Híddisch, Hidatsa Chief*, 1834, watercolor and graphite on paper, Joslyn Art Museum, Omaha, Nebraska, Gift of the Enron Art Foundation, 1986.49.388

between our current culture and history. As I'm looking at regalia and people, I learn he's not even a portrait artist, he's a landscape painter! A lot of these watercolors [depict] these amazing formations and were painted all along the Missouri River. The ones that really struck [me], turns out they're all currently submerged by a series of dams all the way up the Missouri. How do you reemerge those landscapes? How do you celebrate a relationship to place? And then he's painting [these geological formations and] they're calling them "white castles," or "churches" [fig. 8]. But they're made of stone and earth. *That's* the original castle. *That's* the original church, and you're miscommunicating it. I'm trying to build this narrative about belonging to a place, and is there a way [to do that] through art and cultural context. I belong to this place—that's something that's missing in a lot of the people who live here [in America]. They have been displaced, and then that displacement keeps impacting all of us over and over. Even the people who belong to the place are displaced, removed, made sedentary, not allowed to evolve or shift or change. Thinking about that whole trip up that river that Bodmer and Maximilian are on, all the different cultures that they are meeting and interacting with, they're all complex and related to specific landscapes, even though it's the same river. Their culture is the source material. What are the protocols? What are the taboos? And it's embedded in their culture rather than in a text. It's like that question that the Mandans were so interested in: "What do you eat?" There's so much cultural exchange in that question. It tells you what the land can provide. It tells you how you prepare things.

All these different cultural points are condensed and consolidated into a catalogue of watercolors and some writing by Maximilian. Those become source materials for

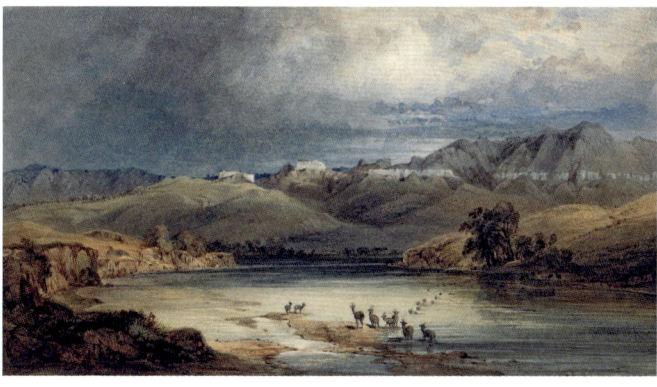

Fig. 8 Karl Bodmer, *White Castles on the Missouri*, 1833, watercolor and graphite on paper, Joslyn Art Museum, Omaha, Nebraska, Gift of the Enron Art Foundation, 1986.49.176

CANNUPA HANSKA LUGER AND MICHAEL BARTHELEMY JR.

this—hard air quote—"Indigenous population" or "American Indian," and it flattens out our culture into a continuous sub-genre of a population, the vanishing ones, right? But they're all distinct, and if you really look at [the watercolors], you can see those variations. I think about that in the context of a museum—one wing or maybe two or three rooms hold the totality of American or Native history in a museum. I'm like, It's so much bigger than that, it's so much deeper than that, it's so much older than that.

So, this exhibition, we landed on referencing *Awa xee* [Dripping Dirt], my clan name.[6] But the relationship of [the words] "dripping earth"—what does that mean? It's an oxy-moron. One aspect of it is fluid, the other aspect of it is rigid. I was thinking about Awa xee in terms of earth lodge rela-tionships and repair. What I understand is that our name comes from the way the lodge begins to leak; the clay and the material starts to run down the inside of the lodge. Then it's the repair [of] the dripping earth.

Have you ever heard tell of the blue glass bead?

MB No, I haven't heard about that, but it does make me won-der about what we were talking about [earlier]: cultural flu-idity as a by-product of contact. I always stress to people, we don't have to actually come in contact with mashíis to feel the effects of them. You have the Mexico City small-pox epidemic [of the early 1500s], and it goes all the way up to the coast of Alaska like a shock wave. We know this from Russian fur traders. Already, we're seeing population decline, we're seeing cultural change, and we're seeing knowledge loss. That's a big thing when epidemic disease hits. There's a lot of cultural loss, a lot of knowledge loss. And then, the specialties.

Consider the nature of your own art, right? You're like, "I get to play make-believe," and you get to play make-believe because you don't have to worry about all of these other factors. Who's gonna grow your food, or who's gonna hunt? The Mandan and the Hidatsa had this very same luxury in the fact that we did so well for ourselves, that our gardens were so [abundant] that you can get incredibly complex in your philosophy, in your storytelling, in your culture, in your ceremonialism, in your art. Right? I'm sure you've seen what they [were] creating in the Knife River period, and even before. And it's incredibly intricate [fig. 9]. And then everything that occurs in the post-epidemic period after

6. *Awa xee*, which directly translates to "Dripping Dirt" in Hidatsa, informed the title of the exhibition, *Dripping Earth*.

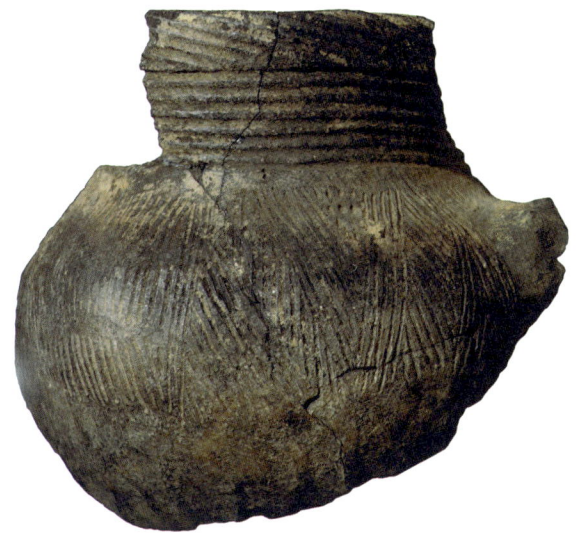

Fig. 9 Mandan Ancestor Artist, Reconstructed Straight Rim Pot with an animal effigy from Scattered Village (32MO31), State Historical Society of North Dakota, 99.10.V9.302.2740

[the smallpox outbreak of] 1837 is incredibly utilitarian. Everything. It's back to basics. It's like, well, I just need to use the damn vessel, you know. We can't have these hyper-stylized animal figures on the rim anymore, we can't put these little owls around the rim, like, we have to think about practicality again—back to basics. Regarding cuisine, we know from the fur trading journals that we had all of these different dishes, right? All these different courses that are being served. And by the time anthropologists show up in the early twentieth century, we're eating pretty basic food, like soups—what is necessary to survive. So I think it's trying to make that distinction between history of survivance versus a history when you're really, truly thriving. And to have something like this glass bead is not far out of the reality. There's a lot of things that we don't understand [from] our contemporary positionality.

I had a student—well, my grandkid—who said, "Grandpa, how do we make those stone hammers?" And I explained that there were specific people that made these stone hammers for the [Stone Hammer] Society. What they would do is call in those ones who wanted those stone hammers made, and they would say, "Go down to the river, and go get that stone. That stone is the thing that's going to change its shape." I think we have this tendency to [think] that people are the ones with power. But we're kind of girasháaci—pitiful—in a lot of ways. We need a lot of help. I think that's again our worldview. The way that the stone hammers were made was not so much this individual crafting the stone. The stone

CANNUPA HANSKA LUGER AND MICHAEL BARTHELEMY JR.

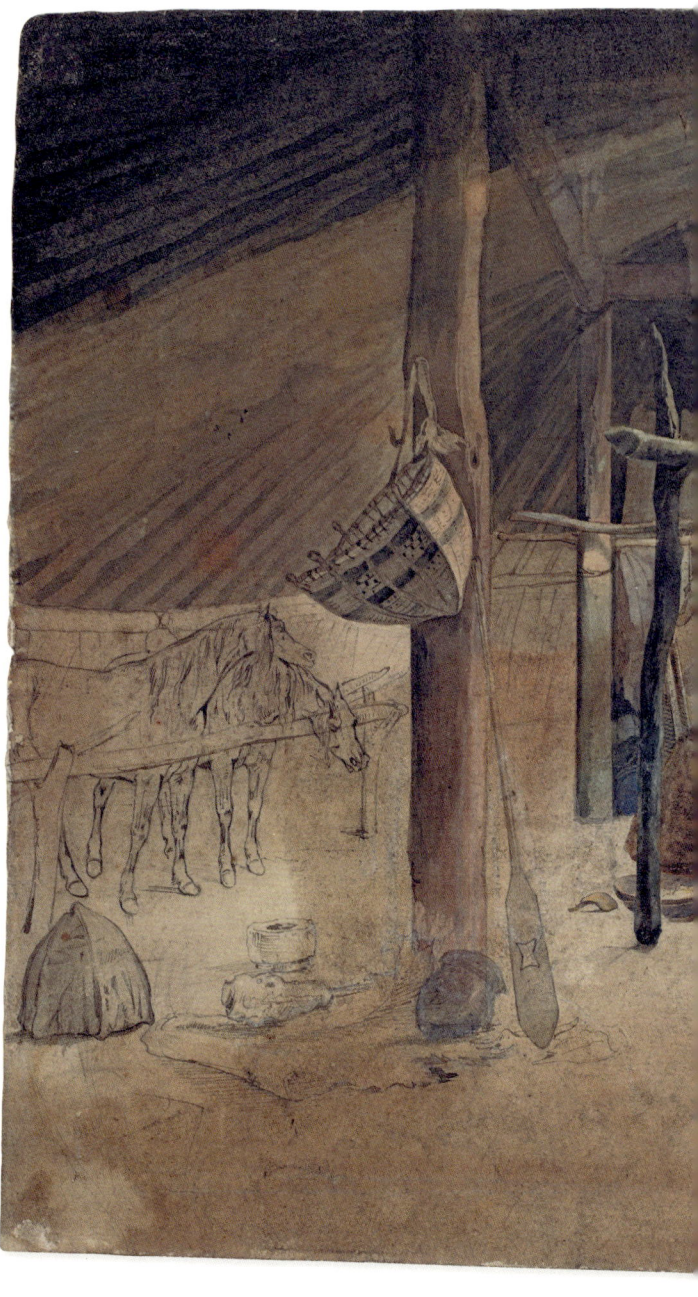

Fig. 10 Karl Bodmer, *Interior of a Mandan Earth Lodge*, 1833–34, watercolor, graphite, and ink on paper, Joslyn Art Museum, Omaha, Nebraska, Gift of the Enron Art Foundation, 1986.49.261.a

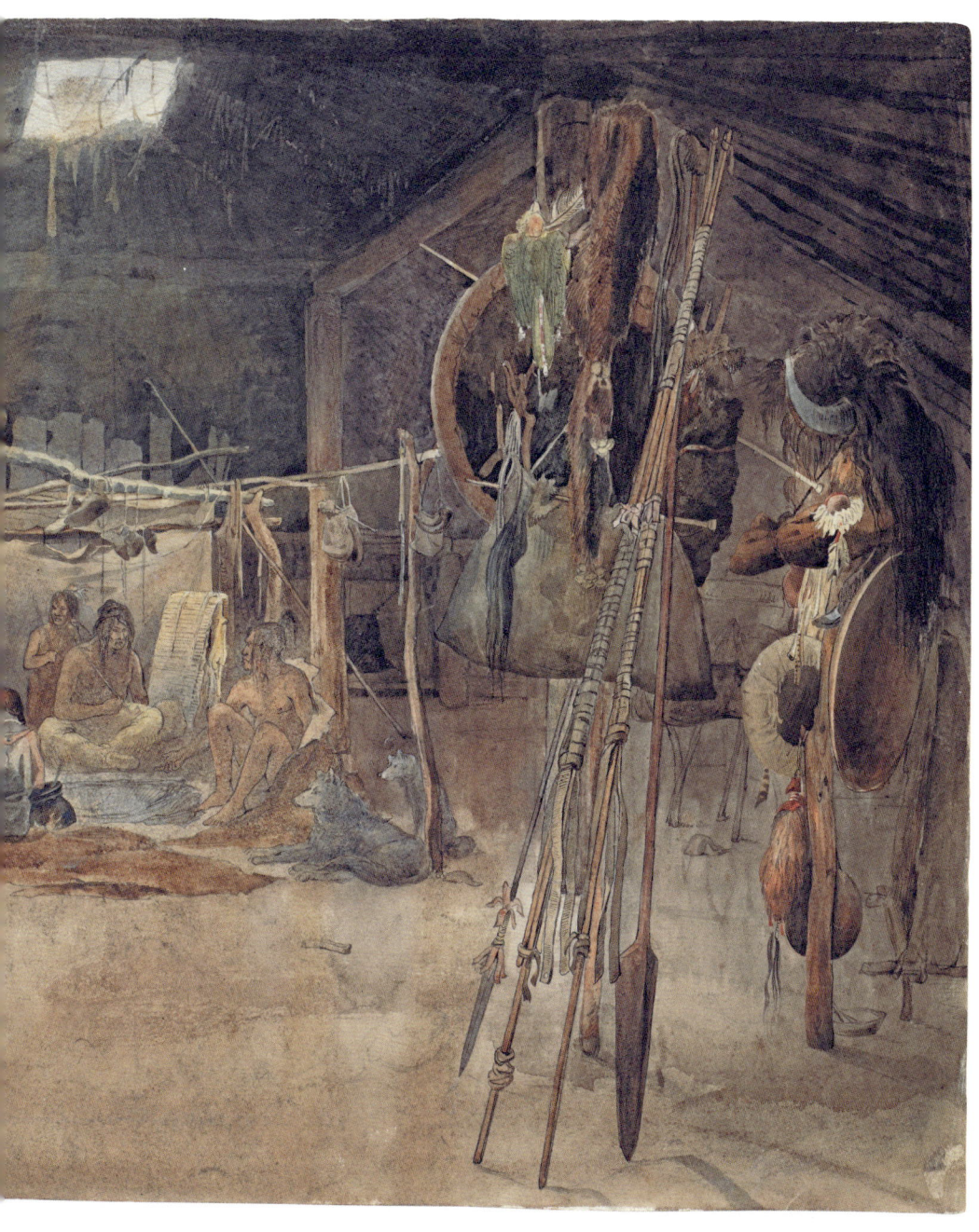

was crafting itself. For four days, they would work that stone in that lodge. It was a medicine and that's why they're just perfectly crafted.

It's also the differentiation between animate and inanimate—we don't really have that. Everything is imbued with essence, with energy, with spirit. Even Spring Boy and Lodge Boy, when they're contending with the No Head, that big monster! They turn themselves into swallows, and they pray to that stone. They say, "I'm gonna heat you up and when I throw you in his mouth, you're gonna get really big." And so they're praying to that stone and that stone is listening. It takes on the attributes of everything else in the natural world.[7]

It's like our trying to describe to mashíis the feelings and emotions that are evoked when we enter into these [ancestral] spaces. It's hard to express in the English language, because it's a foreign concept in the Western understanding. But for us, we get those feelings of place. That's what place is; place is an expression of memory. What anthropologists and archeologists would call "sites" are expressions of memory and experience and things that were learned and things that were brought back to our people.

I was thinking about moving up the trajectory of the river.... When you turn that bend there, remember, and then there's a flat-top view... that's a really important site because that's the home of that white-tailed deer. There's a Mandan story that has to do with that place, where he lived in that lodge, that Mandan boy, and he learned all about [the white-tailed deer's] medicines because he lived in that lodge, he lived in that geographic locale. If we think about storytelling in the earth lodge, and about the transference of knowledge from elders to little ones, you can transport yourself anywhere; whether it's in the terrestrial space or the cosmological, it's the expression within those stories [fig. 10]. They [previous generations] understood they could traverse space and time, and they saw it every year, every season, those stories reminding you of who you were. The very idea of dripping earth, of the lodge space and the fluidity of the transformation of that material—it speaks to the cultural understanding and norms around the animate and inanimate. You do this with your own art. Those things are living because you went through the process of making them. Your thoughts went into them, your prayers went into

7. The twins Spring Boy and Lodge Boy are major figures in Mandan and Hidatsa oral traditions.

AWA XEE

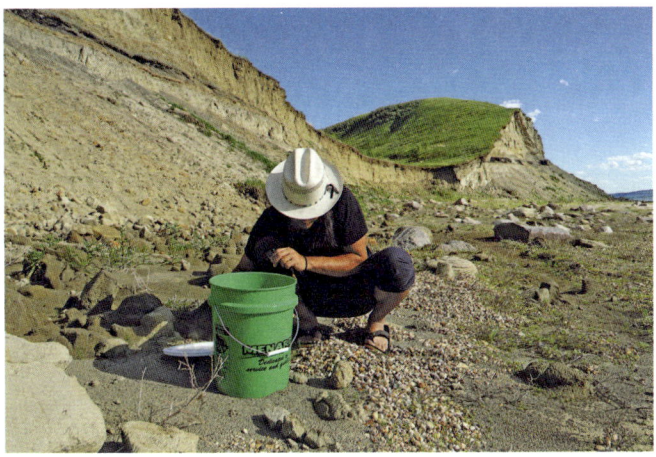

Fig. 11 Luger gathers clay on the banks of the Missouri River near Lucky Mound, North Dakota, 2022, during a Craft Research Fund Artist Fellowship, culminating in the solo exhibition *Mįhą́pmąk*, organized by the Center for Craft, Asheville, North Carolina, August 2022–January 2023

them, your memories went into them, your experiences [fig. 11]. You look at an exhibition and it's an expression of who you are.

Look at all of the material culture. The women made those [cultural belongings] in those lodges, and imbued [them] with their stories, with their prayers. You have to think about the act of creation, the act of making things. And we kind of joke about it in the communities; even making children, right? When we have our little ones, we tell them, "You belong to this place now. You stayed with Grandma and Grandpa, and now you're here, and we're happy that you're here, and you have a place, and you have a role here." The replication of those expressions in the creation of things and making sure that you have good energy and a good mind to be doing those things.

CHL There's this narrative that all the cultures across the globe are presently facing—stories and this sort of knowledge, even through the Western narrative...the gaze, the colonial, the capitalistic, all of those things I'm subject to and participating in, as well. But what's different is, I remember what belonging means and what those material relationships are. When I was in school, the only time that our people came up was in relationship to Lewis and Clark. I have a lot more understanding and knowledge than this one-paragraph reference to my people, and it's the core of my understanding, and it got skipped over. I heard the story [told] differently, and we maintained that story. It made me question everything I was learning in school. If they got that part wrong, what else did they get wrong? The academic

CANNUPA HANSKA LUGER AND MICHAEL BARTHELEMY JR.

tradition of learning is myth building. This myth gets reinforced with every generation that sits in those classrooms
and learns the story. It's hard to dissolve that or correct that
myth. And what I've been thinking is, let's create more stories
in a collective effort to express a broader narrative of the history of this country. As an artist, I'm really interested in how
you shift that mindset. English is a difficult one to do it with,
because the language is built around nouns. Everything's
a thing. Our languages and understandings are relational.
What it does describes what it is. So, I'm presenting a visual
language for people to interpret.

How do you say "buffalo" or "buffalo bull" in Mandan?

MB I know in Hidatsa, it would be "midéegaadi," which is just a
buffalo cow. I don't know what [it is] in Mandan. I could find
out for you, though.

CHL Well, I've been using the Hidatsa word, "midéegaadi." I'm
always shifting who wears the gear, like, the human that's
inside of the regalia, and playing with gender. In this instance,
it's always me, but I like empowering the feminine in the
perpetuation of generations. So, this series of dancers that
I have is called *Midéegaadi*, and they are sci-fi versions of our
buffalo dance or calling ceremonies.… I made this regalia
and filmed it on a green screen and provided very little context behind why I'm doing it.… The green screen separates
my body from the dance, and then we film and juxtapose
the dancers on a variety of lands—wherever we go, we can
do this [pp. 4, 36]. We can film the landscape and let them
dance back on that place. How powerful is the action, the
repetition of it, the maintenance of it?

This project is embedded in research that I had been
doing and relationships to buffalo. I was born in Fort Yates
[North Dakota] and grew up down there and up the river. I
don't know all the stories, but I know the places. I know that
this is my people's place. My dad is originally from Cheyenne
River, but he's enrolled now up in Standing Rock. I always
had that recollection of traveling back and forth from Fort
Yates to Fort Berthold. I remember the Totten Trail, right on
the other side of the bridge over near Garrison. When my
parents split up, that was the point at which the kids would
trade, and I'd go live with my dad or go live with my mom.
That was a fraction of my life, but it was a pivotal moment.
I was fortunate enough to live with my grandpa after my

AWA XEE

Fig. 12 *Wealth*, from the series *Speechless*, 2023, ceramic, synthetic hair, ammunition can, steel, and artificial sinew

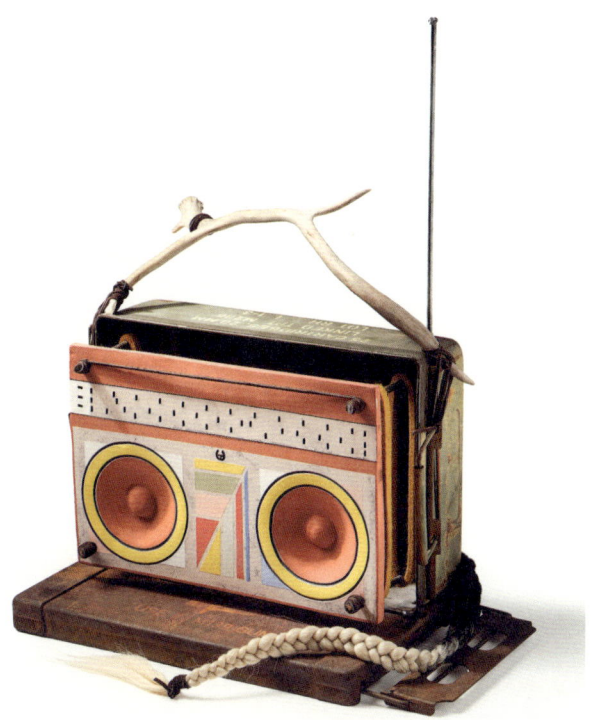

parents split up. I just remember his tinkering and being a junkyard genius. He made my first radio out of plywood and leather, and he taught himself how to do circuitry and [the radio] had vacuum tubes in it [fig. 12]. He had this extensive library and was always learning and educating himself—it was embedded in me that you don't have to go through this thing [formal education] in order to become something, and then that's what you are forever. No. You're alive. Don't tell me who I am until I'm dead. Up until that point, we're still becoming.

I'm really interested in my responsibility as a member of the whole. I gotta sign [my art] and put my name on it. It's got to become a brand because of the system that I work in. It's so contrary to my cultural upbringing, and yet to exist and survive and thrive within the society that I'm currently a part of, I have to do these sorts of things. The question is: Can I alleviate some of that awkwardness for the next person or the next generation?

Clay, she's my teacher. My ceramic instructor at IAIA, Karita Coffey, was wise enough to understand that you can learn from the material. She said, "You're going to produce

CANNUPA HANSKA LUGER AND MICHAEL BARTHELEMY JR.

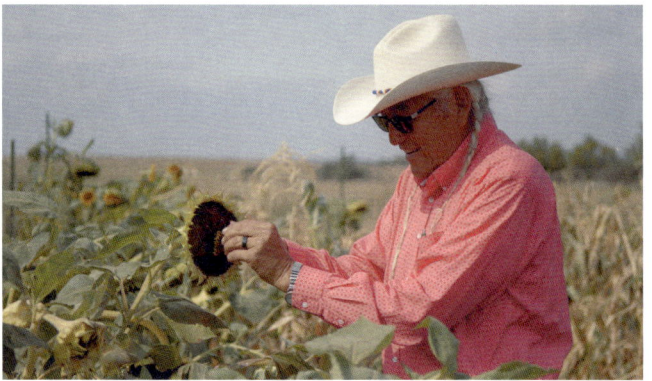

Fig. 13 Still from *Faces from the Interior: Gerard Baker, Michael Barthelemy Jr., Jennifer YoungBear,* 2021, single-channel video with sound, 11 min. 40 sec. Pictured: Gerard Baker in the garden at the Knife River Indian Villages National Historic Site, Stanton, North Dakota

more work than I have on my curriculum, so I'm just going to give you a table in the back of the room, and I want you to knock yourself out. Build anything, build everything. The clay will tell you what it can do. You will learn what it can't, and through the process, you'll begin to understand the material." Clay made me a better human being. Clay was like, "It's not about you. There is a relationship that's happening." As much as I pushed and manipulated and sculpted the material, clay did that right back to me in fundamental ways where I became a lot more patient and understanding around expectations. Expectation limits possibilities. Once I realized that with clay, I started to see it with every material that I work with, which reinforced these cultural contexts [and] more-than-human kinships.

[*The conversation wanders*]

MB I really like what you said, "Don't make a determination about who I am until I'm dead." You're always expressing that idea of fluidity and flux and change. It's learning about new mediums, new things, in the way that you learned about clay [and how to] work it. And it's so interesting, you're echoing all of these things that we're called on through any of our activities. Patience is a big thing I learned in the garden. My older brother, Gerard Baker, put me in this position when he said, "Macúug, this is the last of my sunflower seed, it has to come up" [fig. 13].[8] And then the whole season I'm praying because I can't lose Gerard's seed. It's those things that teach us humility, and it doesn't happen just overnight. Historically, we had this elongated learning experience and always went through the motions of doing and learning. This is something elders are always expressing, too. They're

8. *Macúug* means "little brother" in Hidatsa.

Fig. 14 Stills from *Transmission Fluid 2042*, 2019, from the ongoing series *Future Ancestral Technologies*, 2018–, single-channel video with sound, 2 min. 46 sec. Filmed on the Three Affiliated Tribes (Mandan, Hidatsa, and Arikara Nation) Reservation, Fort Berthold, North Dakota

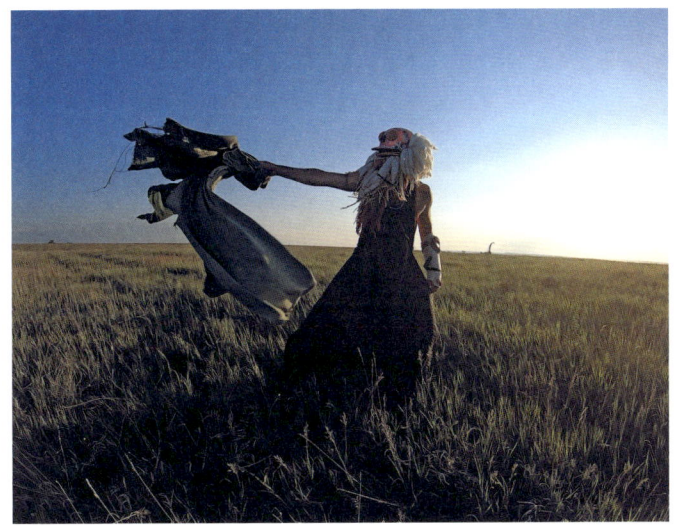

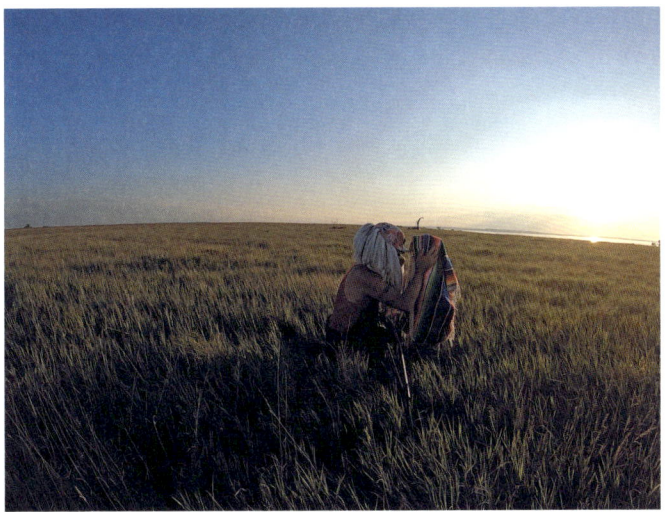

9. *Nuxbaaga* means "people" and can also signify Hidatsa or Indigenous identity. Barthelemy engages this complexity with intention, staking a claim to personhood and holding space for cultural fluidity within a colonized world.

like, "These young guys, they're always in a hurry. Where are they going?" They'll hear one story, and they're gone. And it's the thing that we're contending with—we're trying to get people to learn how to listen. There's even important characters within the narratives that are thinking about the nature of self, the nature of being, the changing of things. But you know as well as I do that everybody's gearing up for the apocalypse, but we already went through it! We already survived it. We're in the postapocalypse now. If that Elon Musk ever makes it to Mars, he should send Nuxbaagas because we'd make it, man, we'd probably live through it.[9] We'd be really cultivating corn, beans, and squash on Mars.

CANNUPA HANSKA LUGER AND MICHAEL BARTHELEMY JR.

CHL I'm really interested in speculative fiction—I call it future ancestral technology, and it's a recognition that time isn't linear [fig. 14]. Everything that I know is because generations before me understood things and were able to pass [the knowledge] along. I would be really interested in hearing more about what has been [our history,] past to present, so that we can speculate and inform [ourselves] and embed it in our far future. How do we time-travel, Grandpa?

MB When we hear stories, we hear different elements because we're in different stages in our life. This process of introspection echoes in that creation narrative among the Mandan when Lone Man, the First Man, finds himself in this place where there's nothing but water, and he begins to wonder, "Who am I and where do I come from?" That sentiment is something that we've carried on. . . . We're at this point where we are, again, really asking ourselves, Who are we? Are we Nueta, People of the First Man? Are we Hidatsa, the People of the Willows? Are we Sahnish, the People from Which All Others Have Come? It's a question that we've been grappling with our entire history. Even considering the evolution of our peoples, there was a time before we were Nueta, and we know that because it's in our stories. There was a time when we became Lone Man's people and lived by those laws in a way that was good for all. It was a transition toward this communal life, this communal system.

When we talk about time travel, I think the lodge space is what transfers us from this time and place to the terrestrial space and the celestial and the place that's down below. That was always [our ancestors'] way of time traveling, their way of echoing back to the past and recounting that this isn't a linear timeline or linear space. This is something that you know, everything is in motion all at once, and we see patterns and we're trying to acknowledge them. This repetitive process is even in the winter counts.[10]

[*Hidatsa elder Harry Sitting Bear comes up in conversation*]

MB Harry and I were talking about landscape and stories embedded within place. We ended our conversation reaching the Colorado Plateau. I said, "Harry, is that our territory?" And he said, "You know, I don't think we have stories there." He led me to the idea that there is no boundary, there is no territory. It's where our stories are. It's the same thing for the

10. Winter counts are pictorial calendars painted on buffalo hide, customarily created by Indigenous people in the Plains region. Each year is represented by a single image that symbolizes an important event. Often, the images are arranged in a spiral pattern.

Fort Laramie Treaty of 1851. It's a document that we're just wedded to, we're obsessed with that map—it's even on our flag for Mandan, Hidatsa, and Arikaras. [During] the whole treaty negotiation, it's people having two separate conversations. The US military are trying to figure out the territorial boundaries. Every single tribe [responds with] an exercise in [defining] who they are by talking about who they have come to be. US military cartographers ask Red Roan Cow, the Mandan, "How would you describe the land of the Nueta?" [He responds], "Well, our land shall extend so far as the buck brush will grow and the antelope go." He's talking about the narrative of Lone Man, and the US military is trying to figure out how to put that on a map. You go down the line, and all these tribes are talking about their coming into being, coming into place. And it's not so much us imposing our will over space; the landscape has claimed us, and this is how we see ourselves.

Everything that we do as Indigenous researchers, in Indian Country, is always in opposition to what has already been written and what has already been done. Even the misunderstandings within Indian Country itself, the appropriation of myths, ideas that have been imparted by the outside culture. You talk to the young kids these days, and they think that Fort Berthold is the only space, the homeland. And I'm like, "We're in the hunting territory, man." We're nowhere close to where the villages are, and for them it's a hard idea to conceptualize. We need to give them perspective. Cannupa, I think you are really reaching back to this idea of [being in] these spaces that are historically mashíi spaces, and you've put Indigenous voice [back in]. You've [created an] Indigenous installation [and are asking], "But what do I do with it and how do I give back?"

Whenever we look at ceremonialism, we look at those ones that brought things back. We think about Black Wolf, a Mandan who brought back the rite of eagle trapping and the rite of fish trapping that he purchased from the black bears. He was from Yellow Earth Village. When we think about clan origin, [there are] figures like Packs Antelope, who all the [people in the Low Cap Clan] come down from, and he received thunder medicine, and he brought it back for the people to make their lives easier and do good things for the larger whole.

It goes back to these understandings of space and landscape. I'm talking about that Maah Daah Hey Trail, in the

CANNUPA HANSKA LUGER AND MICHAEL BARTHELEMY JR.

Badlands, and the thing that we always were curious about in our house as Mandan and Hidatsa is [the fact] that we've been here since the Pleistocene. We've been here hunting the megafauna. And there are other groups that have come in. The Lakotas, for example, they were latecomers to the region; they came into those places that are inherently sacred by their nature, but not because the Hidatsa said so. When other tribes came into places like Wind Cave, Bear Butte, and to the place where Lone Man landed, there was a curiosity. What did they see in these places, and how did it shape them? That's real wisdom because we had that understanding about landscape.

CHL [Relating this to] speculative fiction, I landed in that position because when I was in school, there were no art spaces for contemporary Native artists. There were contemporary Native artists, [as in], there were people who were alive who were Native people. A lot of the work they were producing, though, was for the market that expect[ed] a certain kind of romantic gaze, something that Curtis put in motion. And to sustain ourselves, we provided that: "Buy my wares, and in that, you will now own a piece of a deep time relationship to this place." A whole market was built around that in the [1920s], and then we perpetuated it for a hundred years. When I was in school, there wasn't a whole lot of places for us to talk about what happened in that last one hundred years, the last two hundred years! I wanted to talk about our being here and now, and present. This conversation was brought up in the seventies—it was brought up from the beginning of time. Who am I? Where have I come from?

[I realized that] the best way to make us present is to imagine us in the future, because I just didn't see it in science fiction, I didn't see it in films. I didn't see it in any sort of context that [showed] that we exist beyond that historical context. And then that historical context was reinforced over and over. You know, *Last of the Mohicans*, *Dances with Wolves*. Anytime a film came out with Native people, it just reinforced this historical narrative. Even the freaking *Avatar* movie!

MB It's *Dances with Wolves* in space.

CHL Yeah, exactly. It was another iteration of *A Man Called Horse*. And I was just like, "Come on!" Let's talk about how

AWA XEE

throughout that whole time we survive, through an apocalypse, through literally the end of the world. So we're gonna make it through this moment, we survive this. We're gonna be in that future space. And for sure we would make it on Mars. As an individual, I'm gonna die. That's a gift. I ain't gonna make it. But the stories, the ways to do things—I can share that with that next generation. . . . Why do we endure? Why does Numank Maxana know that he's not alone?[11] How does he know to look for something that can survive even here and build a world out of what that thing's surviving off of? That's a profoundly different narrative and cultural context where there is no doctrine of discovery. There is a way to sustain yourself here, and you have to humble yourself and ask, and that's a different model.

11. *Numank Maxana* is Mandan for "Lone Man."

MB It's the internal fight in Indian Country over authenticity. A lot of people in the community, they'll say, "Your grandma's really old-time. Grandma's 'really traditional.'" And I knew my grandma. She lived with us until I was a junior in high school, and she never described herself as traditional or old-time. My grandma was very contemporary. She'd talk about playing baseball when she went to boarding school. She was really good at baseball, and she would talk about how at the fair that they had in Elbowoods, there was a guy with an open cockpit plane, and he gave her a ride in that plane, and they flew under that Elbowoods bridge [fig. 15].[12] That was her saying, "I'm modern." It's always the perspective and positionality of contemporary Indigenous people. We're reaching for this "authenticity," which is not really tangible. It's not real. And it's because we're trying to play up something that was created for us by anthropologists and artists at the turn of the century, like Catlin and Schoolcraft, and it's something that we're trying to echo.[13] It's a huge hurdle for Indian Country because we're so scared of accepting that cultural fluidity.

12. Located in North Dakota on the Missouri River, Elbowoods was the central town on the Fort Berthold Reservation. In 1954, it was completely engulfed by the Lake Sakakawea reservoir with the creation of the Garrison Dam.

13. Artist George Catlin (1796–1872) and ethnologist Henry Rowe Schoolcraft (1793–1864).

I know that we're so wedded to our tribal affiliations because it has to do with land. It has to do with these contemporary issues. People in the tribe, they'll come to me and be like, "I looked at my rolls, and there's some grandpa that's a Sioux." And they're kind of shocked by it. But in the 1860s there were a lot of Sioux that showed up, and they wanted to live with us because they didn't want to fight the government. So we were like, "Sure."

CANNUPA HANSKA LUGER AND MICHAEL BARTHELEMY JR.

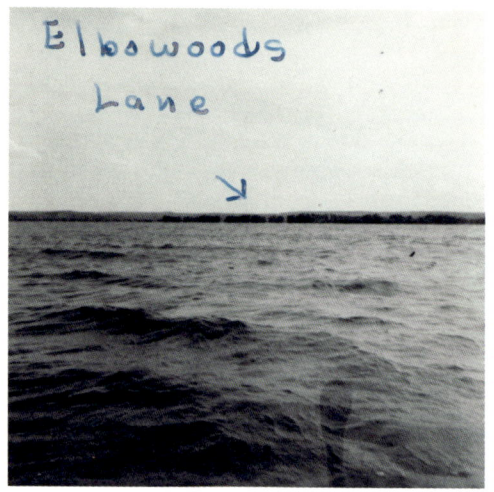

Fig. 15 Elbowoods Lane shown flooded by waters of Garrison Dam, 1954, State Historical Society of North Dakota, 11517-00097

CHL Yeah, yeah.

MB And they stayed with us, and they became parts of our families, parts of our communities. And there's these contemporary kids that are so shocked by this, where they're like, "I thought I was a Hidatsa." Well, you are a Hidatsa. Does that change your being Hidatsa, the fact that you know this grandpa that you have is a Lakota? This is the makeup of you, this is the complexity of you. There's nothing wrong with that, but it's because the outside culture has imposed all of the rules about identity and cultural authenticity and traditionalism.

CHL Yeah, it's far more complex. With that being said, I'm also interested in how you sustain culture with that awareness, and how you inform a population to recognize that this is not a genetic question. This is a culture question. What are you offering? What's your sacrifice for all of us? How do you create that narrative and how do you normalize it?

MB [*nods*]

CHL And then, how you identify yourself and answer the question, Who am I? And where do I come from? It's entangled with a history that's not necessarily your own. How do we collectively move toward recognizing that culture is in flux, that we are a fluid entity? And how do we do that without losing our, I don't know, specialness? Because I feel like that's the anchor point that hamstrings a lot of that sort of thinking.

AWA XEE

We talked about [how] my grandfather was very forward thinking around all of that, and aware of his culture of this context, and was looking at, like, okay, what I've seen in my life is this influx of people. You know, my grandmother, a Norwegian woman, absorbed into the community, being a part of it, participating, making those sacrifices to belong to the culture. It's not about your blood, it's about what do you do when they ask, "Who are you and what have you come from?" And they're not noun answers, they're verb answers—they're action. That's actually what describes who you are and where you've come from. How do we generate that sort of knowledge and that sort of awareness outwardly and influence the totality? Because I think that is the sustainable future that we're all imagining and hoping for. It's more than hope. It's an action. What are you doing, and how does that become who you are and where you've come from? And these are the challenges. For me, art's a great way to play with that. Who are you and where have you come from? I ask that of this fluorescent pink yarn [*gestures to materials in his studio*]. What are you going to share? How are you going to hold a story that's relevant to our present, but actually tells a story about our past to our future [fig. 16]? Can I do that with the materials that I have access to presently? And how is that not just an extension of what we've been doing from time immemorial?

14. A complex, multiday Mandan ceremony about self-sacrifice and community introspection.

MB   You're raising one of these major questions about cultural revitalization and retention and moving forward. And I know your grandpa [Carl Whitman Jr.] was really determined to bring back the Okipa.[14] And I know one of the dissenting voices was my own grandfather, Paige Baker, [as well as] his brother, Philip, and grandpa John Yellow Wolf. I understand both of these positionalities. I know [your grandpa] was trying to bring back the Okipa from the understanding that it's an introspective exercise, it brings all the Mandan together, and it begs these larger philosophical questions. And it's memory and remembrance. Whereas Grandpa John and Grandpa Philip and Grandpa Paige, I think they thought about the complexity of what we needed in order to do the Okipa. We don't have the bundles anymore, we don't have the Corn Priest like we used to. We don't have those that are Buffalo Bulls, those that are part of the societies. I understand where both sides were coming from in this era of the mid-twentieth century, and [their] thinking about

CANNUPA HANSKA LUGER AND MICHAEL BARTHELEMY JR.

these larger ideas of cultural retention. In that moment, [they were] thinking about who are we as Mandan? How do we revitalize? How do we make it functional? We're constantly contending with that, and we haven't had a larger tribal introspection.

You have younger folks [saying], "I'm a Hidatsa," "I'm a Mandan." And it's like, well what does that mean? What does that mean, to be a Hidatsa? What does that mean, to be a Mandan? What does that mean, to be an Arikara? You know, they have a hard time describing what that might be. How do we retain culture? How do we retain the elements of what is "us" without ceremonialism? I think that that's one of those elements that's missing that prevented us from doing that larger introspection. I'm always trying to get people to think about these ideas [of] being and belonging, cultural connection and community connection. It's symbiotic. I always talk about concentric circles of belonging. The smallest circle is the lodge grouping, and from there it's the clan. Then it's the age grade society, and then it's the larger tribal group. And then we have the natural world. If we think about the nature of our relationality to these concentric circles, it's symbiotic in the sense that there's obligation there. There's an acknowledgment by both parties, even in the natural world; [even when we] talk about animals and [natural] elements as relatives. I always pose to people at conferences: If you rock that community in your bio, if you go to the soup hall and there's a community gathering, who will claim you? If you don't have anybody who will claim you, then you should go get reacquainted with that community, because you have plenty of relatives.

Even the way that we referred to ourselves before we got mashíi names was always based on kinship. Nobody really used their names, because your name was [for] when you went through ceremony. You always talk to people based on how you relate to them. For all of us, whenever we go out and acquire these skills or these gifts, we're always thinking, How do I bring these things home? How can I make an impact on community? How can we enrich our people? These [questions] are not something we're creating in the contemporary. We're copying something that has always been done, and it's our way of time traveling.

CHL Also, where is our agency? Because we're locked in this system that allowed us to be this grouping of people

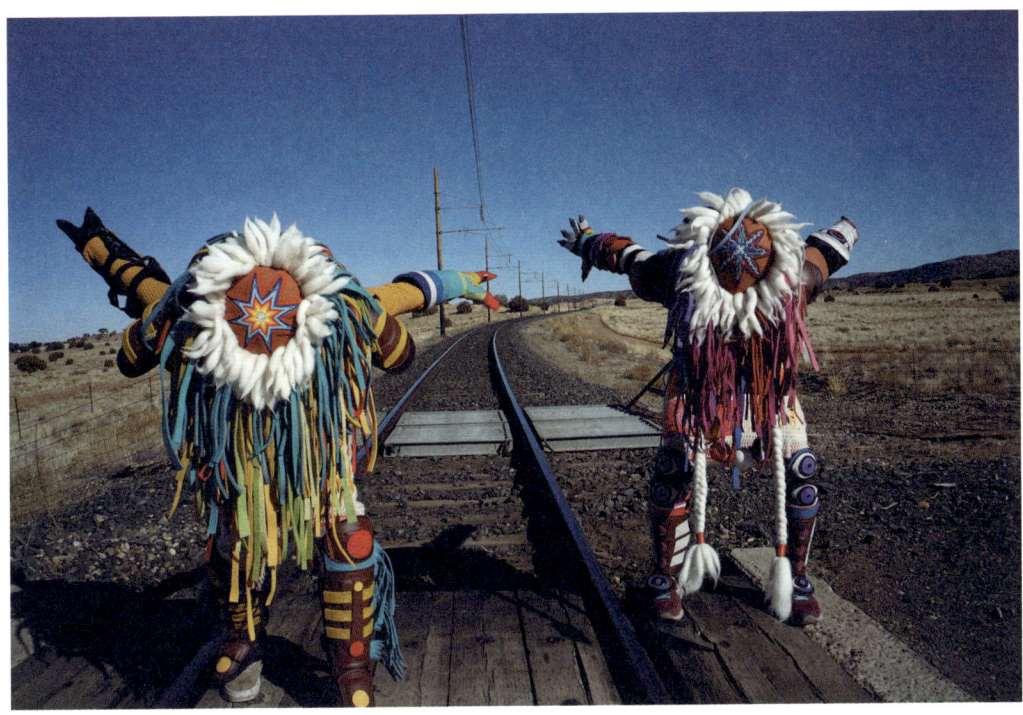

Fig. 16 *The One Who Checks and the One Who Balances*, 2018, from the ongoing series *Future Ancestral Technologies*, 2018–, ceramic, beadwork, surplus industrial felt, riot gear, and afghan blankets

positioned in this site on this landscape, right here, through the United States treaties that were broken over and over. Is there a space in which we have the agency to generate "us"? Now we're the new us. And these questions that I'm constantly asking are so contrary to the models that I grew up with. My boy was born in Taos, and I'm like, "You ain't Taos, homie," but [my kids] are so New Mexico in their upbringing because I don't have enough time or space to come back home and allow them to experience that deeper. I can't get them enrolled because of the oil, you know what I'm saying. So, what are they, and who are they? I can teach them everything about my cultural context, but it's pretty much rooted in the river. I live on a mountain. I don't live on a river anymore. My context has shifted. How and when do we allot ourselves—and these are big, hard questions—the agency to become the people, the human beings, in relationship to whatever place we're in? How have we done that throughout history? And how has that described who we are at that moment of the reservation period? How do we sustain culture? We also recognize that it is in flux. When your protocols and your taboos align with a group, and you're contributing to that whole, how is that not another group? The scary side of that is, it really undermines a lot of the policies that allow

CANNUPA HANSKA LUGER AND MICHAEL BARTHELEMY JR.

us to be who we are in [relation] to the United States government, and that's where [things get] tricky around enrollment. Who do you belong to? All of those questions get really complex, and I think complex is what we've always been, versus a singularity.

MB I'm a very typical grandpa in saying that, you know, there's a story. There was a group of the Mandan that broke off, and they went north, up into what would later be Canada, and they were gone for a long time. And they came back to the Heart River complex, and they stayed with the Mandan that were there, and they noticed that the language had shifted a little. Even their customs had become a little curious. And again, that group, they took off and went north, and they left for a time. They came back to the Heart River region again, and they stayed with Mandan that were there, and they noticed that the language had changed to the point where it was hard to understand them, and their customs had changed, and even the way that they counted their kin had changed. And again they left [for Canada], and they went north, and they were gone for a long time. They came back to the Heart River region and really spoke differently, to the point where people could hardly understand them. It was a different language almost, and the [ones who stayed in the Heart River region] traded with them, and treated [them] well, but they began to be suspicious and wary of those who had left because they were different. And again, those Mandan, they went up north and were gone for a long time, and here, they say, on that fourth time when they came back to the Heart River, [the two groups] were enemies.

You're talking about these new communities where, with these changes, they didn't understand each other. Then, through that mistranslation and misunderstanding, they ended up fighting each other. I remember my grandpa Delvin Driver used to tell that story, and he wouldn't give any commentary or context for it. He would just tell that story, and then kind of sit there for a while. We would all sit there and think about it. It's an interesting reflection on the nature of changing and being. But I know there's always a bringing back to the landscape. My grandma used to say we're kind of like water birds…we always find our way home, always make our way back somehow. Again, it's the cultural memory embedded in place.

AWA XEE

CHL   Yeah, may our shared language always allow us to continue to communicate, right? Even if it's English. Definitely allowed me to speak to folks that we probably never would have talked to.

[Cannupa and Mike realize that it is time to wrap up]

CHL   I want to ask a question, actually. Grandpa, have you ever heard any stories about giants? One thing that I want to embed in this exhibition is a giant version of us. I want our culture to seem too big to fit inside of a museum. And so, my giantism is really in the style of the winter count: More important ideas are bigger. This isn't a perspective thing, it's a scale of importance. But I've never heard any stories specifically of giants, outside of some of those Lodge Boy and Spring Boy stories.

[Mike shares a few stories]

CHL   Maybe every couple of months, we could set up a time to chop it up and talk stories. I see myself holding back in this [conversation] where I want to know more. This has been great for me, thank you, Mikey.

MB   Of course, I'm more than happy to do it. There is something I want to tell Cannupa, because he's my grandson.

[The recorder is turned off, and the conversation continues]

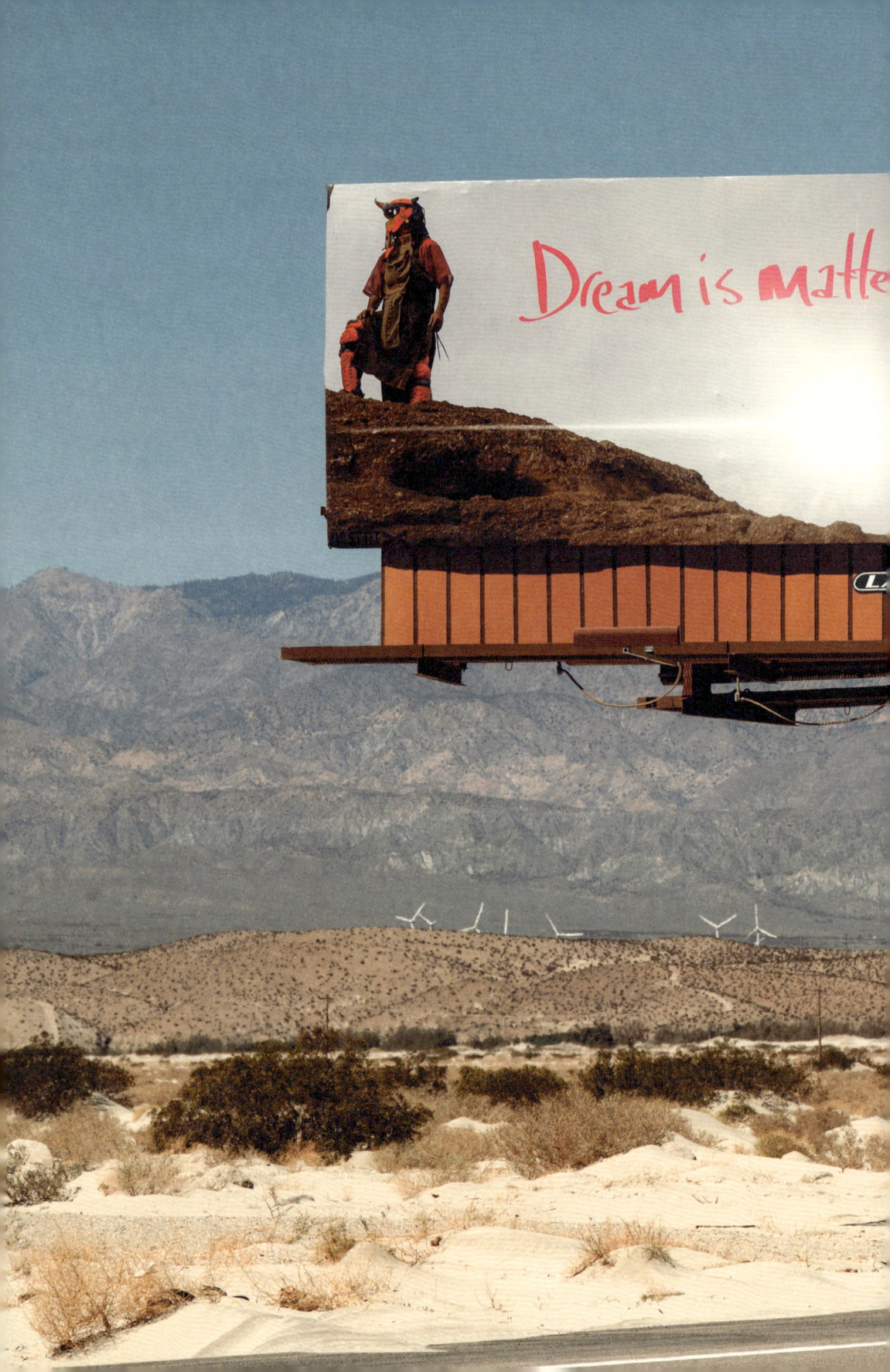

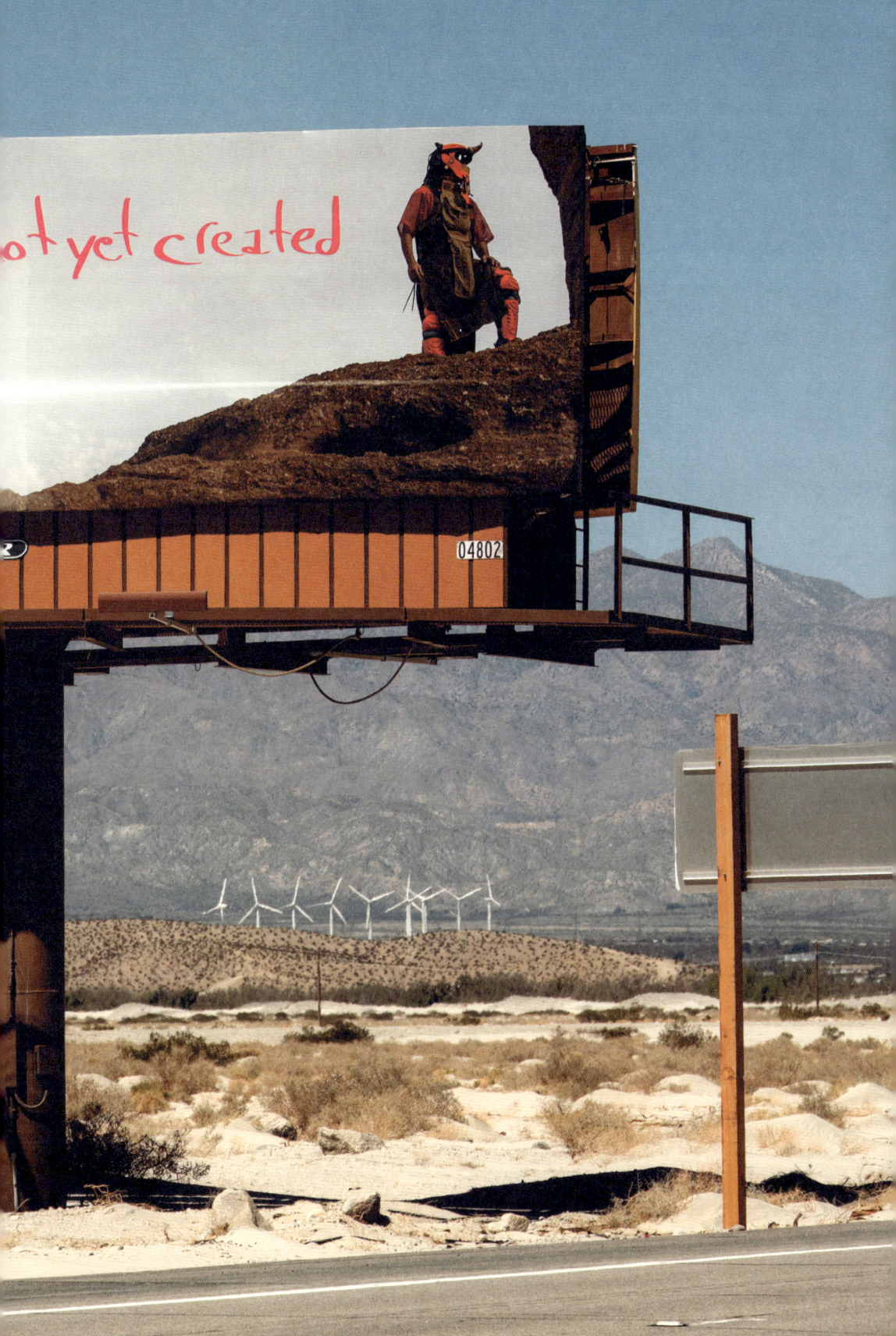

Exhibition Checklist

All works are by Cannupa Hanska Luger (Mandan, Hidatsa, Arikara, and Lakota, b. 1979)

Midéegaadi – Bone, 2021
from the ongoing series *Future Ancestral Technologies*, 2018–
mixed-media bison regalia
installation dimensions variable
Albuquerque Museum, Museum purchase made possible by the Frederick Hammersley Fund for the Arts at the Albuquerque Community Foundation and the Albuquerque Museum Foundation

Midéegaadi – Muscle, 2021
from the ongoing series *Future Ancestral Technologies*, 2018–
mixed-media bison regalia
installation dimensions variable
Albuquerque Museum, Museum purchase made possible by the Frederick Hammersley Fund for the Arts at the Albuquerque Community Foundation and the Albuquerque Museum Foundation

Midéegaadi – Fire, 2022
from the ongoing series *Future Ancestral Technologies*, 2018–
mixed-media bison regalia
installation dimensions variable
Gochman Family Collection

Midéegaadi – Light, 2022
from the ongoing series *Future Ancestral Technologies*, 2018–
mixed-media bison regalia
installation dimensions variable
Courtesy the artist and Garth Greenan Gallery, New York

Midéegaadi – Lightning, 2022
from the ongoing series *Future Ancestral Technologies*, 2018–
mixed-media bison regalia
installation dimensions variable
Courtesy the artist and Garth Greenan Gallery, New York

Midéegaadi – Thunder, 2022
from the ongoing series *Future Ancestral Technologies*, 2018–
mixed-media bison regalia
installation dimensions variable
Courtesy the artist and Garth Greenan Gallery, New York

Midéegaadi – Water, 2022
from the ongoing series *Future Ancestral Technologies*, 2018–
mixed-media bison regalia
installation dimensions variable
Private Collection

Remnant, 2022
from the ongoing series *Transportable Intergenerational Protection Infrastructure (TIPI)*, 2015–
tipi cover made from ripstop and deadstock fabric
196 × 312 in. (497.8 × 792.5 cm)
Courtesy the artist

Nuxbaagaʔihdia: To Go Forth, 2024–25
from the ongoing series *Future Ancestral Technologies*, 2018–
repurposed afghan blanket, industrial wool remnants, and yarn
head, without stand, approx.: 72 × 70 × 38 in. (182.9 × 177.8 × 96.5 cm)
gloves, with stand, height, approx.: 60 in. (152 cm)
Courtesy the artist

Nuxbaagaʔihdia: To Return, 2024–25
from the ongoing series *Future Ancestral Technologies*, 2018–
repurposed afghan blanket, industrial wool remnants, and yarn
head, without stand, approx.: 72 × 70 × 38 in. (182.9 × 177.8 × 96.5 cm)
gloves, with stand, height, approx.: 60 in. (152 cm)
Courtesy the artist

*A/V Presentation: Past, Present +
Future of FB Res*, 2025
digitized slides and audio from
the Whitman Family Archive and
archival images
Courtesy the artist

Irabágu, 2025
ceramic
various dimensions
Courtesy the artist

Máadiraxbi I, 2025
wood, including willow collected
in present-day North Dakota
boat, approx.: 18 × 72 × 72 in.
(45.7 × 183 × 183 cm)
paddle height, approx.: 60 in.
(152.4 cm)
Courtesy the artist

Máadiraxbi II, 2025
wood, including willow collected
in present-day North Dakota
boat, approx.: 18 × 72 × 72 in.
(45.7 × 183 × 183 cm)
paddle height, approx.: 60 in.
(152.4 cm)
Courtesy the artist

Nahxíbi I, 2025
from the ongoing series *Future
Ancestral Technologies*, 2018–
repurposed afghan blanket
and various fibers
approx.: 84 × 108 × 6 in. (213.4 ×
274.3 × 15.2 cm)
Courtesy the artist

Nahxíbi II, 2025
from the ongoing series *Future
Ancestral Technologies*, 2018–
repurposed afghan blanket
and various fibers
approx.: 84 × 108 × 6 in. (213.4 ×
274.3 × 15.2 cm)
Courtesy the artist

A Nation, 2025
from the ongoing series *Future
Ancestral Technologies*, 2018–
ceramic, steel, whitewash,
and detritus
height, approx.: 192 in. (487.7 cm)
Courtesy the artist

… We Are Its People … , 2025
multi-channel video projection
Courtesy the artist

Bone as Remarkable Landscape,
2025
from the ongoing series *Future
Ancestral Technologies*, 2018–
eight-color lithograph
edition of 7
38 × 26 in. (96.5 × 66 cm)
Courtesy the artist and Garth
Greenan Gallery, New York

Fire as Remarkable Landscape, 2025
from the ongoing series *Future
Ancestral Technologies*, 2018–
eight-color lithograph
edition of 7
38 × 26 in. (96.5 × 66 cm)
Courtesy the artist and Garth
Greenan Gallery, New York

Light as Remarkable Landscape,
2025
from the ongoing series *Future
Ancestral Technologies*, 2018–
eight-color lithograph
edition of 7
38 × 26 in. (96.5 × 66 cm)
Courtesy the artist and Garth
Greenan Gallery, New York

Lightning as Remarkable Landscape,
2025
from the ongoing series *Future
Ancestral Technologies*, 2018–
eight-color lithograph
edition of 7
38 × 26 in. (96.5 × 66 cm)
Courtesy the artist and Garth
Greenan Gallery, New York

Muscle as Remarkable Landscape,
2025
from the ongoing series *Future
Ancestral Technologies*, 2018–
eight-color lithograph
edition of 7
38 × 26 in. (96.5 × 66 cm)
Courtesy the artist and Garth
Greenan Gallery, New York

Thunder as Remarkable Landscape,
2025
from the ongoing series *Future
Ancestral Technologies*, 2018–
eight-color lithograph
edition of 7
38 × 26 in. (96.5 × 66 cm)
Courtesy the artist and Garth
Greenan Gallery, New York

Water as Remarkable Landscape,
2025
from the ongoing series *Future
Ancestral Technologies*, 2018–
eight-color lithograph
edition of 7
38 × 26 in. (96.5 × 66 cm)
Courtesy the artist and Garth
Greenan Gallery, New York

Census, 2025–
steel and ceramic
80 × 132 × 48 in. (203.2 × 335.3 ×
121.9 cm)
Courtesy the artist

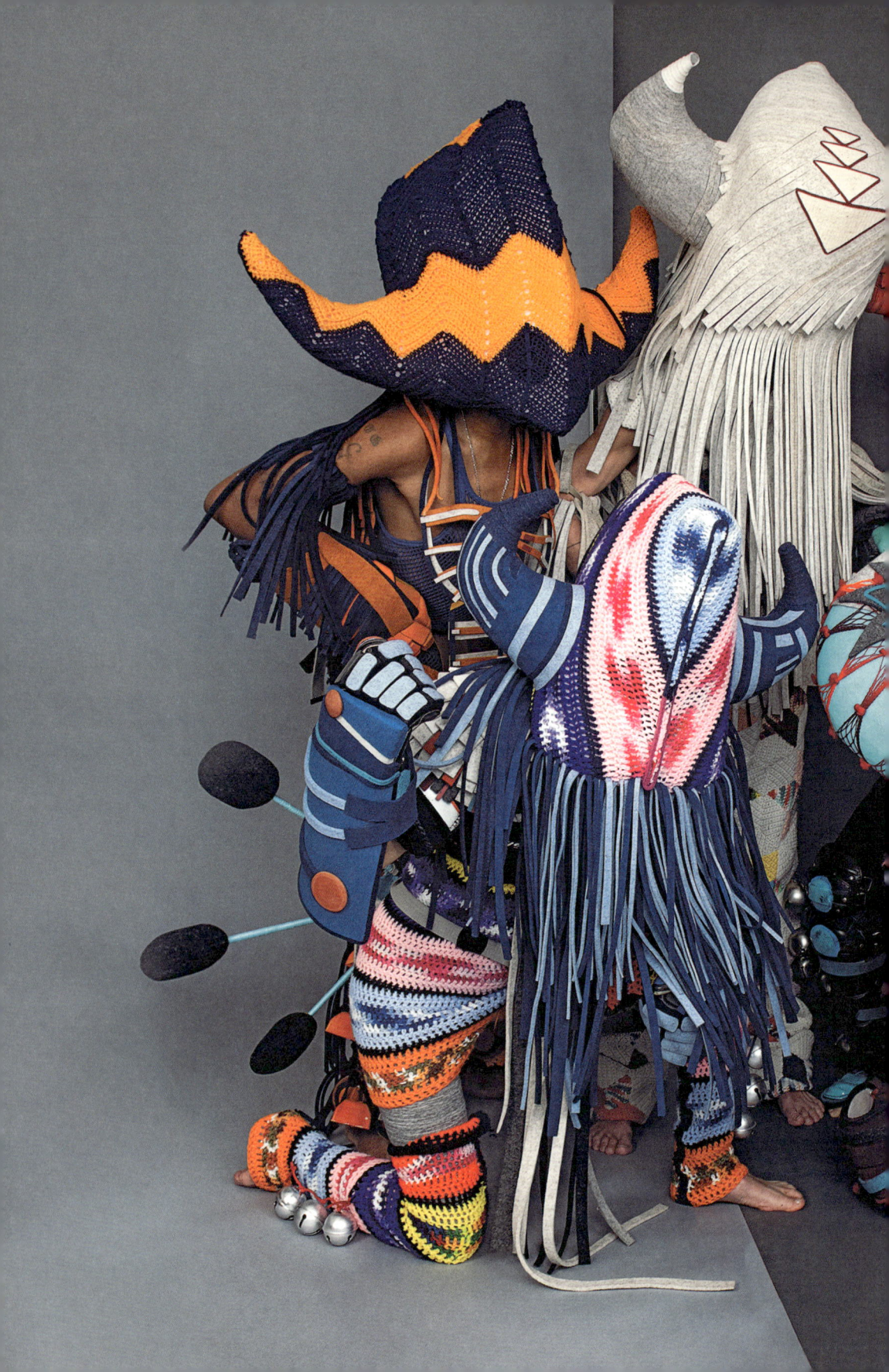

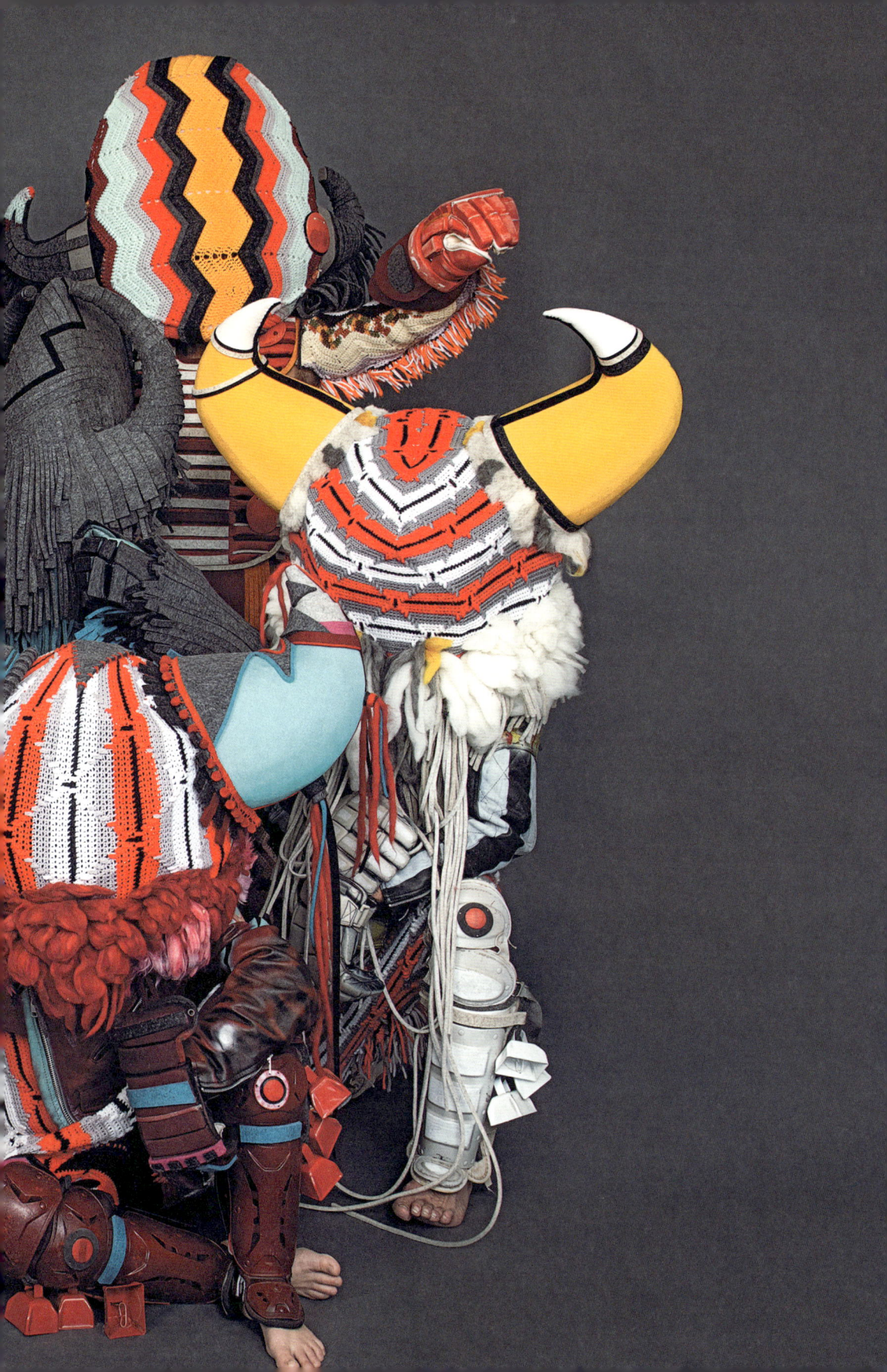

Selected Exhibition History

2025
Desert X 2025, Coachella Valley, California

Sharjah Biennial 16, United Arab Emirates

2024
Breath(e): Toward Climate and Social Justice, Hammer Museum, Los Angeles (traveled to Moody Center for the Arts, Houston, 2025)

Broken Boxes: A Decade of Art, Action, and Dialogue, Albuquerque Museum, New Mexico

Future Imaginaries: Indigenous Art, Fashion, Technology, Autry Museum of the American West, Los Angeles

Preoccupied: Indigenizing the Museum, Baltimore Museum of Art, Maryland

Whitney Biennial 2024: *Even Better Than the Real Thing*, Whitney Museum of American Art, New York

2023
14th Shanghai Biennale, China

Cannupa Hanska Luger: Speechless, Nevada Museum of Art, Reno

If the Sky Were Orange: Art in the Time of Climate Change, Blanton Museum of Art, Austin

Indian Theater: Native Performance, Art, and Self-Determination since 1969, Hessel Museum of Art, Bard College, Annandale-on-Hudson, New York

The Land Carries Our Ancestors: Contemporary Art by Native Americans, National Gallery of Art, Washington, DC

Undoing Time: Art and Histories of Incarceration, Berkeley Art Museum and Pacific Film Archive, California

You're Welcome, University of Michigan Museum of Art, Ann Arbor

2022
Mįhą́pmąk, Center for Craft, Asheville, North Carolina

Reunion, Amarillo Museum of Art, Texas

Water Memories, Metropolitan Museum of Art, New York

2021
Each/Other: Marie Watt and Cannupa Hanska Luger, Denver Art Museum, Colorado (traveled to Peabody Essex Museum, Salem, Massachusetts, 2022)

2020
Displaced: Contemporary Artists Confront the Global Refugee Crisis, SITE Santa Fe, New Mexico

Form and Relation: Contemporary Native Ceramics, Hood Museum of Art, Dartmouth College, Hanover, New Hampshire

2019
Place, Nations, Generations, Beings: 200 Years of Indigenous North American Art, Yale University Art Gallery, New Haven, Connecticut

2018
Art for a New Understanding: Native Voices, 1950s to Now, Crystal Bridges Museum of American Art, Bentonville, Arkansas (traveled to Nasher Museum of Art, Duke University, Durham, North Carolina, 2019; and Memphis Brooks Museum of Art, Tennessee, 2020)

2017
Monarchs: Brown and Native Contemporary Artists in the Path of the Butterfly, Bemis Center for Contemporary Arts, Omaha (traveled to Museum of Contemporary Art North Miami, Florida, 2018; Contemporary at Blue Star and Southwest School of Art, San Antonio, Texas, 2018; and Nerman Museum of Contemporary Art, Overland Park, Kansas, 2019)

Selected Bibliography

Cotter, Lucy, ed. "Making as Future Survival: A Dialogue with Cannupa Hanska Luger." In *Reclaiming Artistic Research*. Berlin: Hatje Cantz, 2024.

Dunnill, Ginger, and Josie Lopez. *Broken Boxes: A Decade of Art, Action, and Dialogue*. Exh. cat. Albuquerque: University of New Mexico Press, 2024.

Gibson, Jeffrey, ed. *An Indigenous Present*. New York: BIG NDN Press; DelMonico Books, 2023.

Iles, Chrissie, and Meg Onli. *Whitney Biennial 2024: Even Better Than the Real Thing*. Exh. cat. New York: Whitney Museum of American Art, 2024.

Kaino, Glenn, and Mika Yoshitake, eds. *Breath(e): Toward Climate and Social Justice*. Exh. cat. Los Angeles: Hammer Museum; New York: DelMonico Books, 2024.

Luger, Cannupa Hanska. "A Letter to Vine on the Virtues of a Good Blade." In *Of Living Stone: Perspectives on Continuous Knowledge and the Work of Vine Deloria Jr.*, edited by David E. Wilkins and Shelly Hulse Wilkins. Lakewood, CO: Fulcrum, 2024.

Luger, Cannupa Hanska. *SURVIVA: A Future Ancestral Field Guide*. Brooklyn: Aora Books, 2025.

Luger, Cannupa Hanska, Eden Pearlstein, and Apsara DiQuinzio. *Cannupa Hanska Luger: Speechless*. Exh. cat. Reno: Nevada Museum of Art; New York: Garth Greenan Gallery; Brooklyn: Small Editions, 2023.

Lukavic, John, Jami C. Powell, and Namita Gupta Wiggers. *Each/Other: Marie Watt and Cannupa Hanska Luger*. Exh. cat. Denver: Denver Art Museum, 2021.

Powell, Jami, ed. *Form and Relation: Contemporary Native Ceramics*. Exh. cat. Hanover, NH: Hood Museum of Art, Dartmouth College, 2020.

Quick-to-See Smith, Jaune, heather ahtone, Joy Harjo, and Shana Bushyhead Condill. *The Land Carries Our Ancestors: Contemporary Art by Native Americans*. Exh. cat. Washington, DC: National Gallery of Art; Princeton, NJ: Princeton University Press, 2023.

Scott, Amy, ed. *Future Imaginaries: Indigenous Art, Fashion, Technology*. Exh. cat. Los Angeles: Autry Museum of the American West; Seattle: University of Washington Press, 2024.

Turner, Dare, and Leila Grothe, eds. *Preoccupied: Indigenizing the Museum*. Exh. cat. Baltimore, MD: Baltimore Museum of Art, 2024.

Contributors

Cannupa Hanska Luger (Mandan, Hidatsa, Arikara, and Lakota) was born on the Standing Rock Reservation in North Dakota and is an enrolled member of the Three Affiliated Tribes of Fort Berthold. He lives and works in New Mexico.

Karin Campbell is the Phil Willson Curator of Contemporary Art at the Joslyn Art Museum.

Annika K. Johnson is the Stacy and Bruce Simon Curator of Native American Art at the Joslyn Art Museum.

Taylor J. Acosta is the chief curator and director of collections at the Joslyn Art Museum.

Michael Barthelemy Jr. (Mandan, Hidatsa, and Arikara Nation/Tongva) is the director of Native American Studies at Nueta Hidatsa Sahnish College in New Town, North Dakota.

Alisha Deegan (Mandan, Hidatsa, and Arikara Nation) is the tribal relations specialist in the National Park Service Office of Native American Affairs in Stanton, North Dakota.

Paul Farber is the director of Monument Lab in Philadelphia.

Josie Lopez is an independent curator and art historian in New Mexico.

Steve Tamayo (Sičaŋǧu Lakota) is an artist and educator and the founder of Bluebird Cultural Initiative in Omaha, Nebraska.

Photography Credits

Front cover: Photograph by Wendy McEahern, Courtesy the artist and Garth Greenan Gallery, New York

Back cover: Photograph by Shayla Blatchford (Diné)

Endpapers: Photographs by Wendy McEahern, Courtesy the artist and Garth Greenan Gallery, New York

p. 2: Courtesy the artist

Frontispiece and pp. 10, 67–79, 162–63: Photographs by Brandon Soder, Courtesy the artist and Garth Greenan Gallery, New York

pp. 4, 92: Photographs by Ginger Dunnill, Courtesy the artist

pp. 6, 14, 17, 43, 46, 58–59, 64–65, 83, 94–95, 99–100, 128: Photographs by Shayla Blatchford (Diné)

pp. 44–45: Photograph by Michael Hull, Courtesy the artist and Times Square Arts

pp. 62–63: Photographs by Gabriel Fermin, Courtesy the artist and Garth Greenan Gallery, New York

pp. 86–87, 90–91: Courtesy the artist

pp. 105–17: Photographs by Wendy McEahern, Courtesy the artist and Garth Greenan Gallery, New York

pp. 118, 122–25: Photographs by Z Long

pp. 126–27: Installation photograph by Justin Deegan, Original photograph by Gabriel Fermin,

Courtesy the artist and For Freedoms

pp. 158–59: Photograph by Lance Gerber, Courtesy the artist and Desert X

Dripping Earth
Figs. 1, 19: Photographs by Ginger Dunnill, Courtesy the artist; fig. 2: Photograph by Black Box Photography, Courtesy the artist and Center for Craft, Asheville, NC; figs. 3, 5, 10, 13, 14, 16: Photographs © Bruce M. White, 2019; figs. 4, 17: Photographs by Shayla Blatchford (Diné); fig. 6: Courtesy the artist and Garth Greenan Gallery, New York; fig. 7: Courtesy the artist; fig. 8: Courtesy the artist and Garth Greenan Gallery, New York; fig. 9: © Whitney Museum of American Art / Licensed by Scala / Art Resource, New York, Photograph by Ron Amstutz; fig. 18: Photograph by Gabriel Fermin, Courtesy the artist and Garth Greenan Gallery, New York; fig. 20: Photograph by Z Long; fig. 21: Photograph by Jeff McLane, Courtesy the artist and Garth Greenan Gallery, New York

Studio Notes
pp. 47–53, 54–55 (bottom), 56–57: Photographs by Shayla Blatchford (Diné); pp. 54 (top, detail), 55 (top, detail): Photographs by Wendy McEahern, Courtesy the artist and Garth Greenan Gallery, New York

Fiber
Fig. 1: Photograph by Shayla Blatchford (Diné); fig. 2: © Ann Hamilton, Photograph by Ian Reeves

Practices of Place: The Monuments of Cannupa Hanska Luger
Fig. 1: Photograph © Frank Schulenburg / CC BY-SA 4.0

The Giant
Fig. 1: Photograph by Carole Raddato / CC BY-SA 2.0; fig. 2: Photograph by Jörg Bittner Unna / CC BY 3.0

Living Landscapes
Fig. 1: Photograph © Bruce M. White, 2019

Of the Beings That Roam the Earth
Fig. 1: Photograph by Nicholas Knight, Courtesy Public Art Fund, New York; fig. 2: Photograph by Z Long

Awa xee: Cannupa Hanska Luger and Michael Barthelemy Jr. in Conversation
Fig. 1: Courtesy the artist; figs. 2, 9, 15: Photographs courtesy State Historical Society of North Dakota; fig. 3: Photograph by Lance Gerber, Courtesy the artist and Desert X; fig. 4: Courtesy the artist and Garth Greenan Gallery, New York; fig. 5: © Zig Jackson, Courtesy the artist; figs. 7, 8, 10: Photographs © Bruce M. White, 2019; fig. 11: Photograph by Ginger Dunnill, Courtesy the artist; fig. 12: Photograph by Wendy McEahern, Courtesy the artist and Garth Greenan Gallery, New York; fig. 13: Photograph by Jon Hustead; fig. 14: Courtesy the artist; fig. 16: Photograph by Chip Thomas, Courtesy the artist

This book is published in conjunction with the exhibition *Dripping Earth: Cannupa Hanska Luger*, presented at the Joslyn Art Museum, Omaha, Nebraska, November 15, 2025–March 8, 2026.

Library of Congress Control Number: 2025940810
ISBN 979-8-9925162-5-8

Published by Joslyn Art Museum, Omaha
joslyn.org

Distributed by University of Washington Press
uwapress.uw.edu

Produced by Marquand Books, Seattle
marquandbooks.com

Edited by Kristin Kearns
Designed by Ryan Polich
Typeset in Auroc Text and Easy
  Grotesk by Brynn Warriner
Proofread by Tanya Heinrich
Color management by I/O Color,
  Seattle
Printed and bound in China by
  Artron Art Group

The typeface used in the Studio Notes is Hanska, designed by Cem Eskinazi and based on Cannupa Hanska Luger's handwriting.

Front cover: *Thunder as Remarkable Landscape* (detail), 2025, from the ongoing series *Future Ancestral Technologies*, 2018–, eight-color lithograph

Back cover: *A Nation* in progress in the artist's studio, 2025

Front endpapers: *Thunder as Remarkable Landscape* (detail), 2025, from the ongoing series *Future Ancestral Technologies*, 2018–, eight-color lithograph

Back endpapers: *Bone as Remarkable Landscape* (detail), 2025, from the ongoing series *Future Ancestral Technologies*, 2018–, eight-color lithograph

p. 2: Lucky Mound, North Dakota, 2022

Frontispiece: *Midéegaadi – Water*, 2022, from the ongoing series *Future Ancestral Technologies*, 2018–, mixed-media bison regalia

p. 4: Luger filming with green screen for *Midéegaadi* video series, 2022

pp. 6, 43, 46–56, 58–59, 100, 128: Stills from the artist's studio, 2025

p. 10: *Midéegaadi – Light* (detail), 2022, from the ongoing series *Future Ancestral Technologies*, 2018–, mixed-media bison regalia

pp. 14, 17: Luger working on *Irabágu* in his studio, 2025

pp. 44–45: Installation view of *Midéegaadi*, Midnight Moment, Times Square Arts, New York, April 1–30, 2025

p. 57: *Light as Remarkable Landscape* (detail), 2025, from the ongoing series *Future Ancestral Technologies*, 2018–, eight-color lithograph

p. 92: Still from *Mįhą́pmą̨k: A Way Home*, 2022, single-channel video with poem by Cannupa Hanska Luger, narrated by 'io Kahoku Lahuikoa Luger, age ten. Filmed on the cut banks of the Missouri River, Lucky Mound, Fort Berthold Reservation, North Dakota

p. 118: *Bison Bead Project* workshop held at the Joslyn Art Museum, Omaha, Nebraska, February 6, 2025

pp. 126–27: Installation view of *We Survive You*, 2021, from the ongoing series *Future Ancestral Technologies*, 2018–, in Mandan, North Dakota, November 1–31, 2021. Completed for LANDBACK. Art, in collaboration with NDN Collective, INDÍGENA, and For Freedoms

pp. 158–59: Installation view of Desert X 2025, Coachella Valley, California, March 8–May 11, 2025. Pictured: *G.H.O.S.T. Ride (Generative Habitation Operating System Technology)*, 2025, from the ongoing series *Future Ancestral Technologies*, 2018–, nomadic land installation and video documentation

pp. 162–63: Editorial photograph of *We Survive You – Midéegaadi*, 2023, featuring seven mixed-media bison regalia made of repurposed materials

Unless otherwise noted, all works are by Cannupa Hanska Luger, © Cannupa Hanska Luger.

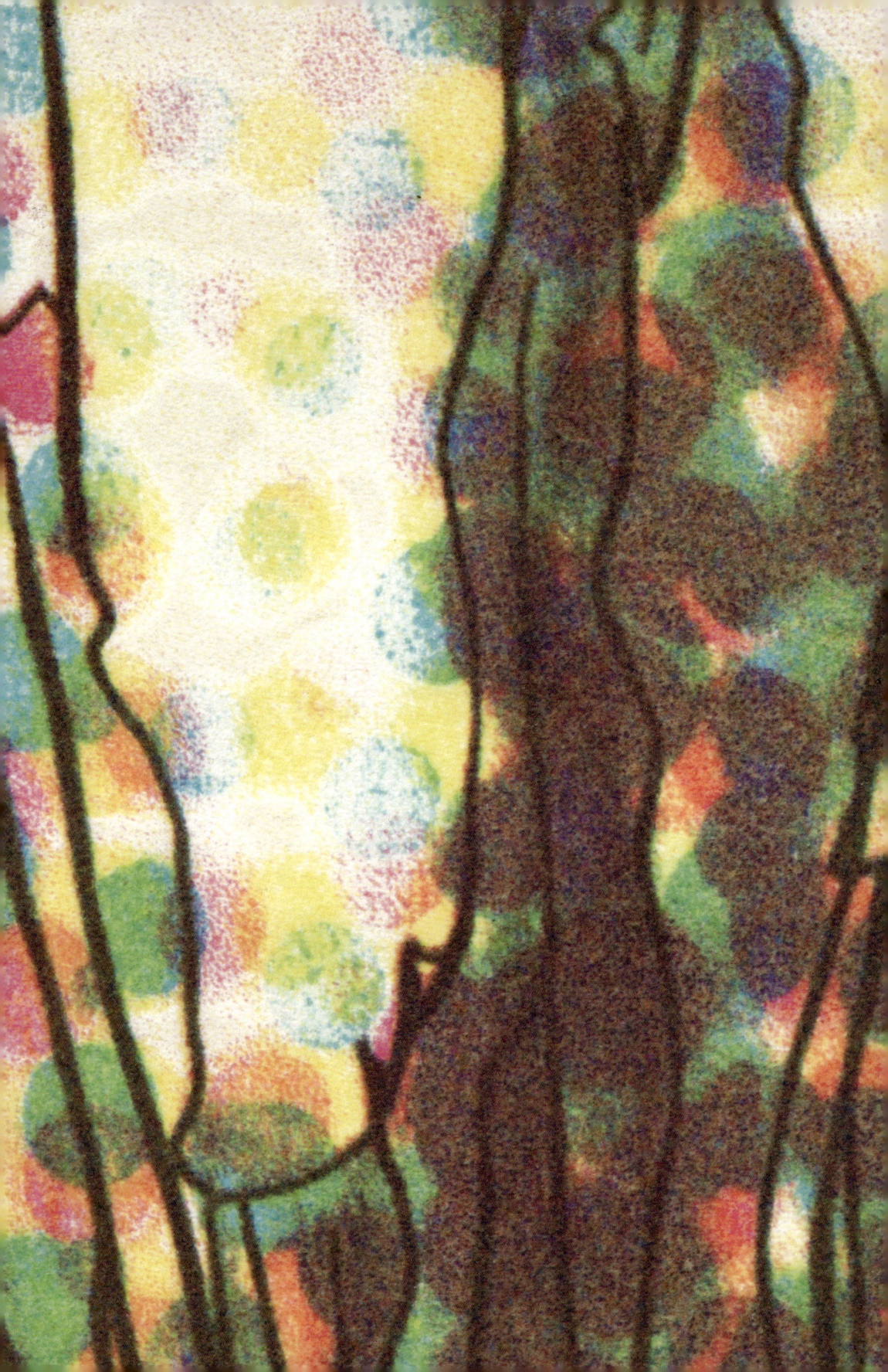